The Changing
Urban School

ROBERT THORNBURY

The Changing Urban School

METHUEN & CO LTD
LONDON

First published in 1978
by Methuen & Co Ltd
11 *New Fetter Lane, London* EC4P 4EE

© 1978 *Robert Thornbury*

Phototypeset by Western Printing Services Ltd
and printed in Great Britain by
Richard Clay (The Chaucer Press), Ltd.
Bungay, Suffolk

ISBN 0 416 55020 7 (*hardbound*)
ISBN 0 416 55030 4 (*paperback*)

For Mary Lou and our children,
Richard, Clare, Jane and Paul

Contents

Acknowledgements

The author would like to thank Harold Silver for his advice and support at various stages in the preparation of this book; to Jane Armstrong at Methuen for final editing; and to Clare Cheasty and all those who helped with the typing.

The table on p. 27 first appeared in Jack Barnes (ed.) *Educational Priority 3*, 'Curriculum innovation in London's EPAs'; London:HMSO, 1975; reproduced with the permission of the Controller of Her Majesty's Stationery Office. The table on p. 99 first appeared in *The Times Educational Supplement*, and that on p. 181 in *New Society*, London, the weekly review of the social sciences. The cartoons on pp. 5, 22, 87, 88, 94, 100, 105, 111, 114, 119, 130, 132, 135, 143, 150–1, 153, 159, 165, 167, 170, 179, 182, 184, 196, 206, 207, 208 first appeared in *The Times Educational Supplement*; those on pp. 9, 81, 83, 86, 146, 149 in *Teachers World*; those on pp. 44, 67, 70, 74 in *Punch*; and those on pp. 34, 198 in *The Architects Journal*. Every effort has been made to contact the artists concerned, though unfortunately this was not possible in every case. The author and publishers are most grateful to those who could be reached for permission to reproduce. The views and opinions stated in this book are those of the author, and do not necessarily coincide with those of his employer, the Inner London Education Authority.

Introduction

In stressed cities all over the world the contemporary urban school seemed a confusing and disturbing place to the newspaper reader or parent of the 1960s and 1970s. Conflicting reports from teachers, children, journalists, government departments and educationists aroused general interest and concern simply by begging the question: what really does go on in schools? In Britain the Great Education Debate, officially initiated by the Prime Minister in 1977, formally put questions of the kind that everyone was asking: what is wrong with schools? Who is to blame? Who, if anyone, is right in their analyses and answers?

This book cannot provide answers to all these questions – no one can quantify educational neglect; but it attempts to give a composite portrait and an explanation of the urban classroom over two decades, and to show what went wrong. It confronts the administrator with the scarcely credible newspaper report and the headmaster with the problems of the increasingly influential 'silent' figures – the caretakers and 'helpers' – who play such an important if unnoticed part in the running of the school. It considers not only what and how children are taught, but also the conditions in which they are taught and those in which they live, which vitally affect their achievement. The stance throughout is uncompromising on how awful many schools and classrooms have been. The teacher is not a psychiatric nurse, the classroom is not a therapy unit. The school should not be a territory of protection rackets and wary, frightened or aggressive children, staffed by harassed adults chafing at a resented career and poor pay.

The book begins by looking at the school in its wider setting. Some of the misguided attempts to provide a better education for educationally deprived urban children are considered in Chapter 2; following chapters outline the social conditions which meant that such short-sighted strategies were born to fail. Chapters 6 to 8 discuss the school as a whole – its construction, running and management, and the effects these have on the life of those who work in it; Chapters 9 to 12 survey the enormous field of changing theories, projects and practices in curriculum. The teaching of English is taken as a case study to show how the pursuit of desirable objectives sometimes resulted in the destruction of social control or curriculum stability because of untimely innovation. Chapter 13 looks at reactions to radical techniques and the new call for accountability. Chapter 14 considers the reactions of the urban child to inner city conditions, and the various attempts that have been made to help him, both from within the school and from without. The book ends by looking at social mix as the means of combating urban disadvantage, at policies that may help to improve it, and in particular at the part that teachers and schools can play in achieving it.

I have never forgotten my first week as a young teacher fifteen years ago in an inner city comprehensive school belonging to Britain's largest urban authority. On the second day the book stock given to me for a class of 'remedial children' consisted of thirty brand-new bibles. These were provided by the County Hall; the school had nothing to give me, so great had been the previous term's destruction. Ten of the children needed special educational placement, one was psychotic and the remainder presented a formidable galaxy of problems. The school suffered repeated spasms of fire-raising. Professional life was nasty, brutish and short – many teachers left each year. Individual departments achieved social order, but often by violent means. Cliques among the staff complained to cabinet ministers in secret after-hours meetings that the school was a disaster – yet it was one of the most expensively staffed, best resourced and most carefully designed inner city schools in the country. In painting a turbulent picture in my first chapter, therefore, I have not exaggerated; I have presented a simplistic cartoon of the urban classroom jungle as it stirred the popular imagination, because it makes a good starting point for the following chapters, which have attempted to deepen the reader's understanding, and my own, of what really was happening and what must happen in the future.

1 Classroom crisis and teacher stress

What was the pathology report on the British urban classroom as 1980 approached? It was a portrait in the cities and large towns of schools in tumult. Indeed, in the conurbations of other advanced countries, such as the US, Australia, and Canada the crisis in the urban classroom was causing widespread alarm.[1] Urban education in Britain in the 1960s and 1970s was devastated by demographic landslide and ravaged by epidemic maladjustment. Some 21 per cent of boys and 16 per cent of girls in the inner city playground exhibited aggressive and abnormal behaviour. Juvenile crimes of violence multiplied seventeen times in the twenty-five years before 1977. Schoolchildren in London and other major cities were often a year behind the national average in reading attainment at eleven years.[2] Not only were playgrounds hazardously menaced by disturbed children, the school curriculum was visibly distorted. Yet such endemic maladjustment among urban children ruled out special educational treatment as too expensive. The cry rang out, disguised as enlightened policy; 'contain your problem children' in the ordinary school. Perhaps, as the teaching profession uneasily claimed, schools merely reflected the deterioration and quality of urban life. But beyond doubt, in London, Glasgow and many urban authorities the schools system, especially in new comprehensives or multi-ethnic neighbourhoods, was on the edge of total collapse.[3]

Urban crime statistics showed soaring violence among 14- to 17-year-olds and younger children as well, most markedly in the inner cities. Among teenage girls the flowering of unisex violence and resort by the authorities to high security imprisonment were clearly documented. Cannabis, amphetamines, glue sniffing, occasional heroin addiction, and lunchtime drinking sessions among older children all obtruded on teachers and taught in the urban classroom.

Parents and the general public, relying on newspapers and the gossip of children for their picture of the urban classroom, listened to hair-raising tales.[4] Playground stabbings, the murder of a street trader planned during playtime, muggings by alienated West Indian teenagers at lunchtime, the teenage suicide following persistent bullying – any of these were easily believed. The long, hot summers of the mid-1970s in the capital city witnessed school and street riots among pupils. Shops displaying stern notices refused to serve schoolchildren, as pilfering exceeded profits. Juveniles shoplifting during lunchtime unprecedentedly found themselves pursued back to their school gates by a police helicopter.

Schoolchildren dominated the criminal statistics. A Scotland Yard study of housebreaking trends between 1973 and 1975 aimed to spot target criminals who could be put under observation and eventually arrested; but the police researchers found that over half of the 37 per cent increase in London burglaries were committed by children aged 11 to 15 years. Police also found that most juvenile crime was committed between noon and 3 p.m. – when children should have been in school.

Behind the daytime crime wave among schoolchildren, according to popular belief, press comment and the confidential mutterings of teachers was the untimely raising of the school leaving age. A monumental professional blunder led the teacher unions in 1973 to insist on ROSLA, the 'raising of the school leaving age'. Within three years the teaching profession was to make a complete volte-face. By 1976 liberal heads of comprehensive schools, and the *Black Paper* enthusiasts, as all along, were publicly urging exemption schemes for early leavers, or even lowering the school leaving age to 14 again.[5] Truancy became particularly bad as ROSLA exacerbated teacher stress at a time of acute staff shortage and part-time working by schools. London secondary schools in 1973 reached the point where each morning the education officer had on his desk a list of twenty schools likely to close down that day through staff shortage.[6]

Despite whitewashing school attendance surveys, which fondly showed an average 89 per cent attendance in city schools, inquisitive journalists nevertheless alleged that secondary school attendances had dropped enormously. After all, as an anonymous education officer wrote, an official 89 per cent attendance could still mean that 54 per cent of the children truanted at least one morning or afternoon each week.[7]

Fire-raising in urban schools was a growing trend. In 1973 in Britain there were 89 major school fires with total damage amounting to nearly £6m; whereas ten years previously the annual figures had been 18 such fires costing £½m.[8] Most school fires in the conurbations of Merseyside,

'We've called you in to help with this appalling problem of truancy.'

Manchester, Birmingham or London were deliberately started by young people at weekends or the evenings, and bomb or fire hoaxes during the school day were even more common. A contemporary primary school which had taken two years to build could be a smouldering wreckage barely two hours after the fire-bug had struck.

Vandalism in urban schools was pandemic and astronomically costly; an estimated £15m of damage was done in 1977. In 1974 the ILEA Chief Architect cited one comprehensive which spent £50 per day – £1,000 per month – on repairing broken glass alone.[9] Visitors to new urban school buildings were shocked at their rapid deterioration – ranging from the graffiti on the corridor lockers, or the orange peel and coke cans in the biology pool, to the conflagration which had gutted a staffroom or stockroom. Glasgow education officials estimated that

[6] two new primary schools each year could be constructed with the money they spent on repairing vandalism. Such statistics were mostly conveyed in confidential reports to education committees, for most policy-makers and teachers feared that publicity would have an immediately contagious effect in making school damage worse. Unfortunately this low-key approach also inhibited anti-vandalism campaigns. So glass continued to be smashed in classroom windows or false fire alarm calls, playground seats survived a week or two, and only constant vigilance by patrolling teachers prevented pipes being pulled away from walls or lavatories stuffed with anything to hand. A school might well employ a full-time plumber, glazier or carpenter. There was no such thing as a safe cloakroom. Children distrusted other children; secondary pupils, especially in the larger comprehensives, carried their coats and satchels everywhere.

Little, apparently, could be done about disruptive or violent pupils. Despite constant horse-trading between heads on the principle 'you take my problem and I'll take yours', very often there was nowhere else to send an unruly teenager. Suspension was an option frequently denied to heads of secondary schools on grounds of legality, professional pride or political acceptability. 'Don't rock the comprehensive boat'; teachers were warned, or 'don't say you can't cope, it will hinder your promotion.' The suspension of primary pupils was unthinkable. Special school places were scarce. The vagaries of professional politics, social work fashion, educational and children's legislation loaded the problems onto ordinary schools. The two persistent vandals who broke into the headmaster's study, ruined the carpet with ink and used his desk as a lavatory were accepted back after several weeks. An assaulted teacher might writhe in embarrassed anger: he could do nothing when the convicted offender, given a supervision order but sent home because no residential place could be found, sauntered nonchalantly back into the classroom.

Despite police complaints about the lack of burglar alarms in schools, many education authorities found it cheaper to replace stolen or vandalized school property than meet the high premiums and security demands of an insurance policy to protect the school. Not uncommonly in the newer schools, one master key, easily stolen from a teacher's desk, fitted every room or cupboard. The complexity of the school caretaker's task was much increased under such circumstances, particularly in the large secondary schools where expensive science laboratories, closed-circuit television or audio-visual aids rooms were an Aladdin's Cave for the thief. Tactics like rationing keys, setting up vandal patrols, laminating windows, or painting drainpipes with non-drying paint to mark the clothes of the intruders all proved remarkably ineffective. The problem was so chronic in Newcastle that

its education officer declared that society had turned full circle to a
scale of vandalism and arson characteristic of 1900, when anyone in the
city hiring a school for a wedding or function was required to employ
two policemen to keep order.[10]

Education was news. A second wave of books appeared, following
those of the early 1950s which had exposed the 'blackboard jungle' in
secondary modern schools.[11] Television offered sharp, timely
documentary coverage of educational issues. The slow progress of the
Tyndale enquiry was prominently featured on television news and
media coverage could make an academic research controversy about
the 'progressive' primary classroom a matter of popular concern.[12] The
comic possibilities of the urban staffroom and classroom, or the daily
saga of a school caretaker's life were sentimentalized in television
serials. Leila Berg's highly-coloured book about the ill-fated Rising Hill
comprehensive school,[13] at the beginning of the period under review,
or the realistic portrait of life in a comprehensive in 1975, given by
Hunter Davies in *The Creighton Report* ten years later,[14] were as grip-
ping as fiction. There were cliff-hanging accounts in the educational
press of the threatened survival or HMI inspection of the progressive
secondary school Countesthorpe College. Trendy editorial teams
flooded the market with messianic paperbacks by the radicals of US
urban education.[15]

Local newspapers were eager for educational 'stories', especially
those featuring rows over comprehensive plans, the debate about
educational standards, the multiracial classroom or progressive
primary school. One newspaper was accused of being an *agent pro-
vocateur* after smuggling a reporter (herself a qualified teacher) into a
teaching job at an unruly London comprehensive.[16] A sensational
exposé of classroom conditions followed this 'inside story'. More sustained, less inflammatory coverage was given to the urban school by
newly-launched magazines like *Forum*, which was committed to
unstreaming and comprehensivism, by the sociological weekly *New
Society*, which began life in 1960, or by *The Guardian* newspaper, widely
read by teachers, which introduced regular education pages. Journalists were heavily criticized for their unbalanced reportage.[17] But they
complained that inside the school system too many people had given
up conceding the truth and got into the public relations habit of playing
down bad news. Teachers were urged not to cry 'stinking fish', so as
not to make the job even more intolerable. Inspectors remained mute,
for reasons we shall discuss. Politicians murmured 'don't rock the
comprehensives'.

Of course all schools, especially the city comprehensives because of
their size, were like the curate's egg – good in parts. Calm might reign
in the science block, while across in the school-leaver's huts a teacher

[8] battled for classroom co-operation from raucous young adults. It was as difficult to find out whether a school was really any good as to assess the professional competence of a family doctor. You found out by word of mouth, or the hard way.

With all the conflicting reports and impressions, no one in the end could tell how serious and widespread the urban school crisis really was. No national reporting system assessed the schools. HM Inspectors were allegedly more active in inspecting lavatories than classrooms. Heads and senior staff hesitated to confess that they were losing their grip, they and the politicians shamed young teachers into collusive silence. At national level, synods of researchers, evaluators, curriculum developers and policy advisers, convinced that there were purely educational solutions, academically disputed issues of questionable relevance while an urban earthquake rumbled beneath them.

Teachers were under stress. A Cambridge researcher in 1975 monitored the cardiac rate of teachers experiencing crises of classroom control.[18] A Friday afternoon with difficult fourth formers could raise the heart rate from 70 to 120 beats a minute. Actuarial records for 1976 showed that deaths among men teachers had more than doubled, and early retirement on a breakdown pension was three times more frequent than it had been ten years earlier.

At the height of the staffing shortage, newspapers jovially reported that the biggest truants were teachers themselves.[19] Even hardened Australians, men 'supply' teachers sent to a different school each morning to cover staff absence, were unable to quell classroom turmoil – and were going home to bed in the afternoon with 'battle fatigue', or sliding off to the cinema. Educational psychologists pointed out that truanting pupils received counselling and social work help, while for the teachers there was nothing. The psychologists put themselves forward as staffroom therapists with whom teachers might discuss their professional traumas and disturbing classroom experiences.

Marked reluctance by teachers to begin or continue their careers in the city schools was nationally observed. Teachers from elsewhere in Scotland would not go to work in tough Glasgow, which by 1972 had 10 per cent permanent vacancies in its secondary schools. Similar reluctance to undertake urban classroom teaching was widely reported, not only in British cities, but also from New York, Sydney, Auckland and Toronto. The effect of teacher shortage in distorting the curriculum and school timetable was more devastating than crude statistics suggested. Technical, craft, mathematics and science teachers were virtually unobtainable: even head of department posts were left unfilled.

British urban teachers had fallen badly behind in pay; the relative

salary position of all teachers had been falling steadily since 1936.[20] At
that time a teacher's salary was 91 per cent of that enjoyed by a member
of parliament. In 1967 it had fallen to 43 per cent. A young teacher
starting in 1973 would work for ten years before achieving the average
manual wage. A Ruskin College research project, commissioned by a
national union, showed that teachers were earning less than other
professionals throughout their careers, the gap being especially wide
among the over-35-year-olds.[21] It was the 25- to 40-year-old teachers
who led the diaspora from the urban classroom, and indeed from the
teaching profession itself. Women teachers complained they had to
delay babies until they were too old to enjoy them. Some young
teachers, wincing under pupil gibes that they could earn more as a
waitress or minicab driver, took such jobs.

'. . . and if you promise to stay for a whole year we'll give you a Scale 5.'

A 1974 survey found large numbers of teachers among the young
professionals joining the middle income flight from cities.[22] This was a
phenomenon which had been observed world wide. Teachers gave as
their main reasons for leaving the city and the urban classroom: marriage and housing difficulties, promotion, dissatisfaction with teaching or their schools, and need to widen their experience. Like other
white-collar employees, teachers were refusing attractive urban posts
because of inflated housing costs and the stress of the commuter
life-style. Their average daily journey to work was, for instance, $17\frac{1}{2}$
miles in London.

By 1974 teacher turnover in London was so high that one teacher in
three was leaving each year. London's turnover, at 29·8 per cent, was
twice the national average. Urban classrooms could only be staffed by
enticing young, inexperienced college leavers temporarily towards the

bright lights of the capital. But they soon left, for marriage, easier jobs, or because they faced a housing crisis. Most teachers were not born locally, or resident locally during teacher training, and therefore did not qualify for public housing. Indeed, some did not want the 'social death' of council tenancy. The cheap bedsitter disappeared as the private rented sector shrank, hastened by Government legislation, and property prices boomed. Yet the extraordinary inflation of house prices during the late 1960s made it at first difficult, and later impossible, for poorly paid teachers to get an initial foothold in the housing market. Some squatted. But most, reflecting an occupational preference for house ownership, sought teaching jobs in the countryside or outer suburbs where they could afford to buy a house. Many teachers, as well as politicians, administrators or inspectors who were parents, moved their families out to the suburbs, considering that children were not safe in the playground and did not learn any more in the urban classroom. Even a payment awarded nationally to teachers working in the disadvantaged urban classroom, or the additional London allowance, failed to dissuade teachers from deserting the cities.

The renamed training colleges, or 'colleges of education', expanded and boomed with activity during the early years of staffing crisis. Many new colleges opened. But most of the colleges were placed deep in the countryside or the remote suburbs. Paradoxically, although dozens of academic courses were designed and numerous books on curriculum were written by college lecturers, contact between colleges and experienced urban teachers in their classrooms was negligible. Colleges were too preoccupied with their own expansion and the need to convince their university colleagues that educational studies were academically respectable.

The colleges and university departments churned out wave after wave of young teachers who nevertheless annually deserted the urban classroom in such numbers that the training task seemed endless. That comfortable assumption was painfully reversed when in 1976 the government imposed drastic cuts in initial training places and began closing down many individual colleges. Even as late as 1973 LEA recruiting officers were globe-trotting in search of teachers. Ecstatic advertisements offered teacher training to mature entrants for city schools – attracting police officers, miners, nurses, hoteliers, actresses, opera singers and countless housewives with teenage children. These enthusiastic recruits, having been promised employment in a fruitful second career, were cruelly left outside the school gates upon qualifying in 1976, when full employment opportunities for the urban teacher vanished almost overnight.

During the years of stress the young woman teacher, arriving in the city and confronted by a turbulent classroom, was dismayed to find

she had completely lost contact with her college. She was a professional orphan on an educational conveyor belt. She was a cypher on
the hieroglyphic timetable of some giant comprehensive; or, dropped
anonymously into a volatile multi-ethnic primary school, was given a
task for which she was quite unprepared. Young teachers in surveys
complained that they had not been taught at college to teach junior
children to read. Their culture shock was profound when, in the
classrooms of decaying cities and industrial towns, they met children
who invited them genially to 'Fuck off' and appeared unteachable.[23]
Yet the young teacher found her senior colleagues themselves were
often under such stress and so demoralized that they could offer little
professional help in the early months of classroom life. The important
James Report into teacher education in 1972 castigated the 'professional negligence' of headmasters and senior staff.[24] Young teachers
were given full timetables, difficult classes, a cursory chat and an
occasional cup of tea, instead of receiving a proper programme of
support in their first year. The James Committee prescribed instead
that each young teacher be released from the classroom for one day a
week in the probationary year; to prepare lesson materials, observe
other colleagues, learn about the urban background or just draw
breath. It also recommended that experienced teachers should be
given a term's secondment every seven years to research, work in
industry or convalesce by travel. But the economic crisis delayed action
on this valuable report except in a few experimental education
authorities. So young teachers continued to be propelled into the
urban classroom as pedagogic cannon fodder.

Young teachers were now a majority in the urban classroom, often
sharing the pop culture, fashion interests and politics of their own
pupils. In 1974 63 per cent of London's teachers were under 35, and 34
per cent were 21–25. Not surprisingly, professional manners and style
changed emphatically during the urban classroom crisis. Fastidious,
even objectionable, demands traditionally made by head teachers concerning the appearance, dress or deportment of younger colleagues
were no longer heard. Young teachers had a limited amount of spare
cash and could not afford party dresses. Anyway the primary classroom was a messy, practical arena suited to working clothes. An urban
head teacher could not afford to criticize the class teacher, for whatever
he, the parents or the pupils themselves thought privately, any barely
competent teacher was a valuable colleague whom you certainly didn't
go out of your way to offend.

Undeniably, these trends occasionally led to problems of classroom
authority and control, or confusion between personal and professional
identity.[25] The fashionably militant or sexually provocative young
teacher of teenagers ran the risk of inflaming passion, mutual infatua-

tion or classroom indiscipline. Love affairs between young teachers and girl sixth formers gained such press notoriety that in 1975 the National Union of Teachers, other unions following suit, issued guidelines which specifically barred teachers from having sex with their pupils. Officials explained that while it would be hypocrisy to say that 16- to 18-year-old girls were not attractive, young teachers were nevertheless advised to seek their girlfriends away from the classroom.

The indefatigable Marje Proops, a national figure and agony columnist of the *Daily Mirror*, informed her mesmerized readers: 'Teachers have told me how sexy girls pursue them both in and out of school. Schoolgirls have actually asked me to tell them how they can get their teacher into bed. A code for teachers may be a good idea – and reassuring for parents.'

A predominantly youthful, urban teaching profession also placed greater emphasis on women's liberation and sexual freedom. It was not surprising therefore to find homosexuality publicly championed in union meetings; and press publicity for a teacher who had openly held hands and kissed his male friend on the way home from school, and impenitently discussed these sexual proclivities with girl pupils.[26] Yet apart from a glaring minority, most young urban teachers were not professionally irresponsible. Waller has described how a hundred years ago the schoolmistress in the small American town was expected to go to bed early and do her courting only on Sundays. For the young city teacher of the 1970s it was very much the same. She was likely to go to bed early on week nights, restricting her love-life to weekends; but less for reasons of moral propriety than because the daily emotional and physical strain of the urban classroom demanded peak athletic condition for survival.

Changes in professional lifestyle and career patterns, and a generation gap in the staffroom transformed teacher politics.[27] Differences ran deep. Older teachers already owned their own houses, which rapidly gained value during this period; young teachers scraped for a mortgage deposit, while their professional poverty was further sharpened by high rents.[28] The gap in life-style between urban teachers themselves widened continually. Staffroom relationships polarized over such matters as curriculum, discipline, school organization and internal politics. Older teachers, tired after decades of stress, suspiciously resisted curriculum changes and other innovations, such as counselling, proposed by their younger colleagues or even the headmaster.[29] They predicted that the team teaching or mixed ability innovation would be left in their lap after the younger staff proposing them had left for greener pastures or promotion, or that they would have to sustain an experiment they had originally opposed as possibly weakening social control in the school. The departed 25- to 40-year-olds, the 'lost generation' whose chairs stood empty in the staffroom, might have mediated these quarrels and smoothed edgy tempers – but they had gone. The older teachers were often right. Many young teachers leap-frogged from school to school for the slightest promotion or salary advantage. A post of responsibility, carrying an additional hundred pounds a year, could reasonably be expected after a year of urban teaching. If you taught craft, music or religious education in an urban secondary school, you might lead your own department within two terms. Before the war, older teachers resentfully remarked, it had not been unusual to wait ten years for your first promotion.

Not surprisingly, such feverish staff turnover often resulted in teachers failing to identify with the children they taught. Cases were recorded of urban secondary schools where the average length of stay for teachers was seven months. Primary children as well as exam pupils in the comprehensives could suffer as many as twenty changes of teacher in a term, to the disruption of classroom life and curriculum progress. Worse still, the social cohesiveness of each school community was visibly sabotaged.

The hierarchy of headmaster and senior staff, with their administrative duties and comfortable offices, nicknamed the 'gerontocracy along the corridor', was often derided and disliked. At the same time the 'collegial' staffroom, in which the headmaster discussed all policy with senior staff, grew increasingly common, particularly in the larger comprehensive schools. Teachers spent hours lobbying and politicking over school decisions, in a miniature democracy of endless committee meetings and a vortex of after-school bureaucracy. Equally time-consuming, but far less productive, were the staffroom cliques, brewing coffee and dissent on the Bunsen burner in the science lab, in the metalwork shop or housecraft flat.

Inter-generational friction among teachers became explosive when transferred to union politics.[30] The main teacher unions fragmented. An NUT splinter group, Rank and File, formed in 1968, was soon producing its own newspaper.[31] Politically, Rank and File was mixed, containing a high proportion of international socialists, some Marxists and Trotskyists and even a few communists. The active membership of Rank and File, an estimated nucleus of 150 teachers, was concentrated in cities like Liverpool and London. It was they, and young urban teachers in other small organizations, who typically voted their support for schoolchildren on strike. Radical young teachers produced their own samizdat magazines and underground press.[32] The 'new English' movement in London launched *Teaching London Kids*, and other groups, including the educational psychologists, had their publications, with names like *Hard Cheese* or *Black Bored*.

Historical tensions often propel individual heroes into public view;

such was the background of the Christopher Searle affair.[33] A left-winger, teaching English in an East End secondary school, Searle encouraged his pupils to write angry political poems and stories about local life. His headmaster, author of the standard British text on the teacher and the law,[34] thought the respect of pupils for the authority of the school had been weakened. Searle was sacked, then afterwards reinstated, amid much publicity. As time went by, such confrontations became unnecessary. Teachers like Searle, whose perceived commitment to the urban child led them to reject the traditional classroom, were increasingly able to find public employment running adventure playgrounds or alternative schools within the system.

Rivalry between the teachers' organizations sharpened.[35] Three new teacher organizations were formed: the reorganized Union of Women Teachers, the Professional Association of Teachers, and one wholly Welsh-speaking union. The PAT, founded in 1970, soon claimed 6,000 members who disapproved of the militancy of other unions and pledged themselves never to go on strike. Hilarious shotgun marriages took place, made necessary by new laws against sexual discrimination but also improving negotiating strength. One example was the conjunction of the National Association of Schoolmasters, noted for their male chauvinism, and the Union of Women Teachers.[36] By 1977 their membership had grown to 90,000.

Professional combativeness among the dissatisfied teachers grew. During the salary campaign of 1973 feeling ran so high that a rally of 2,000 London teachers at the Central Hall, Westminster turned into a bear garden.[37] Proceedings were disrupted by left wingers who pulled out microphone cables and tried to take over the meeting, bringing on darkness, scuffles, punches and chaos. Executive members could not make their speeches, six Labour MPs prematurely abandoned the platform, and police stood anxiously by – although in the event they did not make any arrests.

Teacher militancy had finally reached fever pitch when in 1974 more than 15,000 teachers marched in procession from Hyde Park to the House of Commons in a salary protest. Price inflation and low salaries had emptied the city classrooms of teachers. The secondary schools system in London and other major cities was in imminent danger of collapse.

The teachers who marched expressed a common viewpoint, and by no means conformed to the popular stereotype of the left-wing agitator. Certainly, control of teacher politics in London and other cities was in the hands of communist teachers, who were thus able to influence policy; but the communist teacher-politicians enjoying power in London, and elsewhere, were classroom traditionalists rather than revolutionaries.[38] They were depicted even by their own Rank and

File, for example, as conventional stuffed shirts believing in both
staffroom and party hierarchies. Following demonstrations by the
teachers in a climate of public sympathy, a major review of teachers'
salaries was authorized. The Houghton Award quickly followed,
increasing the average pay of a teacher in 1975 by 26 per cent. The
salaries of head teachers were boosted by one half; primary heads
joined the top ten of British professional salary earners. Comprehensive headmasters commanding £10,000 per year achieved the
economic status of managing directors.

But Britain was suffering from a chronic fiscal crisis. Inflation still ran
at 20 per cent in 1976. Schools all over the country began to complain
that a 70 per cent rise in the cost of paper left insufficient money for
basic materials;[39] yet the crisis dictated ever greater scrutiny of public
expenditure, especially in education, which already took the major
share of local authority spending. Furthermore, the teachers, whose
salaries were the largest item in any education budget, had now
become an expensive commodity. Fewer urban teachers were needed
in the cities with their declining population. Low resignation rates,
coupled with attractive salaries, meant that teaching posts were easily
filled. Promotion opportunities dried up overnight and teachers
moved less frequently. The number of teachers actually employed, or
training as students in colleges, was drastically reduced. For the first
time in two decades there was a labour market which favoured the
employer.

At the same time the public and professional mood hardened, particularly in government circles, where a groundswell among the electorate and employers was felt. Demands were heard that the relatively
well paid teaching profession should expose itself to public and inspec-
torial accountability. There were strong pressures even from the moderate left for a curriculum counter-reformation, more attention to
standards, and the assessment of pupil and teacher performance.

2 The EPA myth

Debate on the urban classroom crisis circled around confused concepts of educational equality and opportunity. Teachers, politicians and administrators examined innumerable real or imaginary constraints allegedly leading to classroom failure or success. Explanations ranged from family size to lead pollution in cities. But for the thirty years after 1945 British educational sociologists were obsessed by the links between social mobility and the schools.[1] Why did so few sons of dockers climb the educational pyramid to Oxford or Cambridge? Academic achievement in the classroom, well paid professional or Civil Service employment and the elitest life-style were regarded as the highest good that education could obtain.

Unfortunately, in pursuing a meritocratic dream even in the comprehensive school, educationists looked at the classroom concomitants of urban crisis, rather than studying employment, housing or population strategy. Consequently educational 'solutions', myths and palliatives were extemporized to paper over widening cracks in the walls of the urban classroom. Psycholinguistics, compensatory curriculum, the EPA myth, managerialism, open-plan or system building: every avenue, it seemed, was explored by crowded bandwagons except the urban street itself.[2]

Geographical patterns of educational inequality between inner cities, conurbations, regions, suburbs and countryside corresponded to the map of social class.[3] The commonly accepted formula for analysing social class was a classification devised by the Registrar General in

1911 for comparing differences in life expectancy according to occupation. It was agreed that any social class label equated only roughly with
income, status or 'morality'. When should an occupational group, for
instance, change social class category? In 1975 the best paid one-third
of manual workers earned more than the lowest paid one-third of
professional workers. Did the high wages and affluent life-style of the
car worker, asked sociologists, make him middle class? In 1975 the
Registrar General altered social class categories, promoting barmen
and bus conductors into Class 4. School teachers were left in Class 2
with a hotch-potch of non-manual workers including sales managers,
farmers and the Prime Minister.

The Registrar General's five broad categories in social class in 1976
were:

Class 1 762,000 families: professional men (and company secretaries)

Class 2 3,145,000 families: including creative artists, airline
pilots

Class 3 7,745,000 families: skilled workers and restaurateurs

Class 4 2,966,000 families: semi-skilled workers (warehouse-
men and barmen)

Class 5 1,205,000 families: unskilled labourers, ticket collectors
and stevedores.

Variations in the educational achievement of children according to
where they lived geographically could be convincingly linked with
their social class rating.[4] The percentage of local children entering sixth
form or the university could be predicted from the social class composition of the local education authority. Indeed, the wisest advice
to an unconceived child was: become the son of a professional or
managerial person in the suburbs, Home Counties or a country town,
but do not choose as your birth place a council estate, immigrant
neighbourhood or most parts of the inner city. Suburban Solihull, for
instance, outstripped all other education authorities in 1973, in having
36 per cent of its geographical population in Class 1. Solihull also
won the higher education stakes that year, 18½ per cent of pupils
gaining university places. Privileged boroughs and counties contrasted sharply in their track record for examinations when compared
with deprived LEAs in the conurbations of the north or the inner
cities.[5]

Understandably, but missing the main target, the Child Poverty
Action Group and other British lobbyists accused the schools system
of apparently increasing or perpetuating inequalities between rich
and poor. Differences in the achievement of children from different
social classes enlarged during the years of compulsory schooling. The

lobbyists were concerned for instance that the General Household Survey in 1973 showed that the child from an unskilled background was fifteen times more likely to be a nonreader at 7 years of age than the child from a professional background.[6]

No one was helped by the varying definitions of disadvantage or deprivation which held the stage. An extreme moral relativism was revived and popularized by cultural pluralists and sociologists of knowledge, for whom everything became a matter of how you saw it, echoing an exclamation of Gandhi, who on seeing the slums of East End London in the 1930s remarked, 'But this is luxury compared to Calcutta where they sleep on the streets'. Sociological study of the combat behaviour of US soldiers in the second world war had given rise to 'reference group' theory.[7] Individuals, it was argued, perceived themselves as deprived or privileged only by comparing themselves with people whom they saw as important. Some sociologists therefore went so far as to assert that all cultures were equally valuable, there being even a rich 'culture of poverty'. A concept of 'relative deprivation' combined neatly with this theory of cultural pluralism.[8] Adherents argued that any notion of educational deprivation, deficit or disadvantage was as damaging as the belief that penicillin or piped water were essential to civilized living.

Such sophistry apart, some compassionate and intelligent campaigns did change the official view of deprivation or disadvantage. Persistent efforts by protest groups succeeded in achieving recognition for minorities like the 'one parent family', where disadvantaged children faced difficulties formerly not appreciated.

By any commonsense definition of disadvantage, regional inequality hit hard in the classroom.[9] Urban school children in the inner cities and northern conurbations had the dice progressively loaded against them. Living standards and educational provision rapidly deteriorated towards the north of England;[10] average wages, unemployment figures, the length of doctors' or hospital lists, the amount of derelict or substandard housing all compared unfavourably with the wealthier south. There were fewer sixth form places, nursery school places or new school buildings in progress. Education authorities in these deprived regions and conurbations also suffered from the self-perpetuating momentum of a cycle of disadvantage. An impoverished urban authority like Wigan, with a local tradition of early school leaving, found that its rate support grant and central government assistance were calculated bewilderingly on past achievement in encouraging pupils to stay on at school. But they needed more not less money to create an educational climate favourable to extended schooling.

Teachers in the classroom remained surprisingly ignorant of the

anger and anxiety frequently expressed by local politicians and educational administrators in council chambers and committee rooms up
and down the country over Whitehall's deployment of the 'rate support grant'.[11] Yet this cryptically titled annual subsidy was crucial to
local government, and especially education departments as the
heaviest spenders. Local government income for educational purposes
traditionally had two sources: a) a domestic rate, raised locally; and
b) the rate support grant from central government which came in two
forms: i) a direct subsidy to the ratepayer and ii) a resources element,
bringing local authorities with rates income considerably below
average up to a reasonable level. Until the early 1970s the poorer urban
education authorities were often hard-pressed in finding money for
their schools. Local factors of industrial activity, social class composition and housing tenure patterns inevitably influenced the financial
performance of each education authority.[12] If the product of a penny
rate was low, the rate support grant was low and the classroom
suffered. But in the early 1970s both the local rating system and the rate
support grant were at last redefined and calculated using a formula
which favoured the urban education authority.

Even then, the rate support grant was not the major influence
in determining what money was spent on children, classrooms
and schools. Local authorities themselves enjoyed considerable
powers. If their political convictions and electoral support persuaded them, politicians on the education committee could spend
as much money as they could raise locally on the classroom. The
top spending urban education authority, Inner London, enjoyed
an unusual privilege after its formation in 1965, which allowed an
education rate precept to be issued without any direct accountability
to the voters.

Variations in local authority spending on classroom materials and
books during the years of cost inflation were revealing.[13] In 1970 the
Association of Education Committees recommended that up to 1974
primary children 9 years old or younger would need £4.25 each spent
annually on classroom materials, and a book allowance (not library
books) of £2.20. Similarly, they recommended that secondary children
would need £7.50 each spent on materials and £3.50 for books. Depressingly, there was widespread failure to achieve that minimum standard, and the resulting inequalities were considerable. In 1971, Welsh
primary children in the depressed seaport of Swansea had only 59p
spent on their books, while neighbouring children in Montgomeryshire received £4.06. Montgomeryshire was not a disadvantaged urban
education authority: but neither was its social class structure dominated by managerial or professional parents or industries providing
lucrative rates. Simply, in Montgomeryshire parents and authorities

were willing to dip generously in their pockets for their children. Five years later, in 1976, discrepancies between education authorities, not necessarily favouring rural but generally favouring suburban children, were just as great as ever. The 1976 league of spending for the national primary classroom showed Inner London leading, with £15.40 for each primary child, followed by rural Powys with £11.21; and Cumbria the lowest with £5.18. Gloucestershire spent the least on its secondary pupils, while the ILEA, massively assisted by rates, urban aid, EPA support and fewer checks on its stewardship, again led nationally with an outstanding £36.96 for each secondary pupil; Harrow, the runner up, was far behind, spending £19.65.

Although urban children in the regions, inner cities and deprived boroughs in conurbations comprised the majority of disadvantaged children in Britain, they were not all of them. Distinctive minorities of disadvantaged children were found outside the urban setting. Rural poverty might be uncommon in Britain, compared with the US and its hillbilly farmers, or Australia, where dairy farm workers lived in old cars; but whatever the quality of their classroom life, the children of low-paid agricultural workers in East Anglia and similar counties had to be counted among the traditionally disadvantaged. Gypsy families too – usually found in rural settings but sometimes camping under urban motorways – increasingly aroused anxiety. The six thousand gypsy children, who together would have filled Eton, Harrow and ten other major public schools, were receiving less than satisfactory educational attention.

Mia Kellmer Pringle, whose research was to be influential in revolutionizing professional opinion, declared that one group of children laboured under multiple disadvantage and were virtually 'born to fail'.[14] These children were handicapped by (a) poverty, (b) bad housing and (c) having grown up in a one parent family or family that was too large. Children 'born to fail' were easily recognized. They had often not been given proper care as babies. They had more often needed the special services of a children's department, mental health or education department, were more prone to illness and accident and were on average three-and-a-half years behind in their reading age at 11 years old.[15] Had they been evenly distributed up and down the country, two children 'born to fail' would have been found in each classroom. In fact they were crowded into urban classrooms in certain conurbations and the inner cities. The largest numbers of seriously disadvantaged children were found in Scotland, with one in 10 children 'born to fail', compared with one in 12 in northern England and one in 47 in southern England. Significantly, only one in 25 of the disadvantaged children came from middle-class homes.

Psychiatrists specializing in the epidemiology of childhood illness

had discovered that the inner urban child exhibited a higher than
average rate of psychiatric disorder. The leading British investigator
into childhood emotional disturbance in the community, Michael
Rutter, found one-quarter of inner London 8-year-olds showed signs
of psychiatric disorder.[16] Their symptoms ranged from sleep disturbance, neurotic crying or fear of school to chronic fighting or stealing,
and often culminated in classroom behaviour which made both the
disturbed child and other children unhappy, hampering educational
progress.

Rutter compared the London children, leaving out immigrants, with
Isle of Wight children living in a predominantly rural setting.[17] He
found that only 12 per cent of the Isle of Wight children presented eight
psychiatric symptoms compared with 25.4 per cent of inner London
children. Like the child development researchers, Rutter explained
higher rates of psychiatric disorder among urban children by multiple
disadvantage: (1) family disturbance when the parents quarrelled or
split up; (2) family deviancy, when mothers had psychiatric disorders
or fathers had criminal records; (3) social circumstances, where London families were large and their homes more often overcrowded; (4)
unsatisfactory school experiences, through a high turnover of teachers
or influx of immigrant children. Later Rutter added that, in his view,
the quality of the school itself played an important role.

The late 1960s were years of national debate, verging on hysteria,
over reading standards and literacy. Repeated surveys of inner city
children showed that too many of them were retarded or backward in
their reading skills. Some 32,000 inner London 8-year-olds tested in an
official literacy survey between 1967 and 1969 proved poor readers
twice as often as the average British school child.[18] The average
8-year-old in inner London was six months behind the national average upon entering the junior school. There was evidence that national
performance in examinations was deteriorating in the conurbations
and improving elsewhere.

Among many reasons suggested for the low urban achievement was
a possibility that 'the intelligence or reasoning ability of London children generally is lower than that of children elsewhere'. This tentative
hypothesis, with its implications for urban classrooms everywhere in
the country, was politely ignored or dismissed as frivolity. In 1968 the
fallacy that disadvantaged children lived in identifiable geographical
districts and attended certain schools had not yet been questioned. The
simple genetic model of a 'cycle of disadvantage' had not yet been
challenged, nor had the genetic argument for self-renewal in the urban
classroom been exposed as a misconception. Thus for reasons explored
later, no outright diagnosis was made of the damaging effects of social
class migration.

[22]   Any such diagnosis, after all, would have repudiated a sacrosanct myth of the elasticity of intelligence of the social composition of school intakes. It would have threatened to revive the inaccurate metaphor of 'pool of ability', the idea that the amount of intelligence in the population was globally infinite. Intelligence, the prevailing view ran, was a flexible attribute, not fixed like a number plate to your forehead at birth. You could do wonders with 'less able' children. The suggestion of a ceiling of attainment lowered aspiration and was fatalistic. An optimistic view of children's potential, however misguidedly held, was an essential working belief for the easily demoralized teacher.

'We will have to have it enlarged so that everybody can have their name on.'

The question that seemed most pressing to the educational mandarins was: how could teachers in their classrooms interrupt the vicious circle of urban poverty and low educational achievement? The influential Plowden Committee of 1967,[19] reporting on primary schools, praised highly the informal British classroom and its curriculum. The committee proposed a completely new intervention strategy for urban primary schools of 'positive discrimination'. Experimental projects,

extra-favourable treatment and resources should be given to schools in
designated 'educational priority areas'.

The first 'action research' EPA project to be initiated had a derisory budget. A sum of £175,000 was allocated for a first wave of EPA projects, in five centres: London, Birmingham, Liverpool, West Riding and Dundee. Solutions might not be easy, claimed A. H. Halsey, professor and sociologist who had specialized in researching education and social mobility; but during the three-year life of each project, innovations might be discovered which would be constructive for planning a long-term programme. The government also made £16m available for rebuilding primary schools in 'educational priority areas', giving priority to inner city rebuilding in all subsequent school improvement programmes; a policy which proved ill-advised.

Teachers in 'schools of exceptional difficulty' qualified for extra pay, and, later still, for 'stress' payments. LEAs were given discretion to create additional senior teaching posts in schools which they regarded as being in the EPA category, and powers to assist schools in downtown neighbourhoods with extra staff, equipment, ancillary help or even minor building.

The Plowden Report suggested eight criteria for identifying 'educational priority areas': social class composition; family size; overcrowding and sharing of dwellings; supplements in cash or kind from the state; poor school attendance and truancy; children unable to speak English; retarded, disturbed and handicapped pupils in the schools; incomplete families.

Government circulars suggested further factors, such as 'multiple deprivation', when several disadvantages combined in a poor general environment. Urban education authorities themselves had considerable discretion in building up EPA criteria. In Liverpool the education department collaborated unusually with other social services in compiling an 'Index of Social Malaise', a comprehensive list of deprivation factors; this list included, in decreasing order of importance: crime – theft: possession orders; electricity board entry warrants; children deloused; unemployment; crime – assault; welfare conference cases; crime – burglary – debtors; crime – miscellaneous; adults mentally ill; and job instability.

The leading figure in the Liverpool EPA project, Eric Midwinter, came to dominate the national scene through his colourful personality.[20] Formerly a college of education lecturer, he brought flair, enthusiasm and an evangelical sense of mission to his project; he became known as 'the man who brought music-hall into the classroom', or even 'Mr EPA'. He wrote prolifically, spoke movingly and was a fertile, endlessly energetic innovator. Midwinter and his team provided a play-mobile and teaching kits for Liverpool pre-school children. Primary children learned practical maths in a classroom supermarket installed by the Tesco chain. Midwinter, pursuing his favourite theme of 'the community school', involved Liverpool parents and public in a 'Support our Schools week', with motorcades, giant mardi-gras puppets marching down the streets, and the guest appearance of the comedian Ken Dodd. Urban children, asserted Midwinter, should have lessons and exams on how to run a football team, rent a flat, deal with angry landlords, cope with being on the dole, or deciding how many children to have.[21]

Midwinter claimed to be a progressive radical working within the system (he consequently opposed the Liverpool free school – free school supporters in turn stigmatized him as a pawn of the establishment). A. H. Halsey, as national policy co-ordinator, manipulated the strings of central government, but Midwinter's extraordinary charisma caused the Liverpool project to dominate the national stage and educational media. In the long run, however, his constant theme of the community school and corresponding curriculum, widely influential during the EPA epoch, tended to lead teachers to a naïve preoccupation with educational solutions.

The Midwinter emphasis on community schools, linking the classroom, the teacher, the college of education, the family and the total economy was reflected in a flood of provocative publications from Liverpool. In a first EPA Project Report Halsey, bemused by the superficial sparkle of the Liverpool project, asserted that the EPA intervention strategy had been highly successful.[22] It was an error of judgement; the uncritical advocacy of Halsey and others diverted fashionable academic and political opinion, and crucial funds, towards educational palliatives and away from total urban strategy. Teachers, administrators and politicians alike had as yet little expertise, compassionate tradition of interest or personal stake in the inner city. So when Halsey offered these seven preliminary conclusions they were therefore widely accepted.

(1) A geographically-defined EPA school was socially and administratively viable.
(2) Pre-school with the active involvement of parents was an outstanding device for raising educational standards.
(3) The community school had powerful implications for community regeneration.
(4) There were practical ways of improving the partnership between families and schools.
(5) There were also practical ways to improve the quality of teaching.

(6) Action research was an effective method of policy formulation
and practical innovation.
(7) The educational priority area was an important, limited part of a
comprehensive social movement towards community development or redevelopment.

Even that final recommendation was not the revolutionary recipe it
seemed. Halsey and his supporters principally had in mind the vigorous community politics being pursued in Liverpool at that time by the
controlling Liberal politicians, and not any total urban strategy.

Not everyone, however, was as happy as Halsey, Midwinter, the
EPA teams and their government patrons. Immediately after the
Plowden Report, the veteran urban sociologist working in Liverpool,
John Barron Mays, attacked the EPA policy as a diversion from poverty, 'like trying to eliminate an endemic disease by making some of
the patients more comfortable'.[23] He was later to be triumphantly
vindicated.

Early opposition to Plowden came from progressive sociolinguists,
philosophers and sociologists who disliked the notions of 'compensatory' education or 'deficit' culture.[24] But their criticisms rested rather
on a narrow platform of cultural relativism than on any case for broad
urban strategy. In particular, sociologists argued that a community
curriculum as advocated by Midwinter blinkered both teachers and
children. This case, elegantly conceptualized by Michael F. D. Young
of the University of London Institute of Education, was bowdlerized
into political crudity by camp followers from the extreme Left.[25]
Regrettably, the academics seemed more interested in pursuing
Florentine vendettas in the corridors of the university than looking at
the urban classroom and its social background.

Early critics also complained that EPA projects failed completely to
investigate the quality of individual schools.[26] Admittedly, a time of
high teacher-turnover, sagging morale and classroom stress made
such sensitive research difficult. Head teachers and powerful unions
could and did sabotage attempts at comparing individual schools, as
demonstrated in the London borough of Tower Hamlets in 1967 when
head teachers halted an enquiry into delinquency in 'good schools and
bad schools'. Indeed, not until 1977 did the HM Inspectorate summon
confidence to rename a document originally called *Common Ground*
and issue it forthrightly as *Ten Good Schools*.[27]

Over a number of years public and professional doubt hardened.
Critics pointed out that only 150 schools, not the 10 per cent or 3,000
schools Plowden had thought would need an EPA rating, benefited by
the EPA building programme. Did not the research evidence in the
USA irrefutably suggest that compensatory educational strategies had

proved ineffective? Housing experts and town planners murmured uneasily, encouraging ministers to start talking about geographical priority areas rather than just educational ones – other people than teachers led a move away from the simple ecology of a model which had so far led the educational world to believe there were classroom solutions.[28]

The concluding report on the EPA projects sharply rejected the entire EPA philosophy, which stood condemned out of the mouths of its evaluators as diversionary and palliative, a piece of research legerdemain. Rigorous scrutiny by Jack Barnes of EPA curriculum innovation in London primary schools produced a politely damning verdict,[29] and Halsey recanted. Barnes had made a paradoxical discovery: accepting the original Plowden criteria for educational disadvantage most disadvantaged children were not found in educational priority areas. Furthermore, most children in the educational priority areas were not disadvantaged. Indeed, the children who did worst in EPA schools were those whose home circumstances were relatively privileged. Halsey, who had throughout seen EPA policy as a meritocratic aid, 'a legitimate attack within the long tradition on social inequality', revised his view, conceding that both the substance and tone of discussion had changed.

But it was in astonishing interviews with 47 primary head teachers of London EPA schools during 1968/69 Barnes uncovered the most disturbing revelation. Experienced head teachers in urban primary schools had completely failed to understand the urban background to the classroom crisis. They had been asked two simple questions. How did they see the EPA problem? And what did they think could be done about it? Barnes reported: 'Although the head teachers perceived the causes of their problem to be social, they all envisaged "educational" solutions to them. Further, the solutions they thought possible were relatively unambitious. Those heads who made suggestions largely wanted "more of the same" '. The classroom professionals like everyone else had neglected a key paragraph in the Plowden report which said, quite succinctly:

> sustained efforts should be made to diversify the social composition of the districts where priority schools are so that teachers and others who make an essential contribution to the life and public services of the neighbourhood are not excluded from them.

Alarmingly for everyone who hoped teachers would take a lead in demanding more coherent urban strategy, their professional elite placed 'changing the social composition of the intakes of EPA schools' unluckiest thirteenth, and last, in their priorities. No more damning indictment of the largest occupational group of professionals working daily in the deteriorating urban setting could be imagined. Teachers might be hard-working and under stress, but they had also branded themselves as complacent and short sighted. They had been indoctrin-

Head teachers' ranking of the Plowden Council's recommendations in terms of their helpfulness

Order		Mean rank
1	No class should have more than 30 children	1.9
2	Children in EPAs should be given a nursery class experience	4.2
3	It should be easier for EPAs to get teachers	5.7
4	There should be one teacher's aide for every two classes in EPAs	5.8
5	There should be extra books and equipment allowances in EPAs	6.0
6	Teachers in EPA schools should have a £120 salary allowance	6.3
7	EPA school buildings should be extensively modernized	6.3
8	There should be more money generally made available to EPA schools	7.2
9	Educational Social Workers should work in EPA schools	7.6
10	There should be more research into the needs of EPAs	8.5
11	EPA schools should have better links with the Colleges of Education	9.4
12	Teachers' centres should be provided in EPAs	10.3
13	There should be changes in the social composition of the intake of EPA schools	10.5

(Barnes, 1975)

ated and conceptually bamboozled by those who should have known better. Government policy and national experts had encouraged teachers to believe in EPAs, and they were professionally and psychologically remote from the important conclusion Barnes now urged upon them: 'The focus for our thinking should not be small areas within the inner city but the inner city as a whole', he declared. The EPA myth, that 'schools could compensate for society' through massive extra resources and educational solutions had been ostracized. But could the teachers, and head teachers, enlarge their urban vision and work to a broader solution?

3 Two housing nations

It was not only high teacher turnover and low professional morale that were at fault; housing and other policy trends had invisibly sabotaged the urban classroom. Unperceived by teachers and shrugged off by urban sociologists, a demographic landslide undermined city schools and community life.[1] It was the same in urban school systems all over the advanced world; social class drift, not straightforward population movement out of the cities for employment and housing in new towns or regions, was the unpublicized villain behind the urban classroom crisis. In Britain government strategy for relieving city stress or over-population by diverting jobs to the 'grey areas' of traditional social neglect and chronic unemployment seriously misfired. Planners, housing experts and teachers unwittingly reinforced the concept of social mobility through housing and schools. In doing so they set off a population exodus which impoverished the cities and larger towns.[2] London suffered the planned loss of one million people and several hundred thousand manufacturing jobs.[3] The capital remained an expanding market for office or services employment, for secretaries or bus drivers; but those were not the jobs the remaining workers wanted or had the skills to do. Other British cities losing jobs offered no alternative employment. Ensuring employment growth in Britain's depressed regions or populating new towns meant firmly discouraging business and industry from setting up or expanding in older cities. Government subsidies for developing economic life, Industrial Development Certificates (IDCs) or Office Development Permits (ODPs) became almost unobtainable.[4]

The densely-populated inner city was abandoned by the younger working class or professional family. These departing parents, moving out to new towns or suburban owner-occupation, had in the past provided community leadership in the cultural life of the urban village. Now they led the diaspora. As Nicholas Taylor wrote, 'the inner areas such as Stepney and Shoreditch, Bermondsey and Deptford, are increasingly being deserted by their traditional artisan leadership and are being left to degenerate into a lumpen-proletariat of hotel porters, kitchen staff, cleaners, the disabled and the unemployed. This raises problems for public participation in planning.'[5] Indeed it did. A property boom in the late 1960s put the average family house in or near the large city almost out of reach for the first-time buyer. Key workers like teachers or social workers, usually born and educated elsewhere, were given low priority on housing waiting lists. Consequently, as the urban crisis heightened most major cities were hit by a shortage of such workers. By 1973 public service jobs offering poor pay for shift work were critically under-staffed. London itself was short of 4,200 bus conductors and drivers, 8,000 Post Office workers and 4,500 policemen as well as hundreds of teachers for its schools.[6] Child population declined even faster than the grown-ups departed, since it was predominantly young families who moved. As we shall see, by 1977 empty classrooms and under-subscribed schools offered a further challenge just as teachers began to enjoy the renewed optimism brought by staffing stability and better salaries.

No one seemed to notice or care about what was happening to urban public housing. The city family in London, Birmingham or Glasgow experienced a falling quality of life. The urban poor, especially immigrants, steadily congregated in the shrinking cities, imposing extra demands on the social services and teachers and giving councils a heavy burden of rent and rate rebates.[7]

Attempts by the strategic planners to revive cities by reducing overcrowding and making them less unwieldy went sadly awry.[8] Population did fall, but at the same time unemployment grew worse, housing deteriorated and the classroom and social work crisis was a gathering avalanche. Population blood-letting was no cure. Highly selective movement of people and jobs defied the intentions of the planners, with jarring impact on housing tenure and social-class structure. Schools were particularly affected.

New town administrators and employers, together with suburban businessmen, welcomed the young office worker, middle-class professional, or skilled worker and his family. The unskilled, the immigrant, the physically or socially handicapped and the elderly were frequently rejected. Outward migration therefore redoubled as this induced bias towards social class drift set off a second wave of flight from public housing and inner city schools. Even more families with children of school age moved out for better schools, jobs or housing.[9] The impact of the economic recession after 1974 was exceptionally severe. Thirty years of town planning had dispersed 400,000 manufacturing and skilled jobs from the London region. More than 250,000 further jobs were lost in the three years 1974–7.

In the US, Canada, Australia and New Zealand the same urban dispersal was observed, often with an even more severe set of complicating multi-ethnic factors.[10] New York City, like London, suffered an employment crisis. Some 700,000 manufacturing jobs disappeared from the city in the decade up to 1976, while the tempo of multiracial immigration quickened. As manufacturing industry or major corporate employers moved their headquarters out of New York, middle income families and their children also left. The taxation base became severely eroded. By 1976 most of the income of the most important city in the wealthiest country in the world was not earned but came from welfare cheques. With the city socially enfeebled and publicly bankrupt, New York politicians had to borrow the pension fund of the teachers to keep essential services, including schools, running.

In New York, Sydney or London a flight of middle income families deserting the urban village left large tracts of the inner city where housing concentrations of ethnic or disadvantaged families living in poverty or under stress quickly built up. The poor family, in these advanced world cities, usually gravitated irrespective of ethnic origin towards the 'difficult' housing neighbourhoods.[11] Each time social and ethnic segregation in housing sharpened, the urban classroom was put under greater stress. Whether in Chicago, Toronto or Glasgow, it was the same. In the early 1960s two-thirds of New York schoolchildren were white; by 1977 two-thirds were black or Hispanic. The principal cities of New Zealand, Auckland and Wellington experienced an influx of Polynesians from the Pacific Islands together with urbanizing Maoris coming into public housing from the countryside to work in motor-assembly plants. In Australian cities socio-economic and ethnic tensions heightened in neighbourhoods where the 'new Mediterranean' immigrants – Greeks, Czechs or Italians – gathered. Teachers commuted in their cars to run immense primary schools in anonymous townships, each containing as many as fifteen hundred multiracial pupils.[12] In the London dockland estate where I lived, first in a tower block and then in a family flat, the demographic landslide could be siesmographed through a variety of signs, ranging from the more trivial graffiti in laundry rooms to the mounting apprehension among parents or fear among elderly tenants.

Multiracial immigration provoked most public anxiety, since the growth of black neighbourhoods was very visible, but later on it was

realized that middle income flight and social class migration presented
the greater threat. Social class or housing segregation was in the long
term more menacing than racial segregation. In New York a minority
white population made racial integration mathematically impossible.[13]
There the skilled upwardly mobile black and Hispanic blue-collar
workers and professionals, the equivalent of London's West Indians
and Asians making good, removed themselves from the rented block,
inner city slum or public housing project to suburban occupation. The
city further deteriorated. In 1976 local residents, desperate to be
rehoused, finished the job begun by marauding gangs and insurance
defrauders in burning out several square miles of private housing in
the South Bronx. Reappraisal was urgently demanded. Why not
accept the all-black US city, but emphasize quality education in all-
black schools? But then the flight of the middle income black family
would have to be halted to provide a reasonable social and intellectual
balance in urban classrooms. Eventually a few educators began to ask
for social mix policies in housing and in employment. However, it was
not until the urban calamity had reached daunting proportions that
such positive urban strategy was urged, By then, all too often, the
social and economic balance of even the all-black city had been
destroyed. Residual mixed populations of lower class blacks and
disadvantaged whites were thrown together in explosive resentment.

International orthodoxy among urban architects, sociologists and
planners had not helped. In Britain after 1945, schemes for widescale
urban renewal and slum clearance followed international fashion.
Urban architects and planners all over the world, admirers of
Corbusier, built huge 'villages in the sky', especially public housing
estates with dramatic skylines of high-rise tower blocks. The bulldozer
demolished row upon row of Victorian red-brick terraces in British
cities. Owner-occupiers and private tenants alike were pushed out of
slum streets to become owner-occupiers in the suburbs, or unwilling
tenants expanding the public housing sector.

British urban sociologists rarely mentioned, and educational writers never, that the US and Britain differ markedly in the scale of their
public housing.[14] In the US by 1975, only 4 per cent of the population
lived in 'housing projects', which were usually considered suitable for
the disadvantaged, or 'problem' families, mostly blacks. Perhaps for
this reason, the sociological and design faults of architectural monumentalism in public housing were dramatized early in the US. In St
Louis, the prize-winning Pruitt-Igoe Housing Project, a vast high-rise
public housing 'village in the sky', had to be blown up with high
explosive shortly after its completion. So great was the vandalism,
crime and devastation after only a year that not even the poorest family

would go and live there. In London, on the other hand, not until 1977–8 did housing politicians begin to demolish the unpopular tower-block flats they could not even give away. The monumentalism of British public housing was echoed in the schools, in the skyscraper comprehensive or prefabricated primary school. There it provoked public and professional revolt.

Britain, unlike the US, Australia or many other countries had a major public housing tradition. But despite this, British urban sociologists since the 1930s had preached sociological fatalism, advocating conservatively laissez-faire economic policy in housing and planning,[15] and praising social mobility as a deserved escape for the hard working and ambitious from the inner city 'zone of transition' out to suburban house ownership. Urban sociologists and their educational counterparts saw no contradiction between such assumptions and the social class drift that ravaged the urban classroom. Unfortunately they failed to realize that the enormous growth of British public housing stock, together with town and country planning laws of unprecedented sophistication, offered British planners an unrivalled opportunity for creative, flexible experiment in urban housing. That flexibility began to be exploited at last in the 1970s, when initiatives in British urban planning began to revive the socially and economically varied urban neighbourhood and classroom.

Politicians of all parties caused irreparable damage by encouraging the electorate over half a century to believe that upward social mobility, even respectability itself, could only be achieved through a change of address. Moving out to the council 'cottage' estate, or the suburban semi-detached houses with their Tudor gables and small gardens was socially desirable.[16] Councillors promoted the merits of 'a property-owning democracy' with subsidized mortgages. But they thus unwittingly precipitated the growth of social divisiveness between two housing nations. For they created a myth which contrasted the respectable owner-occupier with the feckless council tenant. They also made that myth come true; while they expanded public housing enormously they proscribed as heresy the sale of council housing in subtopia. It could be argued that urban sociologists and politicians brought about a silent social revolution, which in fifty years completely transformed patterns of British housing tenure and seriously diminished the possibility of achieving a more democratic society through changes in the schools. Between 1914 and 1977 there was an extraordinary growth in British public housing from 1 per cent to 34 per cent of all housing stock. Amazingly, owner-occupation grew even faster. For while only one family in ten owned or had bought their own house in 1914, by 1974 53 per cent of British families were owner-occupiers. The rate of growth was most pronounced in the thirty years after 1947. The private tenant

and landlord virtually disappeared, pressured by rent acts and other
legislation. There was no intermediate, half way form of housing
tenure to replace the rented dwelling.

Everyone from building society chairmen to the average working
class voter shared the national pride in this phenomenal rise of house
ownership. Only an occasional voice expressed concern that the
suburbs were filling up with middle income owner-occupiers while an
urban proletariat living on deteriorating public housing estates in slum
neighbourhoods steadily grew. Two housing nations, springing up
over a century, regarded each other with hostility across a widening
financial chasm caused by rising house prices. 'As the private landlord
dies out', Colin Ward incisively remarked 'we become not three estates
but two nations, and the distinctions between the two become more
socially and psychologically divisive.'[17]

Regional and social class contrasts in housing tenure were startling.
The level of owner-occupation in the deprived inner city, in the dockland neighbourhoods of London or Liverpool, ran as low as 3 per cent.
But in comfortable seaside towns like Eastbourne, favoured by the
retired middle classes, less than 10 per cent of the housing stock was
municipally owned. Most suburbs, especially, were citadels of
owner-occupation. Social statistics revealed a growing separation in
their housing careers between people of differing educational attainment or social class. The professional worker, or skilled wage-earner
and his family, increasingly owned their own suburban house. By 1977
77 per cent of teachers were owner-occupiers; only 30 per cent of
unskilled manual workers owned a house.

The status of the council tenant and public image of municipal
housing degenerated. Dwindling public esteem and a loss of self-
respect among council tenants had been an inevitable consequence of
political policies and attitudes. Now the council tenant was both
shunned and enviously denounced by those who would not have
changed places with a tower block family for even one week. Professional suburban man, the teacher included, was in no doubt that
council tenancy was 'social death'. He wanted none of it; and financially, educationally and aesthetically he was right.[18]

Public housing had failed to provide a reasonable environment for
family life.[19] Having won international prizes for architectural design,
it then became notorious for its inept management, and the palatial
squalor of its vandalized, uninhabitable tower blocks. Far from having
become the visionary urban 'village in the sky', the municipal housing
estate served to hasten city exodus. Large housing estates increasingly
became rough neighbourhoods characterized by endemic vandalism
and astronomical rent arrears (among as many as one-third of all
tenants). The private house newly built for owner occupation, with

flimsy partition walls, inferior insulation and space standards, compared poorly with council housing designed and fitted to the high Parker-Morris standards. But it was private housing of inferior construction that most families wanted, rather than the council dwelling,

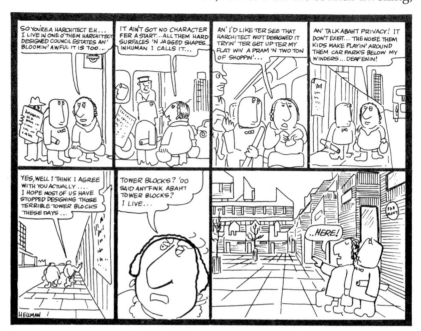

even though built to superior standards, or the imprisonment of a tower block penthouse. Architectural disasters on the grand scale confirmed their doubts. The collapse of school buildings or tower blocks, the scandal of a Ronan Point explosion or the high alumina near-disasters in schools, aroused widespread public and professional misgiving. Eventually in schools and public housing there was a return to traditional approaches, but by then it was almost too late. The sense of grievance and neglect among the council tenantry and schools had sunk deep.

Council tenants were treated more as serfs than citizens. Frequently their lives were administered with patronizing contempt by the petty bureaucrats responsible for day-to-day management of housing estates. There were innumerable stories like that of the apochryphal council tenants who reported an infestation of mice, and was smugly shown printed conditions of tenancy which banned his keeping pets. Municipal paternalism ruled the lives of one-third of British households. Council handbooks issued to tenants urged them, for instance: 'Keep your home clean and tidy. Hang up your pots and pans, put them on a shelf, endeavour to have some method of cleaning as you go

along: do not try and clean the house in one day. Regular bed times for
children and adults except on special occasions.'[20]

Those who applied for transfer to better housing were exposed to humiliating inspection of their dwellings. Respectable tenants disinclined to move, the lady who ran the tap-dancing class or the articulate leader of tenants, were incredulously asked why they did not 'get out'. They were encouraged to transfer or helped to obtain a council mortgage. Troublesome tenants were transferred to particularly stigmatized estates. How were they assessed? A confidential report used by Stockport Corporation officials in 1970 provided a coding system for housing visitors checking up on the standards of council tenants.[21]

(1) VCFFV: very clean and free from vermin.
(2) CFFV: clean and free from vermin.
(3) TOOCFFV: a lower standard than above.
(4) SAS: dirty stove – on suspicion.
(5) DSBF: dirty stove, bugs and fleas.

Pictured as an uncouth, illiterate trade unionist with uncontrollable children, a colour television in his bedroom and expensive car parked in the road, the council tenant was also alleged to pay a derisory rent while being heavily subsidized by more hard-working citizens and owner-occupiers. The myth of public subsidy was discredited by Richard Titmuss and others in the early 1950s, who showed that the middle class family made more use of the welfare state than the average lower income family.[22] In 1975, amid the tangled web of housing subsidies, the average council tenant received £36 per annum, while the average mortgagee obtained £61 tax relief on his mortgage. But by 1977 circumstances had narrowed the gap between folklore and fact. A government report indicated that council house subsidies had begun to exceed by three times the income tax relief paid to owner-occupiers. The house price inflation which in the previous decade gave the owner-occupier a free bonanza and made him a minor capitalist, had further deepened his contempt for the council tenant. But the financial gap in subsidy between them had widened as inflation fed back increased costs into municipal housing. Yet though the tenant might be heavily subsidized the move from renting to house ownership was now almost impossible, as any first-time buyer had to cross a formidable financial chasm, raising a large deposit and finding large mortgage repayments to gain a foothold in the property market. Those remaining in public or private rented housing were left even further behind in the scramble for prosperity. Not surprisingly, a survey in 1977 showed that 78 per cent of public housing tenants aged between 20 and 44 years would like to own their own house, but few could afford to do so.

[36]   Breakdown in traditional patterns of community, kinship and culture followed urban renewal, especially in those working class neighbourhoods where public housing took over. The working class
'extended' family, several generations of relatives living near one
another and giving mutual support, was broken up.[23] For the close,
even claustrophobic kinship and neighbourhood loyalties found in
inner city pubs and on the pavement of the urban back street were not
repeated in the tower block. Urban renewal, ostensibly setting out to
improve quality of life, had destroyed community. That whimsical
kaleidoscope of pigeons, brass bands, darts, football and beer, beloved
of progressive English teachers, was a nostalgic dream in the inner
city. By the late 1960s, however much novelists or sociologists raptur-
ized about cosmopolitan inner city neighbourhoods, with few exceptions they had become territories of dilapidation and shame; like Not-
ting Hill, which had legendarily teemed with community life, but
became notorious for its race riots and inhuman housing conditions.

Researchers discovered what everyone knew: that working class
neighbours on housing estates became strangers to each other. Community spirit and neighbourhood pride rarely flourished; and if they
did they were most frequently found in the immigrant neighbourhood
or street taken over by affluent, middle class families. Most council
tenants became home-centred, having few relatives living locally, little
pride in the neighbourhood and few outside interests. Neither community education nor gimmicks of housing management would really
touch the problem of inner city alienation; the young wife dependent
on tranquillizers, the house-bound pensioner in the anonymous flat
block, the middle-aged couple powerless against teenage vandals or
the comic opera muddles of the housing bureaucracy were common
gossip. Often both husband and wife worked – it was a financial
necessity for many families – so there was little time left for voluntary
association aimed at improving estate or neighbourhood life. Disadvantaged urban parents, if they were both lucky enough to have jobs,
worked long hard hours, leaving little enough time for their children.

Public housing first deteriorated as respectable families, aspiring
parents with young children, were persuaded by housing managers
and economic pressures to move out of the city. But as inner city
estates then slipped downhill, more and more tenants wanted to leave.
Their flight was contagious, setting off a further wave of social class
drift which swelled the flood of planned migration. Each time the
mortgage famine eased or house prices dropped slightly the ripple of
concern went round. 'Respectable' tenants on housing estates and
inner city streets feared that problem families or squatters would move
in next door. The American phenomena of 'abandonment' and 'burning' had arrived in several British cities by 1978.[24]

Each night the television news featured the horrors of life in the [37] housing estates of Belfast. But it was not only in Northern Ireland where police could not patrol public housing estates. Until 1973 London police were legally unable to patrol many large public housing estates as in Southwark, for example, where 15,000 people lived on the vast Aylesbury estate.[25] Vandalism, sexual molestation, break-ins and petty theft were common, yet tenants had to fight for the right to have police patrol. In problem estates an involuntary spiral of complicity arose out of fear. The real facts were disguised. Tenants complained of intimidation by youths or neighbours, but said they were too frightened of reprisals to call the police. Housing managers and police inspectors blandly commented that the reported local crime rates, as reflected in complaints to the police, were lower than elsewhere in the city.

Social stress and hostility were most noticeable in blocks of flats and housing estates built between the wars.[26] Established residents who saw themselves as 'respectable' working class, skilled workers and elderly couples, complained about the influx of 'rough' neighbours moving in, problem, immigrant, families with ill-disciplined children, or unsupported mothers who received a trickle of men visitors. The estate, they said, was 'going down'. The subjective observations of older tenants were confirmed by research evidence.[27]

Decline in morale among British public housing tenants was reflected among the administrators. Research into 'problem' estates showed that housing officers began to neglect day-to-day maintenance if an estate began to look neglected.[28] A self-perpetuating downward spiral was initiated. Lettings officers found that 'respectable' families turned down flats on that estate. Consequently they could only persuade families who had misbehaved or got into rent arrears elsewhere to accept direction into what now became deservedly labelled a 'problem' estate. Temporizing gimmicks, such as a small grant to the tenants' association or distributing free window boxes to elderly tenants were ineffective. Great public housing townships which would have appeared on a world atlas as country towns festered, forgotten, unnoticed and marooned in the conurbations.

Like educationists, housing experts also failed early on to monitor the serious impact of multi-ethnic immigration on public housing. Disturbing statistics were ignored, under-recorded or played down just as they were in schools. In 1971, according to official figures, one in ten Londoners was black, but this was an underestimate. Housing in the capital had absorbed three-quarters of a million Commonwealth newcomers – some 42 per cent of all known immigrants in the country. Other sizeable ethnic communities were concentrated in the provincial conurbations of Leicester, Wolverhampton, Southall, Bradford, Leeds and Liverpool. Urban housing patterns and the urban classrooms were strikingly affected.

By 1970 extremely disquieting reports revealed that many immigrant families were experiencing significant housing discrimination. In London 40 per cent of those allotted to inter-war flats on public housing estates in Lambeth were West Indian families, while West Indian settlement in the borough as a whole was 26 per cent. Immigrant families were being lumped together on older, often 'problem', estates. White families, taking fright, were applying for transfers to other estates; it was alarming to find official action thus making matters worse.

In 1971 a government Select Committee reported on race relations and immigration.[29] It urgently recommended that local authorities should keep confidential housing records in order to prevent bias in 'the housing of the members of ethnic groups'. Two years later, the Runnymede Trust again complained after looking at race and council housing in London that it was time 'all housing authorities looked critically at their role in the process including allocation policies and attitudes of key officials such as housing visitors'.[30] It was not until 1976, however, that the Department of the Environment made a ponderous move: local authorities were asked if they thought ethnic records in housing would help; and, if so, who should compile them?[31]

After a slow start the 'race relations industry' had performed the same volte-face in housing as in the schools over the counting of immigrant heads, but their agitation and special pleading still missed the real point. For the immigrant housing problem was the tip of a larger iceberg. Social and housing class bias was operating against all those urban disadvantaged families and their children, blacks or whites, who were being lumped in problem neighbourhoods, estates or schools. Also, far more serious than any racial segregation in housing was the increasing social class drift among the black immigrant community. Social geographers reported in 1977 that in 30 out of 42 London neighbourhoods with the highest proportion of West Indian born people, the ethnic concentration had grown less.[32] This happened between 1961 and 1971 when the total West Indian population of London had actually risen by 73 per cent. Only the naïve meritocrat could be pleased that a trend towards racial desegregation was destroying communities of varied social class, even if the former social mix had been dominated by West Indian families. But what was now clear was that 'respectable' West Indian families, and especially those in public housing, were taking part in the social class dispersal to the suburbs and owner-occupation.

What had happened? Many inner city families, particularly tenants in public housing, had found after initial apprehension that they were

welcoming hard-working Asian or West Indian families, with agreeable children, as their 'respectable' next door neighbours. But as the
inner city disintegrated, the aspiring immigrant couple and their children had joined the exodus. Both parents took on overtime and a
heavy mortgage in order to buy a semi-detached or terraced house in a
better, mixed working class or suburban neighbourhood. Building
Society statistics showed that, when families were compared and
evenly matched for social class and occupational background, many
more West Indians than whites were buying their own house. Only
housing prices or economic pressures delayed their departure.

However, those rare stratagems which attempted to retrieve socially
varied community in the inner city were regrettably either confined to the private housing market or else misfired badly. Efforts
by the housing associations which sprang up in the early 1960s to
house the homeless had led to trouble in the long term. The housing
associations gave 'problem' families decent housing, cheaply acquired
and converted – but in 'problem' neighbourhoods. Handsome
improvement grants were available in the early 1970s to householders
living in General Improvement Areas (GIAs) to modernize their house
by installing a toilet or bathroom.[33] At the same time the local authority
gave streets in GIAs a facelift, planting trees, landscaping parks and
quietening the traffic flow. The inner city became attractive again in
such neighbourhoods. The heavy cost and physical stress of commuting had taken its toll, and the reasonably wealthy family was thus
prepared to move back in to the city. But, unfortunately, houses in
GIAs and the generous grants which went with them were snapped up
during a speculative property boom either by property developers or
by the individual, affluent middle class family.[34]

A middle class 'gentrification brigade' feverishly bought up Georgian and early Victorian terraces in Melbourne or London, or handsome 'brownstone' houses in Manhattan or the Bronx. These invading
families settled in agreeable neighbourhoods of low-density housing
and tree-lined squares where the middle classes had formerly lived.
Unscrupulous property men hastened the trend, using tempting
offers, bribes and sometimes harassment to persuade working class
owner-occupiers to sell up for a large sum, or in driving out the poor,
or immigrant, families who also occupied these desirable houses in
crowded multi-occupation.

The up-and-coming middle class family soon had a whole house to
itself within striking distance of father's office. They expensively converted a bathroom or added an indoor lavatory, study or patio; the
cellar was once more used for wine, or home beer brewing. Orange
trees adorned the front porch and a foreign car stood outside. Slum
Georgian streets and squares were thus, within the space of a couple of

years, transformed into expensive neighbourhoods which only the affluent could afford to live in. Housing policy had swung the pendulum too far.

It was in the ex-slum neighbourhood and the newly converted street that urban community life flourished. In fashionable Camden or Islington, and their Melbourne or New York equivalents, was found the baby-sitting co-operative, the wine and cheese party for new residents, the bulk buying consortium and articulate parents using the state school system. Indeed, the graduate wives not only took over the street but also the local school, pioneering an elitist form of the social mix strategy. In Camden and some other parts of London they even ventured into the comprehensive school system, either dominating the school via the Parents' Association or laughing off the joking accusation that 'it didn't matter what their kids learnt at school because they could catch up at night in their own homes'. Journalists covering the Tyndale tribunal observed that it was the 'gentrifying' intellectuals of Islington's middle classes who fanned the crisis of the Tyndale junior school in inner London into a national scandal.

Yet social class drift from the cities was obscured, rather than offset, by this trend: the outward flight of thousands of middle income professionals and skilled working class families continued uninterrupted. If two nations, socially divided in their housing, had arisen, the repercussions in urban schools were more complained about than analysed. For instance, there was little research to suggest that social class drift and housing polarization, in enormously exacerbating the classroom crisis, had given the comprehensive schools a difficult start. Teachers knew all about the impact of the 'demographic landslide' in their classrooms. It was they who were assaulted, sometimes stabbed, frequently derided and, worst of all, prevented from actually teaching. They heard from social workers the stories of child battering, juvenile crime, gang affray and intimidation found in the 'difficult' housing estates and slum streets around their schools. It was teachers who could register the possibility of a Maria Colwell tragedy, as indeed did Maria's teacher, often before anyone else; and if not at first hand, then through rumour or the classroom gossip of children and school helpers. But too many teachers, perhaps unwilling to admit the appalling scale of the crisis, or to admit professional defeat, turned their back on the urban neighbourhood. Instead, determinedly, briefly each day they tried to make school an oasis of security for the child. They would not prejudge the child. They would not count the black face. They shared the optimism of the geneticists that the urban community could be self-regenerating. They subscribed to the EPA myth, believing that a treasure chest of extra resources and positive discrimination would provide educational solutions. Or they concluded self-accusingly that there was something wrong with their school and its curriculum.

Anyone who taught in a school, listened to parents in the pub or launderette, or heard urban head teachers bemoaning the decline in their share of able children during this period had to wonder why the teachers did not protest that lack of a constructive comprehensive urban strategy was doing irreparable damage to the urban classroom. But there was not much educational evidence available to help them towards that diagnosis. Voluminous educational research had neglected the explosive links between school performance, housing and social class. No one researched the psychological impact on children from public housing of their parents' awareness of their second-class status as tenants.

Teachers constantly attacked the stereotyping of pupils through streaming, stressing how negative self-image led to poor educational achievement. There was a taboo on discussion of school intakes in terms of their social class composition or housing tenure. Yet in their staffrooms those same teachers commonly spoke in sardonic shorthand of 'the estate children'. Against the background of such teacher prejudice, how could parents so discouraged from any initiative in housing self-management or community education be expected to send to school children who would easily become autonomous learners in the informal classroom?

Close links between urban housing tenure and maladjustment or delinquency among schoolchildren were deducible. When the Institute for the Study and Treatment of Delinquency surveyed school absence in 1974 they found high truancy rates in localities of old and decayed housing, urban renewal or municipal housing of a pre-war type.[35] The researchers reported that, conversely, schools with the lowest truancy rates took children from 'good' housing areas where there was much owner-occupation. Delinquency research showed that 76 per cent of boys from manual backgrounds who were born in 1946 reported that they had committed delinquent acts. But 96 per cent of middle class boys, those rarely found in public housing or slum neighbourhoods, had stayed out of trouble.

Research into housing tenure and reading attainment among primary children attending the same school showed a stark gap.[36] The children came from two adjacent estates, one municipally owned and the other owner-occupied. Only 25 per cent of the children of owner-occupiers lost ground in their reading during the summer holiday, compared with 42 per cent of the council estate children. Furthermore, 36 per cent of the children of owner-occupiers actually improved their reading during the holiday, while only 12 per cent of the children from council housing did so. Obviously attainment and school success were intimately bound up with housing tenure. And as we saw earlier, it was the outer suburbs where owner occupation predominated that sent the most children into the sixth forms and later to the universities.

The confrontation of the two housing nations had been symbolized a long time before, in 1934, in the famous case of the Cutteslowe Wall.[36] That wall had been built deliberately to divide Oxford suburban owner-occupiers from their nearby neighbours who were council tenants. The Cutteslowe Wall was demolished in 1958. But invisibly and symbolically it went on growing: and in 1978 it had reached enormous proportions. The gap in esteem, income, life style, educational experience and housing tenure between the owner-occupier and the council tenant now constituted the most serious threat of all to urban renaissance.

The same deep schism more invisibly split the national classroom. Educational progressives, priding themselves on their democratic vision, had agitated over some thirty years for comprehensive school reorganization. That was now almost completed. But each step towards improving the secondary schools in abolishing selection and setting up comprehensive schools had floundered in the quagmire of the wider social problem. No educational policy would succeed until something was done about housing apartheid. Only a sensitive, vigorous pursuit of social mix for the city and large town could make reasonable urban classroom life possible once again.

4 Multi-ethnic muddle

Educational opinion, in debating urban disadvantage, classroom life and family problems, had invested heavily in educational solutions. But as Harold Silver observed, there was growing doubt that a just society could be arrived at simply through educational reform.[1] When urban policy was seen through the colour prism of ethnicity the key problems were highlighted and intensified. What happened to urbanized New Zealand Maoris or Polynesians, Australian aboriginals or 'new Australians', or the West Indian family in Birmingham was an emotive and highly-charged question; it was also dramatically visible. Undoubtedly there was a close link between ethnicity, black skin and low socio-economic or housing class. In the US, for example, two-thirds of all whites were middle class while two-thirds of all blacks were lower class. So if you wanted to study closely the multiply deprived lower class child you followed round the New York Puerto Rican, the Greek child in Melbourne or the French-speaking child in the Canadian city.

In Britain there was one overriding problem. In many urban schools there was a taboo on the counting of black faces. When immigration first began to expand in the mid-1960s many teachers and education authorities refused to identify or count dark-skinned children. 'I teach them all the same', many teachers claimed. They saw themselves as resisting the racial prejudice of local councillors and politicians who would count heads as a first move towards 'bussing' policy or some other racially prejudiced intervention in the schools. Thus all too often,

[44] despite growing pressure, social disruption and curriculum distortion imposed on the urban classroom by the immigrant invasion, the official policy in Britain throughout the 1950s and 1960s was 'let us avoid racial tension by playing down the presence of these immigrants'. Understandably, discussion became embittered as the years went by and the problems worsened: not just in the schools but also in housing and in society in general. Similar beliefs in the 'melting pot' absorption of 'minorities' or immigrants prevailed in the US and Australia.

Local decision making was not much helped by national policy. There were countermanding circulars, about-turns and much pharisaical posturing at government level. No one doubted that immigrants and their families were constructively employed in driving buses or nursing in the hospitals, but their economic contribution was not rewarded in housing or the schools.[2] The Department of Education

'Goodbye. Our visa's expired. Look after yourself.'

and Science and HM Inspectorate, like everyone else, vacillated according to the policy of the day. Teachers were understandably mystified and left to make their individual response.

How many immigrants were there? According to published statistics by 1972 there were 280,000 'immigrant' pupils in England and Wales,

comprising 3.3 per cent of the school population, most of them concentrated in the towns and cities.[3] The main groups were: West
Indians:100,000; Indians: 56,000; Pakistanis and Bangladeshis: 30,000;
Kenyan Asians: 17,000; Cypriots: 14,000; Italians: 12,000. Occasionally,
additional immigrants arrived; in 1972 several thousand Ugandan
Asians were admitted, and later many Lebanese and Chilean families
sought political refuge.[4]

At first, between 1966 and 1973, the Department of Education and
Science collected information about immigrant pupils as part of the
Local Government Act of 1966, and grants were then made to those
LEAs which had substantial numbers of Commonwealth immigrants
whose language or customs differed from the local community. The
Commonwealth immigrant was defined as 'a person, adult or child
born in another country of the Commonwealth, who had been ordinar-
ily resident in the United Kingdom for less than ten years, and the child
of such a person'. Under this 'ten year rule' LEAs with 2 per cent or
more of such pupils were eligible for grants.[5] The DES definition was
subtly phrased to identify the black faces.

But the figures for the ethnic minority population were constantly
underestimated. There were probably nearer 400,000 such children
by 1977. The 13 per cent immigrant figure given officially for
Wolverhampton or the 9.5 per cent for Birmingham did not record
what the average man in the street would have called members of the
immigrant community.

A more realistic picture was given by the Registrar General's 1972
statistics for live births by birthplace of the mother, which showed that
births to mothers born in the new Commonwealth or Pakistan were at
25 per cent in Wolverhampton and as much as 34 per cent in Brent or
Haringey in London. This statistical gap was reflected in the urban
classroom. In Wandsworth, a borough of immigrant settlement in
inner London, one secondary school in 1976 recorded 39 per cent of its
pupils as official immigrants, while an independent count by the
teachers recorded 67 per cent black faces.

There was considerable concern about the attainment of immigrant
children or the children of immigrants. Literacy surveys in London in
1968 and elsewhere showed disturbing shortcomings in the performance of such children. In 1971 immigrant children, as officially
defined, had in London a mean reading age at least a year below that of
non-immigrants in the primary school. That attainment gap had not
been repaired by 1977. Secondary school leavers of West Indian origin
but fully educated in Britain were also educationally behind most
London children by 1977, in a period of the worst juvenile unemployment for several decades.[6]

What was to be done about the problem? The lack of educational equality for working class children from a British background was already apparent, but clearly the immigrant child born in Britain or recently arrived was even more disadvantaged. In 1963 Edward Boyle, the Minister of Education, faced parents who were protesting at the metamorphosis of Southall into a miniature Asian township. Boyle, basing his judgement on evidence from the US of 'white flight', the turning point at which whites removed their children from neighbourhood schools, advised that no school in Ealing should contain more than 30 per cent immigrants. He promised support for any authority which dispersed immigrant pupils by bussing. Unhappily, no housing stratagem for dispersal was available; 'bussing' was the belated attempt at closing the educational door after the housing horse had bolted.[7] A DES pamphlet on English for immigrants recommended that LEAs should 'if necessary, use transport to disperse the immigrant children round the greater number of schools'.[8] The bussing which aroused so much fury in Boston schools and elsewhere in the US was official British government policy for some six years, but was actually practised only in Ealing and a handful of other education authorities.

Would it not be better for immigrant pupils suffering from educational disadvantage to attend a small, friendly school where a hundred or so children were enrolled; and where there was one teacher for every fifteen children? Would not free transport to school every day and an individualized teaching programme for each child be very acceptable to the immigrant community? That was what the special schools for educationally subnormal children offered.

In a way, it was surprising that the immigrant community did not deliberately make better use of the ESN special schools, in view of their excellent provision and staffing ratios. But instead, by 1969 there was widespread resentment about the large number of West Indian children being allocated to ESN schools. A confidential report in London showed that the heads of ESN schools thought immigrants were wrongly placed in their schools four times more often than other children. Political radicals in the black community argued that this was one more example of the British school system subordinating groups like blacks, women and the working class into an acceptance of an exploited role in society. Political as well as educational capital was made from the fact that many London West Indian children were being unfairly 'ascertained', labelled as educationally subnormal and sent to special schools.[9] For this was certainly happening. In London the proportion of children in special schools who were immigrants rose from 23 per cent in 1966 to 36 per cent in 1969; although in those three years the proportion of immigrants officially recorded as entering ordinary schools only rose by 3 per cent. But why were the West Indian and other immigrant children scoring so low on assessment that special school referral was possible? Explanations put forward included their possible language difficulty or dialect interference, irrelevant curriculum, the low expectation of teachers, the difficulties of white children in relating to black or Asian newcomers in the classroom, poor home background, unstable family relationships, cultural conflict between various ethnic minority communities and the schools themselves and the negative self-image of black children.

A highly publicized debate raged over the London ESN school issue. Part of the problem was the urban staffing crisis. If the ESN schools, with their expensive special provision, had been working effectively there would perhaps have been fewer complaints from black parents. But that was not the case. Despite extra allowances for the teachers, ESN schools were going through a period of poor teacher morale and high staff turnover, with many difficult maladjusted pupils. Defensively, the DES in 1973 issued a memorandum on 'Educational Arrangements for Immigrant Children who may need Special Education'.[10]

The 'ten year rule' system continued to be strongly criticized. The definition was unsatisfactory. The DES admitted that the statistics which were collected did not in any way influence their allocation of resources. However, the returns were used by the Home Office in administering urban aid – those programmes initiated after 1968 which gave 10 per cent of available funds to multiracial LEAs wishing to build day nurseries, or provide language teaching or housing advice centres. The assumption behind the 'ten year rule' was that everyone who had been in the country for longer than that time, including second generation West Indian children, would be culturally assimilated and not present an educational problem. That was the 'melting pot' view of immigration. But when the DES announced in 1973 that the reviled 'ten year rule' would cease, together with all collection of statistics on immigrant pupils, there was an outcry – especially from the leaders of the ethnic minorities.[11] Once more policy making had lagged behind other political trends. Minority leaders now no longer wished to be treated the same as other British citizens. The 'melting pot' or assimilation policy was out of favour, and not only in Britain. The black activists, teachers and community relations officers who had earlier challenged discrimination in labelling black children in schools now pressed for the recording of immigrant statistics to be resumed. In the housing field, as we saw, they had a good case for doing so. And in many schools, they claimed, special help was being forfeited because under the 'ten year rule' the true numbers of immigrant pupils were not being identified. Teachers who pursued policies of 'we treat them all the same' were deliberately preventing special help being obtained for immigrant pupils. But it was not until 1977 that the NUT, the principal teachers' union, reversed its position and agreed to the resumption of counting.

What had been most seriously underestimated was the growing alienation of the second generation of young blacks, especially West Indians, born in Britain. Influenced by an international culture, spread through pop music and the media, they had strong loyalties to the black power movement – sometimes stronger than family or ethnic ties. Black power and black pride hit the schools in the form of demands for a multiracial or 'black studies' curriculum. Combined with a phase of unemployment among young British blacks and existing difficulties in urban classrooms, it created in particular a West Indian problem generation. It was now seen to have been a mistake to assume that the immigrants would integrate easily into British society. The younger ethnic populations, whether in British, American or Australian cities, were not going to follow the example of their predecessors, who had officially assimilated but privately perpetuated their culture, dance and language on Saturday mornings or at weddings. The young now refused to learn to play the game like those dark-skinned graduates of the London School of Economics who had acquired BBC accents, learned to play cricket and eat cucumber sandwiches, and went back to lead nations as members of the political elite.

West Indian bus drivers in Britain complained of their children sliding into delinquency because of the permissive classrooms which were unknown in the West Indies. Back home, they said, the children were at least taught to behave and learn by rough and ready classroom methods, including the Victorian schoolroom tradition of an occasional good beating. They complained that white school teachers, social workers and magistrates encouraged permissive attitudes.[12] Nor was the correct model always offered in the home neighbourhood. In the British city, or Auckland in New Zealand, for example, the problem white family and the newly arrived urbanizing immigrant were commonly put together on the 'difficult' housing estate. New Zealand teachers complained that the immigrant children were copying the poor, delinquent white families in starting early in juvenile crime, vandalism or anti-social behaviour.

At the same time, the West Indian workers and their wives were forced to work long hours of overtime and sometimes neglect their children in order to raise a joint income to buy a house or achieve a reasonable standard of living. Child-rearing traditions in the West Indian community meant that often there was no constant father figure. The recalcitrant West Indian youth took to the streets because he did not get on with his aunt, uncle or mother who looked after him in Britain, and joined a gang of muggers in the tube station.[13] The second generation of black immigrant youths responded both proudly

and deviantly to unemployment, their poor self-image and feelings of
educational disadvantage. Unhappily, in the process of rejecting
school, they often rejected the skills it taught which might have
brought them success in British society. Thus their problems became to
some extent self-perpetuating. Confusion reigned.

While many teachers doggedly pursued their convictions that the
problems of black children were best dealt with under the general
category of disadvantage, others said that those days were over. Official policy continued to be ambiguous. When in 1974 the largest urban
authority in the country appointed an inspector specifically to deal
with the 70,000 black school children in inner London, he was white
and euphemistically entitled Inspector for Community Relations. By
1978 Her Majesty's Inspectorate had one black and one Indian inspector. The professional centre working with London teachers to produce
materials for the disadvantaged ethnic child was called a 'Centre for
Urban Studies'.

Not surprisingly, by 1975 there was agitation and controversy about
this lack of direction. The Home Office had 300 miscellaneous recommendations on this policy area still to consider. The Department of the
Environment had not acted effectively on reports of discrimination
against blacks in public housing. A Commons Select Committee on
Race Relations in 1975 expressed concern that the DES did not have
relevant records or statistics for the number of black students training
to be teachers. It advised the DES to increase its staff dealing with race
relations and to make more use of HM Inspectorate. The Report also
urged that a central fund for the special educational needs of immigrants and their children should be established. An immigrant advisory unit should be set up within the Department and LEAs should
regularly report on their activities. But most of these recommendations
were ignored. Instead a national centre for information and advice on
Educational Disadvantage was set up in Manchester,[14] as it was argued
that the educational needs of immigrants were increasingly compar-
able to those of disadvantaged children in general. The National Union
of Teachers complained that the new unit was only attacking the
problems of disadvantaged whites as an after-thought. They wanted
the phrase 'needs of immigrants' deleted from its terms of reference.
On the other hand, the Caribbean Teachers Association protested that
the unit had originally been their idea and not enough weight was
being given to the problems of blacks. As usual, in this minefield of
social policy, euphemistic, bureaucratic innovation left no one satisfied.

Meanwhile the immigrant and multi-cultural communities expanded rapidly in the conurbations, although the total population of
Britain actually went down 15,000 in the year 1975–6. By mid-1976 3.3

per cent of the population were counted as immigrants. The immigrant community provided one in fifteen of all live births, although the number of immigrants coming into the country had not increased. The immigrant was now defined as a person in the new Commonwealth or Pakistan whose children were born in Britain, including the children of mixed marriages. A major race relations act in 1976 emphasized the need for examining cultural bias in test materials; and for monitoring the allocation of children to ESN or maladjusted schools. It also recommended considering the allegation that entry requirements for higher education sometimes operated against newcomers or the children of immigrants.[15] By 1977 the Community Relations Commission had many local branches supported by local authorities on shoestring budgets. A hundred or so schemes up and down the country assisted adults with language teaching through volunteer home tutors or group tuition. In 1977 the Race Relations Board and Community Commission were merged to form the Commission for Racial Equality. But other organizations, like the Council for Civil Liberties, the Runnymede Trust, or the Schools Council, also continued to be extremely active in the field of multi-ethnic curriculum or policy.

But behind the confusion and occasional hypocrisy lay a major theoretical debate. Indeed, it was for once a lack of theoretical clarity which had created the pragmatic quagmire in which teachers floundered. The genetic debate about the ability of ethnic groups as measured by intelligence test was really the key to policy for the urban classroom.

Educational evidence in Britain and the US had shown that schools were not effective in the way that had once been hoped in increasing equality for the disadvantaged or immigrant child.[16] In 1966 J. S. Coleman working in the US conducted a large-scale enquiry at the request of the US Commissioner of Education into 'The lack of availability of equal educational opportunities for individuals by reason of race, colour, religion or national origin in the US'.[17] Half-way through his research, Coleman optimistically declared that his survey would show a gap between the quality of schools attended by black children and those attended by white. He soon retracted. For in looking at 600,000 children, 60,000 teachers and 4,000 schools, and giving his data sophisticated analysis, Coleman came to the following conclusion: despite any popular myths most black or white American children were taught by similar teachers, in similar schools, with similar facilities and formal curriculum. Furthermore, where there were measurable differences between schools and teachers, they had a negligible effect on the performance of either black or white students as measured by standardized tests. Coleman's shorthand conclusion was 'schools make no difference'. There was one crucial exception. Cole-

man found that the single characteristic of schools which helped
test performance was the presence of 'affluent classmates' or 'social
mix'. The vast research data collected by Coleman was reworked by
Christopher Jencks and his colleagues to produce *Inequality*,[18] an educational bestseller in the US in 1972. Jencks, himself a liberal, was
driven to rebut the fundamental liberal belief that schools could compensate for society. He had always believed that schools were important; but he now concluded that they were only marginal institutions.
He found that poverty was not primarily hereditary. The main reason
some Americans ended up richer than others was that they had more
adequate cognitive skills. More international research subsequently
confirmed this finding. Inequality in educational opportunity was not
responsible for inequality in educational results in any important
sense. In fact, eliminating differences in the amount of schooling
people received would have virtually no effect on income inequality in
the United States. Spending more money on schools would not necessarily raise achievement or increase the likelihood that students would
attend college later. Nevertheless, Jencks thought it was still worth-
while spending a lot of money on schools. He pointed out that people
spent a fifth of their lives in school; and even if it did not affect their
chances of learning to read, getting to college or earning $50,000 a year
when they were fifty, spending more money on schools simply to
make a more pleasant environment with better playgrounds and hap-
pier children was commendable. Jencks informed his US readership
that although education could not compensate for the shortcomings of
society, what was needed was 'what other countries call socialism'. In
fairness, it has to be said that Mosteller and Moynihan, also reworking
the Coleman data during the same period, came to a very different
conclusion.[19] Perhaps, they argued, what Coleman had discovered
was that US society was already more equal than anyone imagined.
And where there was still inequality, if the school was a marginal
institution, might it not be better to spend money where it really would
make a difference rather than on school budgets?

The psychologist Arthur Jensen, also working in the US, argued that
inherited factors accounted for 80 per cent of intelligence, environment
providing merely a surface influence.[20] This explained the comparative
failure, in his view, of the programmes of compensatory or EPA
education. Only such an explanation could account for the poor results
obtained by black and working class children in intelligence tests. For,
Jensen pointed out, numerous studies of pre-school and other programmes, such as Headstart, for the disadvantaged US child had
produced no evidence of permanent improvement in attainment.
True, there were temporary gains of five to ten IQ points, but those
disappeared after the first year of school. Thereafter, the gap between

disadvantaged and other children actually increased. In 1973 in his book *Educability and Group Differences* Jensen produced data showing that black children equalled, if not surpassed, white children in sensori-motor and linguistic development and simple associative learning.[21] But where they failed, compared with white children, was in understanding what they had learnt; in conceptualization, mental manipulation and in some concrete, constructional tasks. They also performed less well than white children in Piagetian tests. Furthermore, even if a bonus of five points was given to compensate the black child for his average lower socio-economic status, an unaccountable gap of ten IQ points remained between white and black children. The average IQ of the lowest, white social class was higher than that of the highest black social class. British educational psychologists commonly agreed that Asian children excelled at mathematics, Jewish children were more verbal, Welsh children sang well and the West Indian was often a superb athlete. The Irish community showed gaps in their achievement similar to those of the blacks or West Indians in Britain. But this, of course, still said nothing about individuals. These were generalizations about populations.

Jerome Bruner disagreed with Jensen's emphasis, putting the figure for inherited factors as low as 40 per cent. But as time went on the progressives, who had so strongly emphasized environmental influences, did more readily admit a considerable factor of hereditability in intelligence. Moderates, like Michael Rutter, nevertheless argued against biological determinism, insisting that there were greater discontinuities than continuities in the so-called cycle of deprivation.[22] No one went as far as the Soviet geneticist Lysenko and his colleagues who in the 1940s had asserted as official party ideology that 'environment was all'; no one, at least, except a few progressives.[23]

Some critics of Jensen and the geneticists suggested that intelligence scores might be contaminated by cultural practice. William Labov, working with Philadelphian blacks, showed that by testing in a relaxed environment a black friendly tester working with a black child, sharing sweets and informal talk, could enhance the test score and the quality of language the child produced.[24] Perhaps, therefore, the American black performed poorly on verbal tests and tests of knowledge because of his inferior educational experience and the wrong testing relationship. Would he not do better on 'culture free' tests?

Jensen responded that blacks in fact did better than whites on tests heavily contaminated with school knowledge. Where they did least well was on pure intelligence tests involving abstract thought. In his view, the prima facie case for US blacks being genetically disposed to lower achievement on IQ tests was established without doubt.

The Clarkes and Rutter, separately reviewing the critical literature on maternal deprivation and early childhood development up to the mid-1970s, rejected the received wisdom of several decades. True, they agreed, deprivation could depress intelligence, but only in cases where deprivation had been extremely severe. Only children who were shut up alone for months, neglected in childhood like animals and severely ill-treated were found to suffer from depressed IQs. Even then they were commonly found to gain over 30 IQ points after only a few months in a good caring home. The conclusion was that the effects of environmental disadvantage on intelligence were rarely permanent.

The IQ test might have provided an early rough and ready guide for Binet or Burt testing children in London or Paris for educational subnormality early in the twentieth century. But intelligence tests had subsequently been misused, in Britain for example, in the hands of educational psychologists and unwary teachers, to stereotype children in selecting for different schools at 11+. The geneticists, in conducting their investigations within such a framework, were using the vocabulary and procedures of an educational caste system. The IQ tests had always favoured the conformist child, although admittedly some had been considerably modified to introduce more 'creative thinking' items. But the suspicion remained that despite a superficial face lift the IQ test was still a device that identified only one kind of intelligence. The comprehensive school enthusiasts of the 1950s in reforming secondary education were mainly concerned to identify the brightest children, concentrating them in the higher streams of the comprehensive school as their first step towards joining the meritocratic elite. As opinion shifted towards unstreaming, that view was abandoned. But even then many local education authorities still used the discredited IQ test as part of their procedures for 'banding' children or constructing mixed ability classrooms.

Although implicitly they perhaps assumed its correctness, nevertheless the meritocrats often rejected the genetic argument as deterministic.[25] They argued that any view of intelligence as fixed and genetically transmitted assumed that educationally backward or retarded children could not have their problems remedied and quickly re-enter the educational mainstream. In advancing such a view, they conveniently forgot for the moment the exceptionally gifted child and the severely subnormal one whose permanent limitations they did accept. They found it difficult to accept that some schoolchildren started and remained permanently behind in the race for glittering prizes and social mobility. For that made the unearned privilege of the meritocrat less defensible. But they did quite rightly argue that an optimistic working hypothesis was needed by all teachers. The possibility of IQ being altered over a period of ten years or generations should be stressed and every child should be encouraged all the time to do his best. But by the 1970s the urban school had considerably changed. There was an ideology of unstreaming which conflicted with the original meritocratic impulse.

Michael Young had satirized the meritocratic viewpoint in 1958 in his book *The Rise of the Meritocracy*.[26] He described a situation in which intelligence was redistributed between the classes and the nature of classes changed. In his book the talented were given 'the opportunity to rise to the level which accords to their capacities and the lower classes consequently reserved for those who are lower in ability'. But as American and British observers began to point out, success in urban society was not based so much on educational achievement as had been expected. By the mid-1970s, in the US, Britain or Australia, all equally hit by economic recession, that was even more true: the monolithic educational pyramid was no longer worshipped. Contestants for social mobility no longer scrambled up the educational steps to the apex of the pyramid – a university chair, a managerial post or a secure position in the civil service. Educational expansion and economic crisis had devalued degree status and educational attainment. Graduate numbers had risen dramatically. Massive involuntary income redistribution in Britain had favoured the skilled working classes at the expense of managers or professional graduates. The landmarks for educational or social discussion had been transformed.

Behind the whole debate lay the implicit but mistaken notion of urban homeostasis.[27] It derived from the biological law of regression generally accepted by geneticists (in common with their psychological or scientific colleagues) which asserted that there was a tendency towards 'regression to the norm', i.e. for everyone to revert to the average. Bright parents would tend to have less bright children: and dull parents would tend to have slightly brighter children. Such a principle accorded with findings on height or other characteristics of physique.

The principle was consistent, too, with the commonsense empiricism of those who emphasized that the so-called 'cycle of deprivation' did not support a view of fixed intellectual inheritance. For if discontinuities in all forms of disadvantage were more common than continuities this would be attributable to biological regression. There was little information about strengths of family continuities where they did occur, as for example in successive generations of severely subnormal families. But the discontinuities were more striking than the continuities as long as a population was static. The privileged of one generation could, just as the folklore said, move from rags to riches – but they could be back in rags again in a few generations.

Contest mobility, in Turner's phrase, which kept open the gates of educational opportunity through school competition, had in fact

increased the amount of upward and downward movement towards
disadvantage or meritocracy. Biological regression, although at first
sight a fatalistic notion, seemed compatible with the beliefs of the child
development progressives and teachers. It also fitted the post-war
arguments of the educational sociologists that there was enormous
wastage of ability in the working class, where an almost inexhaustible
pool of talent was often untapped. Applied to schools or even housing
neighbourhoods, it led to the assumption that social and intellectual
balance would automatically be restored over a period of time by
natural regeneration. All that teachers therefore had to do was to work
hard, helped by extra resources, and to hold on through this temporary crisis.

No doubt the genetic principle of regression would have worked for
the stricken urban school but for a crucial flaw in the argument.
Geneticists, teachers and sociologists had overlooked the headlong
social migration which continuously took away the more able, aspiring
families from the cities. As long as that social class drift persisted, there
could be no affluent classmates and no social mix. The more intelligent
children, who were needed if intellectual desegregation was to lead to
the process of biological regression, were being taken away. Ethnically
it was the same. In 1976 New York's Chancellor of Education asked
'How can you create desegregated schools out of black and white
chips, if people keep on taking away the white chips?' If the flight of
the middle income families continued, whether they were black or
white, neither ethnic nor intellectual desegregation would be possible.

The 'melting pot' theory of immigration was abandoned *force majeure*
in the US cities because of the demographic changes. At first it was
replaced by arguments for cultural pluralism or multi-ethnic curriculum; in Australia and the US, some 'bilingual' children were taught
the early curriculum in their dominant language. But the danger in the
advanced world cities, where discriminatory housing patterns were
increasingly reinforced by cultural separatism and bilingualism in the
schools, was of a balkanization of economic and community life. Bilingual teaching might cement the disadvantaged into their enclaves,
particularly the less able children, who would be tempted not to learn
the language of their 'host' country and would use their mother
tongue. Disadvantaged groups might find themselves locked in 'can-
tonments', from which it would be impossible to break out into the
community for educational opportunities or employment in other
cities, except by transferring from one deprived enclave to another.
There was also a danger of civil commotion if separatism in language,
culture and the schools trapped disadvantaged groups such as French
Canadians or Turkish Cypriots and fomented their resentment. Those

[56] who proposed to strengthen multicultural pluralism by providing bilingual tuition or black studies were therefore playing with fire.

Neverthless, if the bilingual pitfall could be avoided there was something to be said for a multicultural emphasis. The veteran sociologist Kenneth Clarke, who had originally led civil rights campaigns for desegregation, and campaigned for reforming legislation, argued that by the mid-1970s in many US cities school desegregation was a lost cause. Where two-thirds of a city was black or Hispanic, court orders to 'integrate' schools only tilted neighbourhoods into middle income flight. Clarke thought the task should be to achieve 'high quality' education in ethnic or all-black schools. Others were convinced that halting the flight of the middle income family from the city was a more pressing challenge than achieving school desegregation among the poor blacks and disadvantaged whites concentrated in the cities. The dawning discovery in the US that socio-economic mix might be a preferred objective was echoed by Australian and British experience. Whatever the merits of the race and intelligence debate, there was common agreement that the need for socio-economic mix and housing desegregation should take priority.

5 Juggling children and catchments

How were schools organized in response to the urban crisis? There was little attempt by teachers to lobby for overall urban strategy. They looked within the school or the education service for solutions. An attempt was made to enhance classroom life for the average teacher and child through improved resources and managerial techniques. There was a plethora of curriculum innovation in urban schools through the 1960s and 1970s. Experimental reorganization within schools themselves – the integrated day in the primary school; pastoral grouping, mixed ability or team teaching in the secondary school – could all be seen as a reflex response to the chronic social disorder and instability which threatened the urban classroom.[1] Indeed, innovations in school organization or curriculum in urban schools during this period were arguably dictated less by educational philosophy than by a sense of panic. The underlying problem was unavoidable: how to deal with endemic maladjustment, how to avoid or spread out the difficult children.

Why didn't teachers in their staffrooms and their union meetings simply insist upon the suspension of disturbed children, their exclusion from school and the classroom; or separate provision for them in special schools? Why did the teachers not simply refuse to teach children who disrupted the lessons of other children? Why was the epidemic of maladjustment allowed to threaten the success, even the survival of the emerging comprehensives at a time when political considerations made it important that they should prove themselves?[2]

Why did primary teachers moving towards more informal, progressive teaching methods allow disturbed children to put these approaches at risk?[3] Above all, why did teachers allow their educational philosophy and innovatory vision to be sabotaged by the hordes of unruly and disruptive children?

Answers to all these questions are provided by looking at the prevailing climate of professional opinion. Some difficult children were in fact suspended from school. Individual schools embarked on over-repressive policies of discipline. But in general, for reasons of professional dignity, political expediency and educational economy the emphasis was on dealing with the maladjusted in the school.[4] The epidemic was on such a scale that specialist provision was out of the question. The dazed teacher, and compliant head teacher, propped up by extra resources, ancillary staff and often a plentiful flow of temporary teachers, took the advice of government circulars and LEA inspectors. They went along with the policy.

In society in general the official emphasis on a permissive and pluralistic society had weakened the authority of the parent and the teacher. Inside the school the emphasis on curriculum diversity and non-directive discipline weakened the authority of the head and the teachers. No one was as clear as they had been as to what a teacher was supposed to be and do. Sociologists of education declared that the role of the teacher in the classroom had in the post-war decades become more 'diffuse';[5] his authority was more personal and less 'positional', i.e. guaranteed by the fact of his officially being a teacher. There was less ritual and authority in schools, and teachers more often had to earn respect. Closer personal involvement with children pastorally or in subject lessons such as English teaching, reduced social and professional distance, emphasized warmth and informality but sometimes – particularly with so many young teachers in the schools – also dissolved or confused the boundaries of authority. Teachers frequently withdrew from their supervisory posts in the playground and dining hall, as part of their bid for higher status, better salaries and a quiet lunch hour, yet the concept of the teacher as psychiatric nurse and surrogate parent began to gain ground – it was even institutionalized in the large secondary school by the creation of numerous pastoral and non-teaching counsellor posts.

The annual waves of young insecure teachers arriving in the urban classroom were made to feel it was a point of professional pride that they should not admit defeat or be openly outraged by the disturbed children they met during their first few months. As the flight of mid-career teachers occurred more frequently, young arrivals to the staffrooms found there were fewer sympathetic figures who could help them. The head and senior staff were over-burdened or pursued an aloof managerial style which left the young teachers coping with the difficult classrooms. Not surprisingly, some young teachers were pushed towards over-identification with their pupils and altogether failed to establish their authority. Primary head teachers, with their peculiarly diffuse role, complained that they were spending more time as marriage guidance experts than as administrators of spelling tests.

Special schools were no solution.[6] They were unpopular as we saw with the parents of immigrant children. They were extremely expensive, particularly the residential schools, and the size of the maladjustment problem meant it was impossible to place all the children who needed special educational provision. The fifty or so boarding schools for the maladjusted, each taking about fifty seriously disturbed pupils, could make only a negligible contribution. Day schools for the maladjusted, like the schools for educationally subnormal children, did not work well. Staff were often professionally isolated and rarely of the high calibre needed, there being only a small salary addition for the work.

There were conflicting ideas about the curriculum. The fashionable orthodoxies of child psychiatry and child development influenced many teachers of maladjusted pupils to veer towards the psychoanalytical or non-directive techniques. Therapeutic art, self-governing communities and 'acting out' behaviour were encouraged at the expense of a systematically taught curriculum. Many residential maladjusted schools were run as lucrative private businesses, anxious local authorities willingly buying places for their most disturbed children to relieve teacher stress and disorderly classrooms. At the other end of the spectrum, some approved schools were notorious for their physical and psychological severity towards children, which occasionally blew up into a scandal as in the Court Lees case.[7] There was always a danger, too, that placing a maladjusted child in a total community, in an isolated country house with extensive grounds, institutionalized him as a problem child, who would subsequently become a problem adult at even greater cost to the community. Only too often the disturbed urban child graduated through a sequence of boarding, maladjusted and approved schools into borstal and prison. But the day schools for the maladjusted in cities were no more successful. Not only were first-rate teachers difficult to recruit, but the explosive ingredients of childhood disturbance were inflamed by return each evening to the home, emotionally disturbed parents or the provocation and temptations of the neighbourhood and gang life.[8] Nevertheless the utopian rural boarding school was replaced in the 1970s by a new experimental emphasis in the cities on small free schools, sanctuaries and alternative educational units for disturbed children.

Many argued that special educational provision was inappropriate.

When the Warnock Committee began to look at special education in 1975, most experts and virtually everyone in the teaching profession, except head teachers themselves, submitted evidence which argued that children should as far as possible be kept out of special schools. The integration of handicapped or disturbed pupils was the coming orthodoxy. They should mix with normal children and enjoy the benefits of a common school and its curriculum. Children should be special in an ordinary school, rather than ordinary in a special school.

Teachers therefore began to attempt, with creative versatility, to cope with the epidemic of emotional disturbance, encouraged by a climate of opinion which told them that this was their task. Indeed, it was extraordinary how ordinary schools with difficult classrooms manned by embattled young teachers responded as imaginatively and constructively as they did.

The inclusion of large numbers of disturbed children within the ordinary school called for some reorganization. Everyone agreed that disturbed or maladjusted youngsters were best managed in small groups. That meant additional resources, better accommodation and more teachers if poor educational attainment and unruly behaviour were to be remedied or contained. Within both the primary and secondary schools there was a similar response. Nevertheless, even in the most deprived neighbourhood, a school given enough extra resources and support could be astonishingly successful.[9]

In the successful inner city primary school vertical grouping, or unstreaming, grew in popularity. Village schools had traditionally been organized in this way, taking all ages of children and necessarily being unstreamed when one teacher had to work with twenty village children of differing ages and abilities. Vertical grouping provided continuity of relationship and relief from urban stress, particularly where teachers were constantly changing schools. 'Family grouping' resulted in the absence of competitiveness, for older and younger children helped each other. Many varieties of the integrated day were introduced. Generally, this meant that children were engaged in several different activities in the same room. Sometimes children would be directed by the teacher, at others they would have greater freedom of choice. One survey showed that 6 per cent of integrated classrooms allowed children freedom to work around the school all day, only meeting collectively towards the end of the afternoon. Most schools, however, offered more structure than this.

Thus in the urban primary school the organization of teaching groups dispersed the disturbed children and reduced the tension in the timetable and working day as far as possible. Furthermore, with a well-staffed school there was a good deal of withdrawal from the classroom of emotionally disturbed or backward children for special group work in the basic subjects. The 'nurture group' or therapeutic session was also quite common. But, unlike the secondary schools, the primary schools did not pursue policies of systematic remedial department growth.

Inside the secondary school, attempts to manage the increasing number of disturbed children by the reorganization of the curriculum and teaching groups resulted in a phenomenal growth of remedial departments. In the early post-war years, before debate in the comprehensive school had proceeded very far, streaming or meritocratic ability grouping was uncritically accepted. Indeed, Anthony Crosland[10] and other socialist theorists derided any idea of mixed ability, supporting instead the idea of the remedial department in the comprehensive or secondary modern school, since apparently it gave the backward or retarded pupil specially favourable accommodation, teaching and resources. After a period of intensive reteaching in the remedial form, the child could move back, educational or emotional problems solved, into one of the main streams of the comprehensive school. Thus a large comprehensive with perhaps eleven forms of entry might have two or three remedial streams, as well as two or three streams for the academic high fliers expected to take O and A levels and university entrance. As long as there was plenty of transfer of remedial children back into the other streams, teachers were enthusiastic about this organization. Comprehensive schools were often sold by their publicists as institutions where 'he started life as a remedial pupil and now has his PhD'.

The peak of popularity of remedial departments was reached during the mid-1960s and afterwards fell away. A 1971 survey of remedial organization undertaken by HM Inspectorate found that only one-third of the schools had a remedial department or gave remedial help to children, usually with reading, and this was most often in their first year of secondary schooling.[11]

A child could start in the remedial class in the first year, and with intensive tuition make rapid gains and achieve promotion to the higher streams by the end of his second year; so ran the theory. But the 1971 survey showed that although one in every seven children was in need of special help, in some of the 270 schools surveyed as few as 4 per cent were actually getting assistance. 50 per cent of the schools with remedial departments kept the children permanently segregated, often in a separate block with their own curriculum. It was curriculum apartheid in a low-status department. Controversy often circled in the staffroom over whether remedial pupils should do extra reading or mathematics rather than, say, attempting first year French: and whether their differentness was emphasized by their failure to share a common curriculum.

The other approach to educational backwardness and remedial education was the withdrawal of slow learners into small groups. But according to the 1971 survey 20 per cent of the sessions were with individual pupils during lunchtime or a teacher's free period. Only 5 per cent of the staff doing remedial work were specially trained. Certainly, in the emerging comprehensive schools it was just as often the sixth formers who were taught in groups of three or four pupils as it was the less able. Some schools had the strong-mindedness to re-allocate their priorities to help the disadvantaged, but many did not do so.

Experimental work flourished in the remedial departments.[12] Remedial teachers, young, inexperienced and lacking in status or elderly and lacking in ambition, could safely be left to their own devices with these children whose examination results did not greatly matter. There were no curriculum constraints; and it was in the remedial department very often that creative schemes of work experience, community service or integrated studies were initiated. Most of the week was spent on a 'block' timetable as in the primary school, with one teacher teaching several subjects to the class. This was much less unsettling than having the children going round the school on a circuit timetable of many subjects with different teachers for each 35-minute lesson.

However, dissatisfaction gradually grew with remedial departments. Children were transferred to higher streams much less often than had been hoped or imagined. And whereas in the early comprehensives and successful secondary moderns in the cities there had been relatively few very disturbed children, they now became more numerous year by year. Two further developments occurred. The head teachers and senior staffs of schools looked at their successful remedial departments, the block timetable, subject integration and informal classroom methods, the emphasis on group work and talk, and work in the nearby environment, and decided that the principle should be extended. If one remedial class or stream was successful why not have two? Indeed, where increasing numbers of disturbed or backward children were to be given an appropriate curriculum and teaching regime it was necessary to create additional remedial forms. Frequently the additional remedial classes were not rigidly streamed, but all the remedial children in, say, an eleven-form entry were distributed evenly between two or three forms: a miniature unstreaming system for the less able. Very disturbed children were either placed in a sanctuary unit inside the school, or found alternative provision in a special unit or free school.

By far the most important influence on the disappearing secondary moderns and the proliferating comprehensive schools was a major trend towards mixed ability teaching and unstreaming. A number of national researches into streaming in primary and secondary schools had begun to suggest that streaming was educationally undesirable and socially divisive. Colin Lacey[13] showed that streaming created alienation and hostile attitudes towards school among lower stream pupils. Streaming reproduced within the comprehensive school all the socially divisive patterns which had flourished in the old secondary school system. Everyone agreed that pupils were streamed on the basis of weak evidence and that there was little subsequent transfer between streams. Streaming was also a labelling technique, which became a self-fulfilling prophecy, *Pygmalion in the Classroom*, as well-known US research showed.[14] Some schools argued for continuing streaming, but attempted to mystify pupils by carefully labelling their classes with cryptic names or numbers: no one was supposed to know whether they were in the top, middle or remedial streams. But, as Roy Nash found through classroom observation in unstreamed primary classrooms, every child knew exactly where he stood in the pecking order even if no one officially told him.[15] Two important surveys in Britain by Joan Barker-Lunn indicated that it was above all teacher attitude which was the crucial factor, whether in streamed or unstreamed classrooms.[16] Lunn (1970) found no difference between the academic attainments of pupils in streamed and unstreamed primary schools. Following the same pupils to the secondary school (1971) she again came to the same conclusion. However, this second report gave encouragement to non-streamers in particular; pupils from unstreamed backgrounds were found to participate more in the educational life of the secondary school at other times of day and retained more originality. It was noticeable, however, that arguments for unstreaming were more often based negatively on the egalitarian premise that the less able or brighter children did not lose by unstreaming than on any argument for positive gain. Julienne Ford, in a book which is important in any discussion of social mix, looked at social stratification in the contemporary British comprehensive school.[17] She found that middle class children in streamed comprehensive schools were more likely to be taught with other middle class children, and working class children similarly with other working class children. She concluded that children separated by a corridor or a few classrooms, rather than being taught in separate buildings, were still socially divided. A consistently high proportion of children restricted their choice of friends to their own academic stream or its equivalent. Indeed, anyone working in a streamed comprehensive could not fail to be struck by the fact that disadvantaged, often physically smaller children often stood out like a sore thumb in the school assembly – it was like the first world war photographs of infantry and officers all over again. Ford concluded: 'If further research confirms these doubts we must think again about comprehensive schools, at least as now organized.'

But by far the strongest argument for unstreaming in the urban comprehensive school was left unspoken. The growing numbers of problem children meant that remedial classes or departments increasingly became ghettos of disruption and indiscipline in any school where they were introduced. Streaming made social control more not less difficult. Comprehensive school campaigners, or organizations such as the National Association of Teachers of English and the educational journal *Forum* mounted a propaganda campaign to see streaming abandoned. A growing body of opinion urged more unstreaming and mixed ability teaching for the emerging urban comprehensives of the early 1970s.

A revolution had occurred. For several decades most comprehensive schools had followed the advice of London's first education officer half a century earlier: 'put them all together and stream like mad'. They believed, with Crosland, that the mere provision of comprehensive schools would 'provide routes to the universities and to every type of occupation from the highest to the lowest . . . then very slowly, Britain may cease to be the most class-ridden country in the world'. They had agreed with Crosland's added comment that mixed ability teaching was a 'nonsense'. Now more and more teachers joined the growing band of unstreaming enthusiasts.

But many teachers found it impracticable to carry out complete unstreaming in one move. A halfway stage increased the numbers of remedial classes, and forms of academically able children, to create a three-tiered block banding system with a broad middle ability band of several forms. Within each band there would be mixed ability. Each band would offer a common curriculum, which in turn would have common elements provided for all of the bands. But finally there would be a move towards complete mixed ability. At that stage all children followed a common curriculum in mixed ability classes.

The 1971 HM Inspectorate report on remedial provision found that only 18 per cent of schools were unstreamed. By 1973, as the Bullock Report showed, a third of Britain's 12-year-olds were taught in mixed ability teaching groups.[18] Remedial departments were disappearing. Two-thirds of the nation's children now attended comprehensive schools, many of which were moving towards complete mixed ability teaching. The disturbed and disruptive children were being spread across the whole of the year group in a comprehensive school intake. However, mixed ability was usually confined to the first three years of the secondary school. The urban child might now reasonably expect to

be taught from the age of 5 to 14 in a mixed ability or unstreamed
setting.[19]

Mixed ability grouping, integrated or inter-disciplinary studies, could prove a brilliant, timely innovation in the well-run urban secondary school; or, as teachers rapidly found, it could bring educational catastrophe. Distributing the disruptive children across many classes and among many teachers might be an educationally desirable move. But now if a weaker teacher was unable to cope with just two or three children then the work of the whole class could be disrupted. Foreign language teachers frequently complained that unstreamed or mixed ability French teaching was workable for first year pupils but impossible by the third year: they pointed out that 'they can't go on drawing pictures and doing historical work on France while never approaching the language as such'.[20]

An important survey by the ILEA (1976) produced some vital findings.[21] Mixed ability teaching, now introduced in many inner London schools, was generally regarded by the teachers interviewed as a superior approach to streaming. But it was not always an easy move. Generous resources, time and considerable professional commitment were essential in any school attempting a changeover. A number of the mixed ability schools had socially deprived intakes or split sites, and they warned that a move towards reform demanded a positive, common attitude among the staff concerned. Inspectors and psychologists both reported that a majority of pupils seemed to have positive attitudes towards mixed ability teaching. Teachers reported that better social integration was achieved, which gave pupils generally a sense of security and the less able more confidence. Relationships improved between pupils and teachers, and disciplinary problems were lessened in all the schools surveyed. Clearly, spreading out problem children had reduced the impact of their mischief. However, many of the ILEA pupils questioned would have preferred to have been in streamed classes. In schools with high staff turnover where team teaching and other innovations were being introduced there could be a danger that no one teacher was finally responsible for any individual pupil. The emotionally disturbed child, especially the withdrawn or quiet child, could easily be lost or forgotten. A report by HM Inspectorate in 1977 came to some similar conclusions, but expressed many more reservations.[22]

How many schools, having to cope with large numbers of emotionally disturbed children, had been pushed into mixed ability as a palliative, rather than on educational grounds? For some schools, moves towards unstreaming, team teaching and mixed ability grouping weakened an already precarious school structure.[23] It could also be argued that they delayed recognition of the real origins of the urban malaise which had struck the emerging comprehensive schools so ferociously.[24]

Teachers and educational administrators looked outside the school, but accepted the straightjacket in which they were placed. By the early 1960s, at the time of the rise of the comprehensives, social class drift meant that in a deprived inner London borough like Southwark, half the boys entering the first year in a comprehensive school were in the bottom 20 per cent of the national range of ability. A game of juggling catchments became the preoccupation of educational administrators, who desperately tried to share out the more affluent pupils between competing comprehensive schools, and even the remaining grammar schools. Intakes were deteriorating, and neither positive discrimination, extra resources, free schools nor curriculum innovation could counteract the effect.

Yet teachers and administrators tried to make them do just that. Failure to unmask the impact of the urban crisis on the city classroom and the emerging comprehensive schools led to much of the public clamour about standards, a defensive professional stance and finally educational backlash. But the need for social mix was ignored or rejected. Many teachers and educational pundits remained serenely oblivious to the real issues. Brian Simon and some of the more influential proponents for the comprehensive school emphasized the virtues of neighbourhood schools strongly rooted in local community patterns.[25] Dilution of the working class, they argued, would only weaken the solidarity which was necessary if a full-blooded socialist revolution was ever to occur. The meritocrats, concerned only with social mobility in the classroom and the housing market, having dismissed any notion of mixed ability in the comprehensive classroom, had no reason for looking at the social or housing class balance of secondary school intakes. Not even in those areas of the inner cities (e.g. in Bristol's Hartcliffe neighbourhood, London's Tower Hamlets or Glasgow's Priesthill, with up to 85 per cent of housing being public) where the social composition of comprehensives was violently distorted was a lobby mounted. Even politicians responsible for education turned their backs on the problem. They toyed with the suggestion of the Plowden Report that 'sustained efforts' should be made to improve the social composition of schools in EPA neighbourhoods. They still believed that massive EPA resources and staffing would put things right.[26]

The suggested task for the comprehensive school teachers and administrators was not to look at total urban policy but to design an administrative compromise, the 'catchment zone', geographical territory from which children could be recruited for a particular school. Catchment zones should be carefully designed, especially in comprehensive school systems, to draw a range of ability. In Ealing and one or two other authorities, the bussing policy was also adopted to give secondary schools an ethnic range of intake; but those were an

'It's an exclusive little Comprehensive for the children of Shadow Ministers.'

exception.[27] In the smaller urban education authorities the design of the catchment zone was typically on a 'wedge' principle, with catchments extending from the city centre to the periphery, taking in a social and housing mix of pupils from primary schools in different housing neighbourhoods. Each wedge incorporated run-down inner city housing and owner-occupied housing on the suburban outskirts. Efforts were made to frustrate this system, particularly by owner-occupiers who could purchase housing in a more desirable neighbourhood or one with better schools. This could be avoided by a regular review of the catchment areas to maintain social balance. But in fact, as many critics rightly pointed out, catchment areas favoured the middle class. Public housing tenants found transfer extremely difficult to obtain, as did the less well-off private tenant or owner-occupier who could not afford to buy a house in an area served by 'good schools'. The rich could always operate the 'estate agent's charter'. The poor were driven instead to illegal strategies such as giving a false address.[28]

[68]   Another strategy (adopted by six authorities including Hull, Black-
pool, Exeter, and the largest comprehensive system, the Inner London
Education Authority) was banding, labelling children according to
ability before directing them to secondary schools. In London the
wedge-shaped catchment was not feasible because of the huge length
of each catchment. But a large city containing as socially varied a
community as London did in the early 1950s, before urban blight, it was
argued, provided a range of secondary school recruitment. Neighbourhood and borough boundaries could be ignored and viable
comprehensive school catchments which crossed them could be constructed. However, because of a false assumption of urban homeostasis, this strategy only worked partially, and then only as long as the
social class structure of the inner city was not rapidly deteriorating. But
that was exactly what happened. The deterioration in the intake of
many London comprehensive schools in the most difficult and
deprived neighbourhoods, along with the continued existence of the
grammar schools until 1977, meant that both comprehensive schools
competing with each other and grammar schools competing with the
comprehensives, were chasing a diminishing quality of intake.[29]
Authorities like ILEA which used the banding system were therefore
forced to impose 11+ selection tests of the kind that they had just
outlawed in order to identify and then allocate children of varying
ability 'fairly' to comprehensive schools.[30] The ILEA divided children
into seven ability 'bands', later contracted into three bands. This provoked the derisive observation that London children were divided into
gold, bronze and silver, recalling both Plato and the Tripartite system.
    Banding did not work anyway. It provoked a testing and grading of
children, even within the primary school, which stereotyped the expectations of both pupils and parents. Head teachers fought
unscrupulously for a diminishing pool of able children. Indeed, so
much resentment was caused by fighting for intakes among the comprehensive schools that it was decided that head teachers could no
longer be trusted. After 1975 children were allocated to their secondary
schools by the divisional administrators rather than secondary head
teachers. The greatest irony of all arose over the final absorption of the
grammar schools into the comprehensive system. The price paid for
the co-operation of the former London grammar schools in going
comprehensive was that the ILEA, the most progressive urban education authority in the country, had to press a Labour government to
delay legislation which could finally abolish banding, itself the death
gasp of the 11+; for the grammar schools only agreed to enter the
comprehensive system if they could be guaranteed a balanced intake,
which was only obtainable through banding.[31]
    By 1974, ILEA's tenth year of existence, in common with other city

education authorities with declining populations, it faced a new dilemma. Until then, despite a deteriorating quality of intake and a diminishing school population, drawing from a wide geographical territory had kept the large comprehensives up to size, although in some districts they had always resembled giant secondary moderns in their limited range of ability. It had always been argued that large comprehensives gave economies of scale. The wider the catchment, and the bigger the school, the greater the choice of subject options which could be offered. Large schools could have a catchment area juggled so as to recruit a range of ability, thus ensuring a sufficiently large sixth form at the upper end of the school.[32]

But the London school population was due to drop by 40 per cent in the decade 1971–81; in some deprived areas there were soon not enough children to fill the existing secondary school places, and sixth forms in the smaller schools were not considered efficient. The ILEA had two choices, and, to its credit, consulted the parents and public about them. The education officer had suggested a scheme regrouping secondary schools, closing some and retaining the large schools with their own sixth form which had been favoured over the years by policy-makers. Alternatively, schools could progressively grow smaller, when some would die through lack of pupils. A two-year period of intensive public consultation was initiated. But few expected what then happened.[33]

Public agitation showed that the merits of the large comprehensive were no longer accepted. Faced with a choice between retaining fewer large schools or having smaller schools, perhaps run without sixth forms or with shared sixth form centres, the public chose the latter. Everyone had at last, perhaps, obscurely sensed that the revised procedures and reorganization of secondary schools were only educational palliatives aimed at making a fair distribution of a deteriorating overall intake. Many also felt that it was the large, anonymous comprehensives which aggravated conditions of urban crisis.

Parents made their views extremely clear. Education consumers, parents and children, did not like the large comprehensives. In London, parents dissatisfied with the choice of comprehensive schools open to them chained themselves to railings, locked politicians in church halls, sat-in in the Education Officer's room, kept their children at home, set up free schools and carried on a sustained campaign of protest. They wanted smaller, more personal schools even if that meant reducing the curriculum choice.[34]

Administrators and teachers were at last forced to confront the real urban crisis. Thus far they had always played for time. They had up to now worked under the assumption that their administrative strategies were maintaining a range of intake. Now they had to face the fact that

[70] mini-comprehensives in the deprived neighbourhoods would find it impossible to recruit a range of social class and ability. The two nations in housing would be reflected in two nations in the secondary com-

'Haven't I seen your photograph in the school magazine?'

prehensive schools: the contrast would sharpen between schools serving the poor and disadvantaged parts of the city, and those in the prosperous suburbs or gentrified inner city neighbourhoods, which might have a socially balanced intake and their own sixth form. Juggling catchments, as the city population declined and social migration continued apace, had been a conjuring trick that bought time. But it was no longer possible to patch up the system with administrative ingenuity.

6 The day the roof fell in

Urban school buildings had a strong influence on the school life that went on inside them; their design, in any period, reflected the educational ideas of the time,[1] and they could accordingly be a positive help to the whole school staff; too often, however, they proved unsuitable, unsound or unsafe.

The triple-decker Victorian school was a familiar sight in congested urban areas. Solid but inflexible, it treated all pupils alike from ground floor infants up. But immediately after the second world war the picture began to change. The 1944 Education Act, together with a post-war upsurge in the birth rate, gave great impetus to the school building programmes of the late 1940s, and in the next twenty years a number of imaginatively designed and well-constructed schools appeared. Visitors from abroad came to study not only educational method but also the design qualities of the schools themselves.

The period after 1950 saw a return, initially for good reasons, to more compact primary school design. By then there had been a reaction against the large circulation spaces of the corridor and finger plan schools of the 1930s and 1940s, and it had become acceptable to design classrooms on both sides of the corridor. In 1959 a characteristic junior school occupying a city site might have a hall of 2,000 square feet with generous storage and stage facilities, a large separate dining hall, its own library, showers and changing facilities and a garden room or greenhouse. There was a more purposeful organization of teaching space, with five main components: home bases, central resource areas, enclosed or quiet areas, work bays and covered areas. Related changes took place in the emerging middle and secondary comprehensive schools. Science laboratories were no longer equipped with rows of benches facing the teacher. The curriculum emphasis had turned towards the pupil's own investigation and thereby transformed the organization of the room.

But while the architecture of the urban classroom after 1950 displayed some achievements, the general trend was towards disaster. In 1949 the Ministry of Education called for a reduction of 25 per cent in the cost of school buildings, arguing that this was a healthy move. Following that, the Ministry and later the Department of Education and Science kept severe control of cost limits, which by 1970 were well below the national average for building in general and had become extremely constricting.[2] At the same time all LEAs suffered the severe inflation of building costs, without any corresponding relaxation in the cost limits imposed by Whitehall. Although the housing yardsticks, as they were called, recognized regional differences in building housing in the inner cities, the educational cost limits of the DES did not. As a result, the space per child in the urban primary school was reduced over several years from some 42 square feet to 33 square feet, a reduction of 25 per cent. Worse still, school sites for inner city children did not allow for full playing field provision. The ILEA, for instance, was by 1969 paying often unreliable coach operators some £½m per year to deliver children late to over-used, outer suburban playing fields.

By 1977 separate dining rooms had become a thing of the past. Space sometimes had to be used for three different purposes, giving extra chores to staff, wasting time and creating a host of minor problems. Separate libraries were rarely seen in urban primary schools, except where pupil numbers were declining or where resource recesses doubled as teaching rooms. Corridors narrowed, and most seriously, the actual classrooms themselves were shrinking. It was amazing to recall that in the 1940s and late 1950s some education authorities had allocated thousands of pounds to each new school for an original work of art, or for a landscape architect to create an imaginative environment around the school. Frequently architects now found there was no money available for a single tree or shrub. It was extravagantly out of the question to provide a primary school in the inner city with a small biology pool or a unit for housing pets that fitted on to the classroom wall and was accessible from inside and out; and any idea of planting five hundred daffodil bulbs under a group of trees was regarded as absurd educational superfluity.

Some argued that not all the space restrictions forced on architects by financial stringency had been detrimental to good teaching. Un-

doubtedly the cost disciplines could lead to a less wasteful or better-
designed school. Large, pretentious entrance halls were for instance,
no longer seen. The inferior finish on buildings, equipment and general amenities was perhaps not harmful; but the loss of space was
extremely serious, and no one could be pleased with the cheap vinyl
asbestos tiles which replaced the semi-sprung floors of school halls
twenty years previously; with classroom ceilings which were lowered
to under eight feet, or the total absence of cross-ventilation. But by the
early 1970s architects were so straightjacketed by inflation, cost-limits
and site standards, that they could hardly be blamed for the results.[3]
Builders were similarly constrained. One urban authority in 1973 was
unable to find a single contractor to take on a £300,000 secondary
school project. The builders believed quite simply that schools could
not be constructed within the existing cost limits.

Architects were also constrained by fashionable orthodoxies. The
same emphases were found in school building as in public housing.
New building was always preferred.[4] Politicians, education officers
and architects who liked to leave their name on a building were fond of
measuring achievement by the number of school building 'starts' the
education committee had been able to sponsor while in office. The
large, architect-designed project was favoured, especially if it was part
of an urban renewal programme. By the early 1960s, such schemes
resulted in the demolition of many old schools and the construction of
new ones all over the country. That trend was exacerbated by the
Plowden Report and subsequent central government policies. The
planners bulldozed tracts of the inner cities, or, in new towns,
designed and built their Corbusier-like vision of the urban village, with
its futuristic, industrially produced tower blocks and open-plan
primary school or sky-scraper comprehensive complete with lifts and
acres of glass windows. As for consultation with teachers, children
or parents, that was minimal. Had it occurred, money might have been
diverted to provide playing fields or remodel older schools. But the
electorate, conditioned by the experts, believed that only new, ambitious school or house-building programmes represented any kind of
achievement.

Worst of all, an irrational stampede towards open-plan primary
school building was accelerated during a time of economic severity.
Experimental open-plan designs did not have internal walls, and were
thus both educationally progressive and cheap. Open-plan schools,
resembling the flimsy pavilions put up at temporary exhibitions, were
hurriedly assembled in school playgrounds. Hundreds of perfectly
good late-Victorian school buildings were thunderously demolished to
make way for experimental schools of questionable construction and
design. As late as 1971, the then education minister announced a

primary schools improvement programme which meant the destruction of nearly all Victorian urban primary schools by 1978.

'Say what you like, these new schools don't stand up to classroom violence like the old Victorian ones.'

The rapid growth of industrial school building techniques began in 1957. Local authorities themselves designed and organized building systems to put up schools which they claimed were cheap, flexible and attractive. In 1970 the Department of Education issued two booklets warmly approving this novel trend. Soon there were eight consortia with exotic names (ASC, CLASP, CLAW, MACE, METHOD, ONWARD, SCOLA and SEAC) at work building schools.[5] The first of these (the Consortium of Local Authorities Special Programme) started in Nottinghamshire, where school architects faced heavy expenditure on foundations for schools where disused mines had caused subsidence. The architects designed a light-weight building, based on a frame which would move with the ground in the event of subsidence or ground collapse.

Each consortium was a band of local authority architects agreed on a certain philosophy of school building design, placing orders for the component parts with builders and suppliers. The initials of the consortia, and more particularly what they stood for, were unknown to many parents and teachers, yet by 1970 nearly half the total building programme was accounted for by CLASP or systems like it. They became briefly fashionable. Architects assured politicians they could now cost buildings with greater accuracy than by more traditional methods. The schools thus built were flexible, could easily be modified or extended, and the argued cost-benefits were so great that financially sensitive education authorities began to insist on schools built by

consortia. For system-building stabilized building costs at a time of
rapid inflation in the construcion industry. Early on, claims were also
made that maintenance costs would be appreciably reduced, since
pre-painted windows and plastic coated partitions cut out labour
charges. Architecturally, the consortium schools found international
approval. A prize winning CLASP school was exhibited at the 1970
Milan Trienniale.

The fashionable praise was to prove short-lived; not every young
architect was ambitious to participate in school system building. A
generation of architects was emerging who, preferring to design individual schools, did not want to sink their professional identity in
manuals and standard details. Besides, serious technical doubts about
the consortium systems approach to school building began to be
expressed quietly by the whole architectural profession, although the
classroom storm did not break immediately.[6] In 1973 architects began
to announce in their professional journals that something was seriously wrong. They complained that in circumstances of absurd financial restraint the consortia systems represented the worst possible
approach. Consortium building was uneconomical and inflexible,
encouraging architects to skimp on their design work. There were
cheaper and more traditional approaches which would produce better
results. Fierce controversy raged in the microscopic professional world
of school design between working architects and their superiors. The
ILEA, followed by seven other LEAs, decided on the basis of two
different reports to leave the MACE consortium.[7] Interestingly,
although both reports reached the same conclusion their reasoning
was very different. One report, prepared by four job architects, was
highly critical of the system, alleging that it produced poor quality
buildings at higher costs than traditional schools. The other, produced
by the principal architect and the education officer, argued more officially that with a draconian cut back in education spending MACE
membership was no longer economic.

The *Architectural Journal*, giving magisterial judgement on the MACE
system, recited some of its innumerable faults: the poor sound and
thermal insulation, the costliness of ducted warm air heating, the
external wall leaks, failures of concrete beams, impracticality of plumb-
ing units and the lack of choice in finish. The journal pointed out that
MACE construction in some respects did not comply with building
bye-laws or fire requirements, and that structural engineers and
mechanical service experts, resenting a lack of consultation, were
unhappy about many aspects of the system. 'A programme for hundreds of schools in south-east England has been embarked upon
without even building and testing a prototype in use', the *Architectural
Journal* scathingly concluded.[8]

By 1973 misgivings were forcibly expressed by the teachers.[9] The professional associations complained about the rapid expansion of open-plan school building. They feared that local education authorities might be putting up system-built schools with the object of packing as many children as possible into a given space, rather than with any educational philosophy in mind. After all, was it not cheaper to build a badly designed, open-plan school than a badly designed traditional school? Sixty-four local education authorities were questioned in 1974 about their open-plan school building policies, and it emerged that less than half of them had consulted with teachers before going ahead with schemes.

A public storm broke out; in several highly publicized cases new primary and secondary schools built by consortia and using the systems approach came under heavy criticism from their occupants. After one term in the brand new John Milton Primary School in central London, teachers complained to the education authority that their new building, constructed under the MACE system, was in many ways worse than the Victorian school it replaced.[10] Two weeks after their moving in a rainstorm had caused seven roof leaks. Ceiling tiles had disintegrated, and teachers had been fishing pieces of the ceiling out of their coffee. Badly fitted toilets had been repaired six times in a fortnight. Security was poor, even by the low standards of schools: in the first term, there had been repeated break-ins to the school.[11] The heating and air conditioning system did not work; and there was such a shortage of storage space that teachers and parents had bought timber for shelves and an outside shed. A classroom sink had come away from the wall, and the walls themselves were sodden because there was no money for tile surrounds in the sink area, or skirting boards to provide protection from wet floors.

In the summer of 1973, at the official opening of another new primary school in central London, the head teacher startled guests by her outspoken criticism of the design and layout of the school, whereupon the local mayor, as chairman of the school managers, promptly refused to accept formal takeover of the school.[12] In spring 1976, when the first multi-storey comprehensive school built under the MACE system was opened in the London suburb of Lewisham, girls and teachers alternately froze or fainted in temperatures which fluctuated up to 42°C.[13] The industrially prefabricated school building had fresh air ventilation through slit windows while, theoretically, warm air filtered down through holes in the ceiling. But attempts to keep down the costs left out, ludicrously, the extractor fans vital to any such system.

But was the urban child actually safe when working in the school building? A mistress taking a rehearsal in the hall of Camden Girls School in North London in 1973 heard creaking and sounds like falling

gravel on two or three occasions. A girl was sent to look out of the
upstairs window. She noticed a sag in the roof of the hall, and a crack
two feet long was seen at the edge of the ceiling. The same evening, the
hall was used for a meeting of parents. Later that night the roof
collapsed. The subsequent report[14] blamed the collapse on five features of the building, the chief being quick-setting high alumina
cement which had been used to make the beams, probably for speed of
production in the factory; over a period this had lost its strength.
Researchers investigating the collapse of a swimming pool at a school
in Stepney in February 1974 again diagnosed the high alumina
hazard.[15] For some years it had been known that high alumina cement
was dangerously prone to 'conversion', a change within the concrete
that weakened and rotted it; but it was thought this only occurred in
wet or humid conditions. Now building experts confirmed in a Department of Environment circular that a further lethal danger had been identified: 'conversion' could take place under normal conditions and there
was no established method of checking the safety of such buildings.

The DES instructed all LEAs and governing bodies of voluntary
schools to investigate every educational building for which they were
responsible. A danger dossier secretly drawn up at the Department of
the Environment initially listed thirteen and, soon after, two hundred
buildings, mostly schools, where there was an identifiable risk. Later
still, the government announced that four hundred 'high risk' buildings should be urgently checked by engineers. Finally in mid-1974, a
government circular announced that several thousand buildings were
in need of inspection for possibly dangerous structural defect. All
these buildings were at risk because they had used high alumina
cement in load-bearing situations: the government banned this type of
cement until further notice.

Urban teachers had frequently been criticized and rightly, for
injudicious innovation. It is worth remembering that other professionals concerned with the urban school also misapplied the brave technological revolution of the 1960s.

The whole question of urban school safety aroused concern, in particular over accidental fires and arson in urban schools where fire precautions had formerly seemed adequate.[16] Incendiarism occurred most
commonly at night, or during weekends and school holidays. When
schools were in session hoax calls were more common. Senior fire
officers considered that system-built schools in general offered less fire
risk. The means of escape from CLASP schools, for instance, were
assessed overall as safer than those in older school buildings. Nonetheless, there were new technical anxieties. Fires which broke out in
school hours in traditional buildings were usually detected quickly.

But this could no longer be relied upon in the case of system-built premises, where fire might spread quickly through a roof void. In the open-plan school dense smoke could build up very quickly. Craft materials, modern plastic and other classroom apparatus were often especially inflammable. It was for this reason that, in 1974, thousands of polypropylene chairs which could prove a fire hazard were withdrawn from London schools.

A survey by the Fire Precautions Association in 1970 identified three special factors of danger in schools: insufficient or inadequately protected escape routes; insufficiently trained occupants; and inadequate fire warning systems.[17] The ILEA, carrying out a survey in 1969, found fire precaution systems inadequate in over one hundred buildings, mostly older Victorian schools. A major improvements programme was initiated. Experts were uneasily aware that the urban school with its multiplying population of disturbed children now contained many possible arsonists. Special care needed to be taken in community or open school settings where there was considerable freedom of movement or new variety of choice of curriculum materials. Small-scale fires causing injuries to young children could easily occur. For instance, in one progressive open-plan school in inner London, a volunteer teaching children to build small boats driven by methylated spirits turned away momentarily. The children played with fire near the container and an accident occurred. Changing curricula or teaching styles can certainly alter how safe a building is.

In fact, however, 40 per cent of accidental injury to children in school involved not fire but bone fractures. Surprisingly, more accidents happened in the ordinary classroom than in most obvious black spots, such as laboratories, handicraft rooms or domestic science flats. Apart from the gymnasium, the classroom was the most common setting for school accidents, according to DES and other surveys. One piece of school equipment in particular (outside the classroom) was both a hygiene risk and source of fatalities: the roller towel, in its old-fashioned and more modern version, led to as many as four school deaths in one year.[18]

School architecture and design were severely criticized from time to time by public health inspectors. The urban school, they said, was characteristically a Victorian building with pre-Victorian safety standards. Health hazards from faulty school design or building could be extremely serious. Medical statistics showed, for example, that school children under fifteen years of age were six times more likely to be ill with dysentery than the rest of the population of England and Wales. Both hair fashions and informal teaching groups no doubt played a part in the 50 per cent increase in head lice infestation among schoolchildren reported between 1972 and 1977.

School design was particularly censured for insanitary toilet arrangements and a lack of adequate hygiene in school kitchens. In the case of older urban school buildings the problem was linked with a lack of money for minor improvements while they awaited rebuilding. But in new schools, too, there was much to criticize. Many faults could no doubt have been avoided, but LEAs were curiously excused, under existing regulations, from any need to submit school plans to the local building authority for approval (although they sometimes did so on a courtesy basis). Thus the pleasant architectural feature of bare brick wall found in school dining rooms might be fashionable and economical but was not hygienic. Some toilets had 'stable' doors, or even opened directly into teaching areas. Yet such architectural features were banned as hygienically unacceptable in any public restaurant. Regulations which applied to workers in shops, offices or factories did not count for children in schools. The nominal responsibility for the enforcement of school regulations rested with HM Inspectorate. Many thought that the only thing inspectors did was to count lavatories, others alleged that they rarely carried out routine inspections of school premises since they were mainly concerned with educational aspects of the schools they visited. Where the truth lay is a question to which we shall return.

To the children in urban schools the most upsetting feature of the building was an unpleasant school lavatory. A survey conducted jointly by a national newspaper and educational pressure groups in 1974 questioned adolescent pupils about the quality of life in secondary schools. It found that many lavatories were still out in the playground, rather than indoors in the school. Children reported that many school lavatories did have soap, toilet paper, towels, mirrors, waste bins and hot and cold water – but that just as often they were filthy, dark, very cold, badly ventilated and unpleasant, with no sanitary waste bins or locks on the doors. Many younger children were especially frightened by gangs of smokers who monopolized the cubicles. In some city secondary schools a plumber was employed virtually full-time in repairing daily damage to school lavatories.[19] The answer seemed to be to readjust spending priorities and employ a fierce ancillary as concierge.

Urban schoolchildren in their elderly Victorian building were also poorly treated in heating arrangements. Pupils and teachers in urban schools were not protected like other workers under the 1963 Shops, Offices and Railway Premises Act. Virtually no other advanced country in 1978 had heating standards for schools as low as those in Britain. Consequently, many pupils and teachers were working in conditions which would have been prohibited in other fields of employment, despite the common knowledge that accident rates rise as heating temperatures drop. Schools compared badly with prisons or military barracks. A convict, a soldier, a sailor or an airman was legally entitled to have his living quarters heated to a minimum of 18°C. The same applied to youngsters in detention centres or borstals – but not to children in classrooms.

In the mid-1970s professional and public opinion swung round in another direction. Education authorities had been successful in convincing teachers that their Victorian schools should be replaced in the space age. Having listened to the teachers' complaints, having been embarrassed by the public protests of consumers and architects over industrial building systems, the administrators and politicians offered teachers a new choice: a new school or the existing Victorian building remodelled. Most teachers chose the latter. Given the rigid cost limits and site standards, it was better to retain the majestic Victorian castle, with its iron girders and immensely strong construction. Like urban renewal and tower blocks in housing, the large new school was discredited and public and professional opinion favoured small size and remodelling. Thus ornate, solid, towering Board schools continued to dominate the city skyline with their Prussian façades, Dutch gables and brick work, ornamental towers and cupolas. The myth of the educational palace rising newly from the demolition site had been finally discredited: in education committee rooms all over the country a revised gospel was propagated.[20]

There was also a significant shift towards humanizing architecture and design in housing which had clear implications for schools as buildings.[21] Oscar Newman investigated the relationship between 'defensible space', crime rates and vandalism in US municipal housing projects; he discovered that some architectural design conferred anonymity and encouraged negligence, petty crime or vandalism.[22] Other things being equal, there was more pride and care taken where a clear boundary existed between public spaces and 'defensible' private areas. The implications of the new architectural sociology for urban schools were arresting. The small secondary school was the equivalent of the small street or residential close in public housing, where Newman found a greater sense of security and identity. Could not groups of pupils spend most of their time in one or two rooms, grouped to foster community and the sense of 'defensible space', where they might keep their books, clothes and other kits? The bleak corridor with its lockers and cloakrooms, practically designed to offer anonymity to the casual school thief, could well be replaced. Small-scale, identifiable home-rooms would enhance a sense of ownership, create incentives, restrain casual vandalism and encourage pupils informally to exert surveillance over each other. Most of these principles could in fact be observed in the informal classroom and free schools.

It would be naïve to conclude that little was achieved in school

design during the two decades of urban school crisis. There was
outstanding architectural work of great imagination and merit. Comprehensive, middle and first schools with their parents' rooms, resource centres, community education facilities, swimming pools, libraries, theatres, sixth form suites and bookshops exceeded the wildest dreams of previous generations. The British school compared favourably with urban school design in North America, Australia or Europe. Impressive schools were frequently built, as well as the flimsy bungalows of the ill-fated consortia programmes. But if a balance sheet

'If this building gets much older it'll become historic and they'll never pull it down.'

were drawn up for urban school design during the period, the debit entries would outweigh any creditable achievement. However, the heretical notion that architects alone could create educational perfection, or that school buildings could compensate for society, had been dispelled.

7 The caretaker has the keys

In an unsurpassed study of the American urban school, Willard Waller highlighted in 1932 the influence of individuals in the school community who had negligible status but considerable power as influentials or 'gate keepers', among them the school janitor or caretaker.[1] Waller argued that these officially unimportant people played a crucial role in deciding success in the classroom or the relationship of the school with its local community.

Waller's analysis was certainly true for the British urban school half a century later. Numerous new faces appeared in the corridors and staffrooms of primary and secondary schools during the urban school crisis. During a period of feverish teacher turnover, the role and influence of the school caretaker or primary helpers enlarged considerably. Indeed, to understand the urban school of the mid-1970s it is essential to know about the back-stage power and politics of the institution. There was a covert as well as an obvious daily contribution made by the school caretaker, his assistants and cleaners; and also by numerous extras including dinner ladies, school secretaries, technicians, media resource officers, school librarians and others who helped the teachers.

Visitors from abroad entering the British urban school were astonished, especially in the inner cities and some conurbations, at the generous growth of ancillary staffing provided from the late 1960s onwards for teachers working with disadvantaged children.[2] A large comprehensive school attended by 2,000 children in 1977 might have a non-teaching staff comprising: 10 full or part-time clerical workers; some 26 technicians and ancillary helpers; a school caretaker and 6 assistants; 26 cleaners and school meals staff; and extra para-professionals like the school counsellor, librarian, media resource officer and secretaries. Many of these were newly established positions.[3]

". . . and as my secretary, you'll naturally be expected to run the school . . ."

In primary schools the school secretary was a powerful figure. In the emerging comprehensive schools she became a highly-trained administrator, serving the equivalent of a small township as its accounting officer for school journeys, uniform grants, wages for ancillary staff, book allowances and equipment requisitions. Leading a team of three or four secretaries, this administrator also assumed responsibility for crucial curriculum or planning decisions connected with alternative use of resources or the EPA virement schemes (described later). The comprehensive school secretariat might also provide clerical support for the head teacher, senior members of staff, and typing or duplicating services for the various subject departments.

Another new face appearing in London comprehensive schools and sometimes elsewhere, often working closely with the librarian who was now usually a full-time professional specializing in books and curriculum resources, was the 'media resource officer'.[4] A publishing explosion had created not only a wealth of extra books for teachers planning courses, but also a rich variety of 'non-print' audio-visual aids. In London, over a period of ten years, 300 media resource officers were trained for attachment to schools and teachers' centres, where they became responsible for the servicing and supervision of audio-visual aids, and for the creative manufacture and classifying of curriculum resources – slides, photographs and video tapes – not seen at all in the schools ten years before.

The expansion of ancillary staff was a mixed blessing.[5] True, teachers already fully stretched into 'extended professionalization' with many additional tasks were sensibly relieved from pressure. Jobs like supervising meals, administering first aid, tying shoe laces, or handing out paper and paints from the stock cupboard were increasingly taken over, following the Plowden Report, by a flotilla of local ladies in nylon overalls. But sadly, the humanist tradition which saw the teacher as professionally responsible for the child throughout the day was eroded. At worst, this weakened the community and destroyed social cohesion during a critical period for schools. For instance, where teachers no longer undertook school meal supervision, a chaotic dinner hall might be supervised by bewildered helpers whose only professional preparation in the social management of children had been the donning of an overall.

The school lunch hour, where traditionally teachers talked and ate informally with children, deteriorated dismally. Some teachers, out of professional conviction or because they were hard up, still ate their meal with the urban schoolchild and his friends. Others, the public complained, consumed a free meal with colleagues at separate tables or in their own dining room. The abdication of the school dinner as a ceremony, a social and educative occasion, was a major mistake. Only the most progressive schools made successful systematic attempts to see that the school meals supervisors took on a professional role and encouraged talk and civilized behaviour.

The traditional value of the daily school meal had been demonstrated and become accepted during the second world war. For the first time a generation of well-nourished urban, working class children grew up who, despite rationing, received a balanced diet. Thirty years later, there was much dissatisfaction with school meals. The Child Poverty Action Group, attracting headlines and television coverage, typically pointed to the 'stigma of free school meals' being suffered in the 1970s by many disadvantaged children, who were being publicly labelled as 'free meals children'.[6] Some children had to eat at separate tables, others were lined up in a separate queue; yet others were called out in class or were given special cards which they had to produce at the canteen. The egalitarian pursuit of a common curriculum, unstreaming or mixed ability teaching could be undermined in a few minutes by an insensitive dinner supervisor.

But many school meals were substandard. The adverse effects on the health and diet of urban children of poor quality school meals and the

ending of free school milk aroused medical concern.[7] A lengthy investigation in 1975 by Arnold Bender and colleagues in twelve schools in
Brent, a deprived multi-ethnic outer London borough, found that
none of their school meals reached the DES protein target of 29 grammes of meat; and only two senior schools achieved the recommended
calorie target of 880 calories per meal.[8] In other words, urban children
were being undernourished. Professor Bender and his colleagues
uncovered a world of amateurish maladministration dominated by the
whims of individual headmasters and inept lady helpers who produced soggy chips, over-cooked cabbage and could not slice food into
equal portions. Poor quality food was purchased and badly prepared.
In Brent, where the survey took place, school dinners were often the
main meal of the day; many children appeared rarely to eat more than
sliced bread and jam or cereals at home.

While the abandonment of the school meal by teachers was regrettably widespread, individual schools made agreeable innovations.
Most characteristically, the set-piece ritual with a canteen or drill hall
atmosphere was replaced with cafeteria-style seating and service.
Many girls' schools offered slimming salads instead of stodgy potatoes
and puddings. Less acceptably, money-saving moves were made
towards the use of converted plant protein instead of meat. 'Textured
Vegetable Protein' (TVP), a product based on soya beans and widely
used as a filler in meat products, became much in vogue with school
meals administrators.[9] Thus some urban children, already disadvantaged, were sentenced to a diet of vegetarianism, jam sandwiches and
fish and chips, while the school meal was less than ever an event to
look forward to.

In primary schools local helpers could often provide the kind of
permanent emotional attachments which children lacked in an epoch
of high teacher turnover. These primary helpers – street personalities,
aunts or grandmothers, mothers known to other mothers and local
families, as well as to the children – not only supervised the playground, dinner, first aid, or the stock cupboard, or accompanied
children on outings; they also provided a continuity of care and sense
of community where the head and teachers sometimes failed.[10] The
school ancillary staffs appointed in such large numbers after the Plowden Report established their own hierarchy and particular relationships – sometimes delicately balanced – with the school caretaker,
teachers and head. Unlike the school cleaners, their role was not
always clearly definable in the eyes of others. Some ancillary helpers,
such as the nursery assistant, were accountable to one teacher. Some
came in specially for a period of the day to supervise school meals or
the playground. But most ancillary helpers assisted around the school
on a variety of tasks. Over the years, these invading local women

became a semi-professional cadre with their own skills and responsibilities. While at first they worked on simple tasks such as covering library books, by the mid-1970s they were acquiring skills and leader-

'You must learn to delegate responsibility, Headmaster!'

ship in first aid, duplicating, audio-visual aids, organizing playground games and running the school parties or journeys. They had become an identifiable and important group within the school, with mounting influence upon teachers and children.

As Waller had observed fifty years before, the cleaners, helpers and caretaker could often be as important as the head or other teaching staff in determining professional failure or happiness. For the young teacher in her first year a confidential whisper, resigned gesture or raised eyebrow among the ancillary staff experienced in the ways of the school and neighbourhood could signify approval or professional disaster. The local grandmother who after some years commanded the stock room keys or had the ear of the headmistress, had the power of life or death over the young teacher. So did the school secretary who, controlling the telephone switchboard and guarding entry to the head teacher's room, decided who had access to the outside world or the seat of power. The distress of a young teacher whose boyfriend was barred from reaching her on the staffroom telephone could be the last straw. The struggling temporary teacher could be cut down to size, subtly derided, reprimanded by the caretaker in front of the children, sabotaged by a sly, officious helper, or deprived of teaching materials ('there is no more sugar paper this term'). The progressive young

nursery teacher might have to fight professionally with a difficult
cleaner, or a dominating, middle-aged nursery assistant who, having
mothered her own family, had emphatic views on what should happen in classrooms.

But the explosion of ancillary employment identified dozens of
valuable people who brought benefits to the school, contributed skills
and enriched their own lives. When cleaners and school caretaker,
teachers and head teacher, and the band of helpers worked together as
a co-operative team they could be unstoppable. Recruiting local aunts,
mums and grandmothers not only brought the local community, but
sometimes brought Asian or West Indian faces into the multi-ethnic
school. A particular advantage for the community school of ancillary
staffing as opposed to using voluntary help was that in disadvantaged
neighbourhoods 'volunteer' parents often proved to be unemployable
mothers with psychiatric or personality problems. Paid school helpers
could, however, be carefully selected and were financially accountable
for their work and behaviour.

Without doubt, next to the head teacher the key personality in any
urban school was the school caretaker, or the schoolkeeper as he was
known in London schools. Waller wrote of his US equivalent: 'the
janitor is a person of no little importance in any school system . . . his
actual influence is often out of proportion . . . largely this pro-
portionate importance of the janitor is derived from the fact that the

'I'm not workin' a minute after 4 . . .'

'. . . an' I can't be expected to fix the boiler . . .'

'. . . now you've allowed all those kids on me floors.'

janitor is always a member of the local community, whereas teachers belong rather to the outside world . . . Instances of spying by janitors can be multiplied without end.'

Those suspicious reservations of forty years ago were sometimes still applicable in Britain. But the positive espionage of schoolkeepers and helpers in the contemporary urban school became invaluable. As local people, they knew more than carbons of clinic letters or teachers' notes could ever reveal about individual children, families and the neighbourhood.

The schoolkeeper, resident in his Victorian cottage in the school playground, with his cleaners and the ancillary helpers, was an unpaid community social worker, intelligence agency and grapevine for the urban primary school. A quiet word could give the secondary head teacher early warning of neighbourhood tensions, gang or criminal activity. Information about a move by the housing department to shift problem families to a 'difficult' estate, the discreet identification of 'children at risk' of sexual molestation, neglect or child battering could give the teachers the alert. Where there was exceptional family stress, it was often the school caretaker or helper who was able to signal fears or suspicions. After all, the families in question might be relatives as well as neighbours.

So the master spy and uncrowned king of this intelligence fraternity was the school caretaker. Presented to the British television public or in educational periodicals as a joke figure, the school caretaker was literally and sociologically a gate-keeper: he carried the keys of the educational kingdom, potentially wielding enormous power and influence. The school was his kingdom; the assistant keepers were his courtiers, the cleaners his retinue, and the teachers and children often his loyal or unwilling subjects – and the building was controlled by him each evening, week-end and during all of the holidays. If he banned the Brownies or refused to lend the plastic chairs for a wedding party, neighbourhood life stopped in its tracks.

Urban school caretakers faced increasing stress during these years.[11] The annoyance and strain to them and their families of living in a difficult neighbourhood, being seen as 'authority', dealing with intruders, endless broken windows, threats of arson or robbery made a heavy burden. Sometimes their response, a mixture of shop steward patois and guard dog mentality, made matters worse. Unlike teachers they could not disappear at the end of the afternoon to be whisked out to the peaceful suburbs. As the urban school crisis grew stormier, the caretakers became militant. Inner London school caretakers refused at one point, for instance, after a number of violent street attacks, to undertake their traditional task of delivering dinner money to the bank. An increase in threats by children or their parents, intimidation by fly-by-night window cleaning contractors, or backlash from hostility the head or teachers had generated in the neighbourhood added to their frustrations.

Any local newspaper of the time carried press reports conveying something of the menace and insecurity of the urban school caretaker's job. Typical of many such stories, often rating only a few column inches of space, was the story of what happened one night in 1974 to a south London schoolkeeper and his wife returning home after a night out.

> They saw one of the boys urinating in the school gate. Mrs. Baker said, 'My husband spoke to him about it and the lad started taking his coat off to him. We ignored him and tried to get in and close the gate behind us, when the four boys rushed us. One punched my husband in the face and knocked his glasses off. We managed to close the gates and then they started banging and thudding. So I ran in and called the police.'[12]

Court action could not be guaranteed in such cases. On that occasion one boy was bound over and the other fined a total of £15 for assault and being drunk and disorderly.

How did enthusiastic moves towards the 'community school' and community involvement in education affect the school caretaker and his job? Education administrators and head teachers who pushed 'community school' policies, irrespective of the urban setting of their work, were usually safely digging suburban gardens when such outrages as that just described occurred. When one city discussed an ambitious blueprint for community education by means of a series of public consultation meetings, it was the school caretakers, who would be perhaps most affected, who were left out when every other conceivable group in the community was represented. Ironically, while teachers were generating enthusiasm for 'community education' the school caretakers were negotiating a weekly dog meat allowance so that every school might have an Alsatian guard dog. In London, serious anxiety about child rapings, molestation and school robberies led to public agitation for better security in schools even while plans were being formulated for throwing open the school gates for most of each day. Opening the school buildings for intensive use by the community had been a successful tradition in the Cambridge village colleges and in some of the show-piece urban comprehensive schools. The social and educational merit of such schemes was beyond doubt; but as with curriculum innovation, realistic timing was needed when promoting them.

School caretakers therefore faced a rising challenge from vandals, arsonists and thieves taking advantage of the poor security and construction of new buildings. Fire-proofing might have improved marginally, but the flimsy open-plan primary school made effective security impossible. Night marauders easily entered comprehensive school sites which covered several acres. They stole sophisticated audio-visual aids apparatus, motor engineering and welding tools – not the contents of the school safe. Reluctance by politicians and administrators to meet colossal insurance premiums or instal expensive alarm systems often led school caretakers to feel they were not being given official backing. Parents and ratepayers, through their proxy the education officer, preferred to sigh resignedly and dip their hands into their pockets. But it was the school caretaker who was left the vulnerable victim of further 'aggravation'.

The school caretaker, teachers and children, were almost more vulnerable where an open-door policy exposed the school during classroom hours to casual visitors who might be parents, but just as easily could be dangerous intruders. The British urban school system had not reached the point where, as in New York, 4,500 armed guards were employed in school corridors to keep order. But the entering of schools in full daylight by glib or stealthy intruders was a growing trend. Their intention might be the theft of roof lead, petty theft from the staffroom, sexual assault or exposure; invasions of schools by ex-pupils or youths from other schools happened occasionally. In a typical case 'the school secretary noticed two men on the roof. The head was informed but did not have any record of any workmen scheduled to arrive at the school. The schoolkeeper asked for their names and to see their job tickets. They gave their names and the firm were telephoned. The firm had no work scheduled and asked to speak to the men. They refused saying they would get into trouble as they were not supposed to start work yet and then left.'[13]

Given the stress and tension of the job, maintaining a selective recruitment of caretakers proved difficult. In the heyday of the urban school before the second world war, caretakers were recruited from the ranks of ex-servicemen. They considered themselves on a par with the Corps of Commissionaires. Upright men with moustaches, military bearing, precise timekeeping, and dedicated to high cleaning standards, they were much admired – and occasionally feared. But by the 1970s school caretakers complained that their high wages, housing and perquisites were just not worth the irritations and tensions of being marooned in a sea of asphalt in a rough neighbourhood. No amount of money could compensate for the loss of respect, the complaints of wives and the never-ending claustrophobia of the job. Not surprisingly, recruiting difficulties meant that on occasion an unscrupulous school caretaker was employed. It might be that, day after day, the dinner money would be mysteriously short of a few pence when it reached the bank. Weekend possession of an empty building could lead to more unusual pursuits than the caretaker letting his children play in the Wendy house of the nursery class. Police calling at midnight on one caretaker to warn him that classroom lights were blazing found a gang storing away the proceeds of a major bank robbery.

Any visitor wanting a confidential insight into an urban school was well advised to talk informally with the school caretaker. A contemporary memoir by a 76-year-old retired London schoolkeeper eloquently confirmed Waller's analysis:

> Being one practically born on a school in Deptford soon after the LCC took over from the London School Board about 1900, I feel qualified to bring back memories of the fun we had and moments of glory over the years. What has astonished me is the number of supervisors that now seems necessary. Whereas in those days there seemed to be only four or five plus a good Scottish lady who delighted in poking her umbrella in every corner in an inspection, there now seems to be more supervisors than schoolkeepers, but I suppose that's progress . . . I was fortunate in having two delightful headmistresses who had only to be asked to give permission for absence to be immediately granted, and blessed with a capable wife to manage till I got back, (no assistants then under a Grade V as it was known). One still lives near me and calls occasionally. The work accumulated of course till one got back. One perspired on solid fuel boilers with the boiler house door open and there were still buckets of coal to be carried up and down stairs. Incidentally, I had the sweep in last week at this flat and his words were, 'blimey, you still knocking about after 11 years retirement. Must be all that clinker you shifted!' Visiting the few friends left one cannot help noticing the difference. The manual work may be less but the mental effort has trebled at least. The old comradeship is still there even if the status has improved enormously.[14]

Significantly, and in keeping with the times, the London school caretakers negotiated for a change of nomenclature within their 1977 pay round. It was their wish to become known as 'schools services managers'. Traditionally, there had been great pride and sense of community among the school caretaking fraternity. Perhaps it would return as prospects for the urban school revived.

8 Management by mafia or creative bureaucracy

In *The Sociology of Teaching* Willard Waller observed that schools were usually organized on the principle of autocracy:

> The generalization that schools have a despotic political structure seems to hold true for nearly all types of schools . . . . self government is rarely real. Usually it is but a mask for the rule of the teacher oligarchy. It is not enough to point out that the school is a despotism. It is a despotism in a state of perilous equilibrium. It is a despotism threatened from within and exposed to regulation and interference from without. It is a despotism capable of being overturned in a moment, exposed to the instant loss of its stability and prestige. It is a despotism resting upon children, at once the most tractable and the most unstable members of the community.[1]

The most powerful figure in the British urban school was the headmaster. Unlike his Australian or US counterpart, the British headmaster or headmistress (about 12,000 head teachers in the early 1970s were women) enjoyed unlimited, almost monarchical rule by any international comparison. US education experts indeed saw him as often having higher status and enjoying more limelight than the education officer who was nominally in charge of all the local schools.[2]

Not until 1978, with declining urban school rolls and threatened school closures, and professional and public opinion beginning to threaten their impregnable prestige, was the power of British head teachers challenged. Until the mid-1970s the 29,000 primary and secondary head teachers in British state schools, most of them urban schools, had sole and unchallenged control over organization and curriculum. For, whatever their articles of government said, it was the head teachers who decided who would have contact with the school from the local community; what examinations the children would enter; which children would be admitted to the school; and the oversight of their attendance. Head teachers gave final approval, as accounting officers, to nearly all decisions involving the spending of money on books, equipment or the curriculum in general.[3]

Unlike the US or Australian school principals, for instance, the British head teacher was no victim of the education office. No one sent him teachers by overnight telegram or withdrew teachers at equally short notice: at least not until the mid-1970s. For, in varying degrees, the head teacher was responsible for choosing his own staff and having the last word on appointments.

Head teachers could also exercise powerful sanctions in controlling their teachers. They could give them the most able groups of pupils, or the most socially intractable: they could withhold or give special responsibility posts which carried additional salary. Until the mid-1970s the British parent had very little say in the running of the school.

'I wonder what he does in real life?'

During an epoch of classroom and staffing crisis urban head teachers were little troubled by outside interference – from parents, politicians or administrators.

The British head teacher, much more than the classroom teacher, enjoyed complete security of tenure and freedom from teaching commitments during the day. It was almost impossible to sack a head teacher for inefficiency. Several years of bitter manoeuvring were needed, for example, before the head of a Cambridgeshire school was sacked in 1970 on the grounds of inefficiency. Where an unwilling head teacher was pushed out on professional grounds, as in the case of charismatics like R. F. Mackenzie in Scotland or Michael Duane in London, there was usually much media publicity and political skulduggery.[4] Although in theory a head teacher's contract could be ended at three or four months' notice, most education committees were extremely unwilling to use the power they possessed because it meant an unpleasant trial procedure and conflict with strong unions, and there were no satisfactory arrangements for financial compensation.

The usual compromise therefore was for a 'difficult', mentally-ill or miscreant head teacher to be put on permanent salary in a sinecure appointment, in a college, advisory or inspectorate job. Failure in any of those professional settings was considered, perhaps rightly, to carry few adverse educational consequences. No children could be damaged, only potential teachers.

It was almost as difficult to sack teachers for professional shortcomings. Between 1967 and 1970, the National Union of Teachers recorded only half a dozen non-criminal sackings in England and Wales. Criminal sackings were done very quietly, usually through discreet resignation on health grounds. The difficulties involved in sacking teachers were highlighted in the case of the six luckless Tyndale teachers, including their headmaster, who had to be fired for striking rather than for running the school inefficiently. The DES retained a secret 'List 99' of teachers black-listed on various grounds, amounting to some several hundred names. It was alleged to include teachers who encouraged antisocial behaviour amongst schoolchildren on political grounds, as well as those who lost their driving licences or were sexual offenders. Indeed, in 1977 special branch officers were still raiding a number of schools where the political opinions of the teachers had aroused their concern. The 'List 99' remained top secret and professional associations pressed hard to have sight of these clandestine dossiers on teachers.[5]

If only because every teacher willing to stay in a classroom was desperately needed, the work of the teaching profession, and especially head teachers during these years, was rarely assessed, let alone censured, with any vigour or severity by the adviser or inspector.

Ineffectual HMI inspection continued until 1968, but almost no attempt was made to research 'the good school' as opposed to the bad school. Indeed, as we have seen, the essential co-operation of head teachers for that exercise was rarely forthcoming. Only in the mid-1970s did HM Inspectorate begin to criticize the teachers, revive inspection as such or begin to do something about the poor calibre candidates who had been enticed or unwillingly recruited into the teaching profession during the years of public neglect.

In 1976, Richard Peters concluded that the head's traditional autonomy was as inviolable as ever.[6] His powers were still exercised in an authoritarian manner, often at the expense of others – especially junior staff or pupils, and sometimes parents. Sociologists concurred: interviews with heads revealed that paternalistic or totalitarian attitudes still predominated in their own description of the job. Head teachers reported that they valued most those personal qualities and tasks which emphasized their role as leaders. Almost all the 500 headmasters interviewed maintained that the traditional, charismatic and pastoral role of the head was all-important. Gerald Bernbaum did find, however, that the growing size of schools, staff shortages and a shift to comprehensive reorganization had compelled headmasters to play a stronger managerial and administrative role.[7] Even so, headmasters unanimously reported that they would least like to see a successor in their job who was 'currently employed at a managerial level outside education'. Most wanted the next headmaster of their school to 'have a clear set of moral values' and be an active church member. The insularity of urban head teachers also led them into professional paranoia. Large numbers declared 'no one understands my problem'. Michael Steinman, of the University of Nebraska, found London heads contemptuous alike of elected politicians, advisers, managers and governors of schools.[8] As many as 66 per cent of 144 head teachers interviewed in several London boroughs in 1970 thought politicians did not understand their conditions or professional problems. Yet, as we saw, head teachers were just as purblind in neglecting the urban crisis as politicians and teachers.

But by 1977 it looked as though changing circumstances would depose the autocratic head. Teachers' organizations were demanding more say. A major enquiry (Taylor Report) reported on public and parental participation in school management. The growth of the collegial staffroom and the increasing size of comprehensive schools had weakened the power of the head teacher and given the classroom teacher more say. More responsibility was delegated to heads of subject departments, who often took important decisions formerly reserved by the head. The school caretaker and ancillary staff had become more vocal. With declining school rolls, some head teachers became insecure about their authority and even their jobs, for as the [97] pupils disappeared some schools had to close.

Head teachers were no longer easily able to maintain their authority through tradition, ritual and sanctions.[9] Social order in the urban classroom was more difficult, especially in the large comprehensives and where large numbers of unwilling ROSLA pupils, high staff turnover and exceptional social stress compounded in a disadvantaged, multi-ethnic neighbourhood. Activist minorities of left-wing teachers in the staffrooms could also sharpen the misunderstandings arising from a professional generation gap, further threatening the despotism, however benevolent, of the head teacher. Parents and pupil governors were increasingly being appointed to managing bodies in urban schools. A growth of parent and pupil consumerism, especially a drift of sixth formers into further education colleges, constituted a multiple threat to the autocracy, power and even salary of the head teacher. Local authority inspectors as well as HM Inspectorate began to make tough noises about teachers whose performance might be felt to be ineffective. Moderate reformers, as well as controversial education spokesmen of the Right, were suggesting renewable contracts for head teachers. Countesthorpe College in Leicestershire was an extremely *avant-garde* school in which the head teacher's power was devolved. Renamed 'warden', the head of Countesthorpe handed over decision-making to the staff, acting as chairman to a staff committee. The staff of the William Tyndale School considered pooling both decision-making and salary cheques.

What could be the response of the distracted head teacher? Some succumbed to the management myth.[10] Mangement theory, applied to head teachers and schools, proved a pyramid-selling bandwagon.[11] There was a maniacal gleam in the eye of the many converts, newly fluent in managerial jargon, who descended in the schools or returned to their colleagues radiating bogus technology, advice column psychology and conceptual illiteracy. The management mafia, for that is effectively what they were, brought their own jargon, the polysyllabic rendering of the obvious, into schools. Some believed in the gospel of the curriculum – it alone would produce repentant, compliant and educable pupils. With good management, school discipline would no longer be a problem. That particular fallacy often alienated young teachers. Indeed, many teachers quite rightly suspected and opposed the naïve application of management theory to the complex world of the classroom. But it took time for them to do so. And by that time the professional quagmire had been considerably irrigated by the outpourings of the management experts. Sociologists of educational knowledge were also slow in identifying the hidden curriculum behind the management vogue – 'management' was just the latest imperialism to retain influence over the schools and local education authority decision-making channels.

Staffroom notices for management courses arrived like travel brochures, offering expertise to the heads of large schools and departments on individual subjects or even the timetable. Even the wilder shores of group therapy were visited by management enthusiasts. When approaching their innocent victims who were so ready to seek any port in a storm, the management mafiosi, like the Salvation Army, borrowed other people's good tunes. They plagiarized flow diagrams from the mathematicians, the Fog Index from the reading experts and extempore drama from the mental hospitals, especially mimicry of those constipated silences which passed for non-directive psychiatry.

The controversial psychodynamic approach to school life was practised, many thought successfully, by Elizabeth Richardson, who spent three years as an observer and consultant at Nailsea School, a large comprehensive formed from a grammar school.[12] Her analysis described who felt threatened, who changed their minds and who won in the staffroom, but she received a mixed press. Other educationists disputed whether the Tavistockian approach she favoured was just sloppy or, in fact, covertly authoritarian. Richardson saw personal dramas as universal problems, often expressed through the authority or management structure of the school. Teachers working with her made changes in the school hierarchy and method of working, during and after the period of her consultancy. The story of Countesthorpe, as recounted by the staff, showed a similar preoccupation with the dynamics of staffroom life, but with more curriculum emphasis. William Taylor, and other academics who had taught in secondary modern schools, produced in-tray exercises for training in school management and innovation in large secondary schools.

The besieged secondary head teachers were singled out for special blandishment by the managerial mafia. Some were admirably strong-minded. But it was tempting for the head of an urban school under stress to grasp at the managerial fallacy which gave him refuge, and gave him a new style of control. Discussion of the educational philosophy of the school was replaced by a view in which the head teacher saw himself as a troubleshooter whose response to staff debate was 'personnel management'. This managerial style of leadership could lead even the well-intentioned headmaster to exacerbate the problems of his school; he could become typecast as administrative doyen of 'that non-teaching gerontocracy along the corridor'. Despite the addition of two, and sometimes effectively three, deputy head teachers in the larger secondary schools, heads and senior staff, it seemed, did less and less teaching.[13] Sometimes the head and senior

How many periods do they teach?
A TES survey

School and size	Total periods possible	Head	Deputy Heads	Heads of Houses	Department & Faculty Heads	Year Tutor or Teachers	Average Teacher
London Comp. 1,310	36	Cover only	11–15	20	22–27		29
London Comp. 1,380	35	Cover only	4–10	17	28	30	
London Comp. 1,110	35	8 + cover	2–5		26–27	17	29
London Comp. 1,300	35	11	11	24–26	24–26		29
Kent Grammar (boys) 630	40	6	23		32–33		32
Devonshire Sec. Mod. 670	40	5	20		35	33–35	35
Sheffield Comp. 1,600	40	3	6		31	26	32
Sheffield Comp. 2,150	40	0	20		26–32		34
Lancashire R. C. Comp. 1,210	40	0	20		30–32		32
Lancashire Comp. 1,010	35	0	17		30	27–28	30
Lancashire Comp. 1,310	35	6	12–14		28	23–25	30
Berkshire Comp. 1,010	40	2	15		32–33	33	34
Berkshire Comp. (Girls) 1,100	40	6	10–24		31		33
Newcastle Comp. 1,800	40	6	12–15	25	32–35		35
Newcastle Comp. 1,620	40	6	15		32	28	34
Newcastle Comp. 1,400	40	16	11–14		32	28	34
Leicestershire Upper 1,350	35	Cover	12–13	14	28–30		28–30
Leicestershire 11–16 1,450	35	4	19–27		26–29		28–29
Leicestershire 11–16 1,160	40	Cover	12–14	28	32		34

Where no figure is shown, the school has no such post

(*The Times Educational Supplement*, 25 March, 1977)

colleagues were on constant patrol around the school, on call with a pocket radio, ready to deal with intruders or quell incipient riots. But if the management ethos prevailed the senior teachers often remained with their heads down in their administrative offices, while disorder mounted in classrooms and corridors.

'Does anyone on the staff actually teach?'

The managerial trend was a threat more than a benefit. Further suspicion was aroused by the mid-1970s when advertisements in teachers' journals invited recruitment to management courses for promotion. The teaching profession advisedly scrutinized this departure with suspicion. For while many urban authorities were abandoning the confidential report, some began operating a clandestine selection system through residential courses which offered intending heads or heads of department 'preparation for promotion'. This was a most insidious trend, particularly after 1975 when economic cuts, falling urban school rolls and resignation rates had brought more career anxiety into the minds of teachers. After all, in future there would be a longer wait for promotion and it would be harder won. It might be tempting for advisers or inspectors to identify the high flier and mark his card by means of a management course. But no one officially measured actual performance in the school or classroom, particularly in social control, curriculum innovation or the ability to inspire colleagues. Often a managerial system, based on exclusive country weekends and officer selection techniques, threatened to prove more distorting than the confidential reports and telephone calls it replaced. Wise education authorities, as in Australia, offered the urban teacher management training only *after* promotion to a new post. By this careful approach there was no professional malice, and management methods could make a valid contribution.

However, the concept of good management in itself was not unsound. Urban schools were crying out for vigorous management, and where head teachers managed to avoid the dangers of a false emphasis on managerial style they could often successfully introduce new approaches in running the school.[14] An innovative, creative bureaucracy could bring immense benefits.

Inner London Education Authority's Alternative Use of Resources scheme (AUR), for instance, which was increasingly copied by other LEAs, put the school budget under the democratic control of the staff and head.[15] The principle behind the AUR scheme was 'virement', defined as 'the application of resources intended for one end to the purposes of another'. That sounded like financial conspiracy; but in the jargon of the accountant in fact it was the quite legal 'transfer of a surplus to balance a deficit under another head'.

Under the AUR scheme a school staff, consulting with the head teacher, decided on their long-term plans and strategies. How did they want to spend their money? Did they want library books, another dinner helper, more part-time teachers or a minibus? Should they knock down a partition to create a parents' room, spend more on educational visits or buy a colour television recorder? Substantial amounts of money (£6,700 in 1977 for an ILEA primary school with 320 children on roll) were given to teachers to spend as they wished under their AUR budget.[16]

1 Basic staffing

Each school began with some basic staffing unconnected with the AUR budget. In 1977–8 in inner London the ratio of teacher to pupil was 1:18 in primary schools and 1:15 in secondary schools. Some non-teaching staff were provided free by the education authority. For instance, every school with 800 or more pupils qualified automatically for a full-time librarian, or a share from a pool of teachers helping in schools which had large numbers of immigrant children.

2 School allowance

Each school also received an allowance or capitation sum, which was in 1977–8 £11 for each primary pupil and £30 for each secondary pupil.

5 per cent of the capitation sum could be spent under the AUR scheme quite apart from any additional money specially allocated.

3 AUR

A complex calculation was made for each school, allocating money from a global sum for the whole of inner London.[17] That took into account the size of the school roll, individual staffing needs, the position of the school in an educational priority index, and other special factors, based on the advice of the local inspector.

The great advantage of this sophisticated scheme was its flexibility. It involved several important assumptions. First, it assumed that each urban school was individual and different; second that management decisions should be democratically arrived at through professional self-appraisal of the unique circumstances of each school. Third, long-term educational planning was encouraged, for the AUR scheme allowed schools to pay over several years for more expensive items such as the videotape recorder or minibus. Fourth, teachers and head teachers were encouraged, perhaps for the first time in many years, to begin thinking about the cost-effectiveness of classroom activity. Fifth, the decision-making demanded by the AUR scheme involved, if properly applied, democratic discussion of the curriculum and the philosophy of the school. Teachers were compelled to talk about their priorities for the urban classroom. Although the democratic application of the AUR scheme was regrettably not always brought out fully in schools, London teachers were in general delighted with the approach. Imagine, for instance, the pleasure of a secondary English Department consisting of fifteen teachers at last being able to appoint a part-time clerical worker to type stencils and run off duplicating.

Example 1: a primary school

How did a typical primary school in a generous LEA use its resources under the AUR scheme in the mid-1970s? The fixed resources of one primary school were:

> 15 full-time teachers: £3,950 each
> 1 nursery assistant: £3,010
> primary helpers totalling 60 hours a week: £3,600
> a part-time school secretary: £3,050

In addition, £11,500 was available for reallocation under the AUR scheme. The school used that discretion to buy:

1.8* teachers: £3,950 for each full teacher
1 nursery assistant for an additional nursery class: £3,010
1 woman helper for 12 hours weekly during term: £720
1 secretarial helper for 6 hours weekly: £610

The remaining cash was kept for local purchases from the local newsagent or electrical shop or for other emergencies.

Example 2 : a comprehensive school

The primary school could have allocated its AUR budget in several other ways, but in a secondary comprehensive school there was an even larger number of permutations by which the money could be spent. Here are two possible schemes for AUR spending in a comprehensve school with a roll of 1,230 pupils, which received £23,000 under the AUR scheme. The school had the following basic staffing and resources which could not be reallocated.

2 full-time teachers for work with immigrant children
3 full-time clerical officers
1 part-time clerical officer (37½ hours)
1 general assistant (25 hours)
1 full-time media resource officer
1 full-time librarian
1 senior laboratory technician
1 laboratory technician
2 junior laboratory technicians
1 workshop technician
1 storekeeper
1 general assistant for immigrants
(The schoolkeeping staff and cleaners were separately provided)

The school capitation provided £30 per head for each boy and girl, amounting to £36,900, 5 per cent of which could also be spent under the AUR scheme. Thus the school had £23,000 plus £1,845 = £24,845 of AUR, virement or discretionary spending.

Scheme 1

The school could simply have spent its AUR money on, say: 5.1 extra teachers (at £20,145) and 1 laboratory technician (at £2,800) at a total cost of £23,945. Bearing in mind that the school allowance was £36,900, two-thirds of the financial resources of the school would then have remained to be spent on learning materials and equipment.

* i.e. teachers working to 1.8 of a full week.

In the event another more sophisticated scheme, involving a good deal of complex negotiations among the staff themselves, was adopted:

Scheme 2

The headmaster and staff decided to buy fewer books and materials, but to increase the non-teaching support for the school by buying:

    1 part-time 0.6 teacher: £2,370
    1 part-time 0.5 instructor for technical subjects: £1,560
    1 laboratory technician: £2,800
    1 AVA technician: £2,880
    1 shorthand typist: £3,400
    1 storekeeper: £2,950
    1 full-time clerical officer: £3,050
    1 senior clerical officer: £3,280

This total of £22,290 left £35,055 in the school allowance and £2,555 of AUR money which could be used for local purchase and emergencies.

Lively staffroom debate and extensive consultations preceded this decision. The headmaster and senior cabinet of heads of department were lobbied energetically by their colleagues. Staff-room discussion compelled everyone to work out the educational philosophy and priorities of the school against a context of financial realism. Scrutiny of the curriculum, and more particularly the timetable, was the nerve-centre of debate. When a choice had to be made between, say, teaching maths in smaller groups or buying a laboratory technician for the science department, the timetable was an influential factor on its own account as well as reflecting the final decision.[18] The complex timetable hieroglyphics were the key to the politics, power and philosophy, the hidden and official curriculum of each secondary school.

A second scheme of creative bureaucracy which had enormous impact on the urban school was the Educational Priority Area index. Earlier I criticized the EPA strategy for assuming that there was an exclusively educational solution to the urban crisis. Nevertheless, enthusiasm, higher professional morale and better classrooms did result; it funnelled extra money, teachers and learning materials into deprived urban schools. In Inner London and Liverpool researchers devised measures to distinguish between primary schools in order, as Plowden had suggested, 'to raise schools with poor standards to the national average and then quite deliberately to make them better'. Their definitions of educational priority used Plowden criteria (see p. 23). Other suggestions, locally or from Whitehall, were added to build up the indices of multiple deprivation. In Inner London a forty-strong team

'2b are using it for modern maths, 5c for a Mass Media project and
Home Economics want it for a knitting pattern.'

of research and statistics staff constructed for schools an EPA index of ten criteria and measures.[19]

ILEA primary EPA index

Criterion	Measure
1 Social class composition	% of males in unskilled and semi-skilled occupations
2 Large families	% of children in households of 6 or more
3 Overcrowding	% of households living at a density of more than $1\frac{1}{2}$ persons per room
4 Housing stress	% of households without an inside wc
5 Cash supplements	% of pupils receiving free meals
6 Absenteeism	% of pupils absent during first week of May 1967 (in this case)
7 Immigrants	% of immigrants in schools
8 Handicapped pupils	% of pupils in bottom (lowest 25%) ability groups
9 Teacher turnover	% of teachers in school less than 3 years
10 Pupil turnover	% of pupils who have moved during the year

All 850 London primary schools were ranked from highest to lowest, the most deprived school being given the top score. Practical experience resulted in changes to the index. As time went by, pupil absenteeism and housing stress were dropped in favour of two other criteria: 'lack of parental interest' (measured by whether the parent attended the school medical); and 'crowding in the school building' (measured by the number of children occupying each 100 square feet of floor space). 'Teacher turnover' was dropped, because some head teachers kept the EPA rating of their school artificially high, running successful classrooms but encouraging staff to move constantly for promotion, and thus scoring strongly on 'teacher turnover'. A factor of 'teacher stress' was also introduced and then dropped because it penalized schools working well under difficult circumstances. Predictably, the shifting political climate caused 'percentage of immigrant pupils' to be dropped from the EPA index although demands came later for its reinclusion. An important new criterion of 'disturbed children', those identified as abnormally maladjusted on the Rutter Scale, was also later added.

The EPA bonanza was so warmly welcomed in disadvantaged primary schools in London that a secondary school index was planned,[20] which emphasized secondary school characteristics which made teaching more difficult but over which the school had virtually no control.

ILEA secondary EPA index

Criterion	Measure
1 Backward children	% of 11+ children in the lowest ability band
2 Immigrants	% of immigrants in the school
3 Poverty	% of pupils in attendance receiving free meals
4 Large families	% of children in families of 4 or more children
5 One parent families	% of pupils not living with both natural parents
6 Social class	% of pupils with semi-skilled/unskilled guardians
7 Pupil turnover	% of pupils who changed schools
8 Adequacy of buildings	Split site, age of building, tall buildings (lift)
9 Technical studies	% of teaching staff who are handicraft, housecraft, technical teachers

Local education authorities set up teachers' and resource centres, specializing in the teaching of reading, mathematics or multi-ethnic studies. Special concessions were offered to London primary schools, allowing them to buy a wide range of audio-visual aids apparatus at one-third of cost – thus triggering off a revolution in educational technology. The head teacher in the inner city EPA school became a wealthy patron on a scale which made suburban colleagues gasp with envy, even though they would not have wanted to teach the very difficult children.

So generous were the schemes of creative bureaucracy and extra resources which aimed at halting deterioration in urban classrooms that newspapers like the London *Evening Standard* accused the education authority of 'trying to buy themselves out of trouble with resources'.

The powerful chief education officers strongly resisted the logical final step of managerialism: corporate management. Throughout the period of local government reorganization, which between 1964 and 1974 reduced the total number of LEAs to just over a hundred in the interests of efficiency, education officers fought every attempt to put them and their departments under a chief local authority executive.[21] Their motives were mixed: a commendable intention to protect the local educational traditions was mingled with professional insularity and lack of vision. Corporate management meant that each department head, including the education officer, had to justify his share of the budget. But educational need was hard to demonstrate. An urgent case for sewers or roads, when looking at the total responsibility of a local authority, was much easier to present. Social workers could always produce a more heart-rending story than the teachers. And was there not a danger of reviving some system of educational accountability, of 'payment by results'? The education officers headed heavy-spending departments with decades of independent tradition behind them. They were not prepared to be put down by accountants from the powerful treasurer's department, by short-sighted councillors intent on 'cheese-paring' the school budget, by Whitehall civil servants or politicians – or even by fashionable public clamour for improved standards.[22]

In a new climate of growing financial rigour it was inevitable that British educational practice would be affected by the sophisticated planning techniques developed in the US. Economic recession brought a sharp awareness of the need for scrutinizing public expenditure for cost effectiveness. DES papers, like the 1970 feasibility study for output budgeting, began to encourage stricter assessment of expenditure according to purposes and results. They argued that systematic assessment of the use of resources across traditional institutions or departments illuminated policy choices which otherwise remained masked. During the 1960s, when the rate of educational spending (as expressed as a share of growth in the national product) rose each year, a PPB (Planning Programming Budgeting) system helped the DES to allocate resources effectively.[23] Later, with near financial bankruptcy in the public sector, central government found such cost-effectiveness techniques even more valuable when imposing tighter controls, cash limits and ceilings on educational expenditure.

But who, finally, did control the purse strings for the urban classroom? The Layfield Committee of Inquiry, reporting in 1976, declared that local education authorities were and should continue as the financial management for schools.[24] Education, as the largest local service, employed more people than any other department. If the largest part of the local education budget, the salaries of the teachers themselves, was taken over by central government this would lead to a fully centralized school system. Government should pay for services which were wholly national in character. Central government control would deprive local authorities of educational initiative in running schools to suit local conditions.

Despite Layfield, there were growing signs of more curriculum centralism and financial intervention by central government. On the other hand, trends towards central intervention were matched by simultaneous pressures towards increased devolution of school and curriculum control, particularly into the hands of parents.[25] Educa-

tional accountability, community education, and urban curriculum
were becoming closely linked.

Where did the permanent civil servants, the shadowy figures in the Department of Education and Science, stand in relation to control of the urban school? Despite the honourable refusal by the DES, at least on the face of it, to make a takeover bid for the control of the curriculum in schools, from 1972 onwards there were straws in the wind suggesting that their thoughts were certainly moving in that direction.

A highly critical analysis of the DES as a secretive central bureaucracy was made in the OECD (Organization for Economic Co-operation and Development) report on British education in 1975.[26] The DES representatives were quite unable, in their confrontation meeting with the OECD examiners, to meet the various criticisms made. The visitors' team had complained that educational decision-making in England and Wales showed very few signs of democratic participation. Civil servants had immense power in their own right, particularly with such a rapid succession of education ministers as had passed through the DES in recent years. The DES was unnecessarily secretive about its decision-making processes, which appeared to rely largely on informal networks and the 'old boy' system; long-term objectives and priorities therefore tended to escape adequate scrutiny.

The DES civil servants, particularly in the upper tiers, were largely products of the public school and Oxbridge systems – they had little personal experience of the vast state school system they were trying to run. For many years they had worked at some distance, with little impact on the child in the classroom, but in 1976 the then Labour government encouraged them and the resuscitated HM Inspectorate to attempt nothing less than a full-scale *coup d'état* – a central takeover of the state schools.

9 The Curriculum Church

Curriculum policy in the urban school was bedevilled with professional shortsightedness. Not only teachers, but educational philosophers and sociologists, college lecturers, curriculum developers and researchers pursued sectarian obsessions within the new religion. Those responsible for the raising of the school leaving age, the counting of immigrants, compensatory education, or the teaching of reading, all offered conflicting curriculum advice.[1] The growing Curriculum Church was attacked for its secularism in purveying a commodity called 'knowledge' by the deschooler Ivan Illich. The curriculum development movement, indeed, resembled nothing so much as a mad tea party of neo-scholastics. Educational sociologists, project directors and researchers, deschoolers and a host of Marxists all squabbled for funding and influence. They also neglected to consider total urban strategy.

The curriculum prophets offered a range of charlatanism, metaphysics and occasionally useful theology. Their jargon even filtered through to the children. Every schism and heresy found in the Church was reflected in the vendettas they conducted from their armchairs. The progressive pharisees believed only in the supreme importance of the spoken word, in children's talk, creative writing and fluency: or favoured 'direct' spoken teaching of modern languages. The gnostic tradition was maintained by those extreme progressives who claimed to transcend logic intuitively in their teaching. Children would, they thought, spontaneously acquire literacy in their classrooms through being exposed to a rich environment of books. Some progressives subscribed to the Pelagian heresy, claiming that faith in the curriculum among teachers would alone purge schools of sin and misbehaviour. Indeed, most curriculum developers were also Lutheran antinomians.

'Today? Well, actually we had vertical structuring with team teaching in an open-plan environment.'

They believed that the curriculum gospel and not the law of discipline would revive schools. The official dogma of the curriculum papacy, the Schools Council, was that curriculum, not social control, would carry the urban schools through difficult times to redemption and salvation. Put your curriculum in order and other problems would solve themselves. The Sadducees, authors of the *Black Papers* – advocates of the written word and defenders of written examinations – opposed progressivism. They sometimes converted to Jansenism, believing in the total corruption of their pupils by original sin; curriculum innovation was then dismissed as nonsense and, instead, they urged old-fashioned regimes of harshness, ritual and moral rigour. The sociologists of knowledge, noted for over-subtle argument containing just the occasional grain of truth, were the modern Scotists,[2] while the complex Donatist heresy taught that sacraments administered by an unworthy minister were invalid. Sinners receiving them should be denied salvation, although if the same sacraments were offered by a worthy minister then they were valid. Thus it was possible for Labour education ministers to initiate central government interference in the schools of a kind they themselves had majestically denounced when proposed by the political opposition.

Much of the curriculum debate was an irrelevant sideshow to social realities. It was also quite falsely polarized by skilled publicists of both the extreme Left and Right; for meanwhile in the classroom several hundred thousand urban teachers muddled confusedly along holding to the middle ground. Indeed, it was possible to argue, as did Lawrence Stenhouse, that curriculum renewal occurred more often than innovation.[3]

A dozen factors forced the pace of curriculum renewal from the early 1960s.[4] There were international reasons for curriculum reform: superior Soviet achievement in technology and science had alarmed Western educationists; Britain needed metrication upon entry into the European Common Market. In Britain itself, new education authorities, middle schools and the national network of comprehensive schools demanded a fresh look at curriculum. It was argued that the unstreamed, mixed ability secondary school needed a brand new curriculum. The informal classroom movement was strong, especially after the Plowden Report. In a mood of professional confidence, many teachers more often produced their own curriculum materials in schools or teachers' centres – secondary teachers in local groups devised CSE courses and examinations. New reading schemes and audio-visual aids came on the market. Until the mid-1970s, annually expanding budgets allowed schools to experiment with innovation. Professional organizations and ginger groups encouraged experimentation in the curriculum. Teacher organizations for remedial education (NARE) multiracial education (NAME), the teaching of reading (UKRA) the teaching of English (NATE) all sprang up. Parents and teachers formed organizations such as the campaign for comprehensive education (CCE) or the advisory centre for education (ACE) and its magazine *Where*? There was new concern with the needs of the gifted, autistic or the dyslexic child.

Newspaper editors saw that the education industry was expanding,

in crisis, and newsworthy. More education correspondents were
appointed by newspapers. *The Guardian* newspaper launched an education page. *New Society* gave the schools some sociological scrutiny
from 1961 onwards. *The Times Educational Supplement* expanded its
pages, circulation and revenue; its job advertisement pages grew
rapidly with the staffing shortages. New academic journals dealing
with teacher education and curriculum studies were launched. Samizdat magazines, using the more commonly available offset press,
flourished; they had titles like *Teaching London Kids*, *Rank and File* or
Humpty Dumpty, and provided for militants and minorities.

Reviving a climate of excitement over education which had been
stimulated in pre-war politics through the Left Book Club, Penguin
Education Specials offered a stream of de-schooling, radical and
revolutionary paperbacks. These had titles like *The Great Brain Robbery*,
Pedagogy of the Oppressed, *Why Schools Fail*, or *Compulsory Miseducation*.[5]

The Schools Council was nationally responsible for curriculum
development and examinations after 1965, and soon had a hundred or
so projects running, with an annual budget of some £2 million. Jointly
funded by the DES and local authorities, the Schools Council had a
peculiar constitution resulting from the insistence of teachers that 'the
secret garden of the curriculum' was their private monopoly.[6] It was,
therefore, a compromise institution with a majority of teachers nomi-
nated by the unions in its steering committees. This constitution was to
prove most unsatisfactory, but no action was taken until 1977 to
change it. Although in theory the Council was supported by local
curriculum development groups and teachers' centres, it fell victim to a
series of centralist paradoxes. Despite the ostensible commitment to
teachers, 90 or so of its first 125 projects had teams based in universities. The Council was committed ideologically to the view that every
school should have a curriculum determined by the head teacher and
staff. The LEAs, who substantially funded it, joined with teachers in
demanding the Council should not interfere locally with curriculum.
But through its national projects and publications it was obliged to
propagate a consensus view of what the curriculum should be
like.

The Schools Council spawned many new professionals, the curriculum developer, the evaluator, the researcher – an army of meta-
physicians. Like doctors, curriculum evaluators had their own ethic of
confidentiality or disclosure. They wrote and published prolifically,
mostly for each other or the captive audiences of college of education
or Open University education students who provided their salaries.
Teachers in classrooms were much less responsive.

The chief curriculum strategy adopted by the Council, influenced
largely by the US pattern (which showed early signs of failure) was the

paternalistic 'research and development mode'. The Council would employ a few bright teachers or researchers on secondment to study a dozen or so schools. The team would then sit down in a university department and invent a curriculum solution, producing publications

'It was about time that "concepts" came in and "ideas" went out.'

and packages of learning materials. Not until after the mid-1970s was this strategy reappraised. The record of the Schools Council from the point of view of dissemination and impact on ordinary classrooms was remarkably bad. But its labyrinthine bureaucracy together with a conspiracy among LEAs and unions that there should be no threat of curriculum centralism guaranteed its ineffectiveness from the start. Mechanisms of dissemination were available but not used. Teachers' centres were sponsored by the Schools Council and proliferated with astonishing ease under LEA management. They sprang up all over the educational map after 1965, when the newly formed Schools Council issued a blueprint which saw them as a network for creating and diffusing curriculum development.[7] By the early 1970s there were 600 teachers' centres in Britain; in 1965 there had been only 20. The jumbo jet visitors from other countries invariably asked to see both 'an open school' and 'a teachers' centre'. But teachers' centres were little used for curriculum dissemination.

After 1965 the editing and publication of national curriculum materials was semi-monopolized by the Schools Council. Strangely powerless to enforce its curriculum edicts through dissemination in LEAs, the Council did erode the traditional entrepreneurial freedom of the educational publisher.[8] Publishers put a brave face on their predi-

cament. Joint projects with the Schools Council, they claimed, cut
development costs.

Publishers and equipment manufacturers in general lost less ground than might have been imagined. They commanded a large home market because of the choice enjoyed by the British teacher. There was an even larger international English-speaking market for their own products. The information and textbook market expanded rapidly, especially in the developing countries, and was extremely profitable. The British teacher thus enjoyed an *embarras de richesses* in school books, audio-visual aids and equipment. Unlike, say, many US or Australian teachers whose curriculum straitjacket often meant choosing one book out of four prescribed texts, the British teacher, apart from the constraints of the school-leaving exams (or 11+ tests where they remained) had complete curriculum freedom.

The curriculum debate continued aimlessly. Some thought that confusion itself was a virtue – this was a pluralistic, rich society in which there were many answers rather than one. Certainly, the teaching profession was fundamentally split over classroom aims. 1,500 primary and middle schools teachers interviewed for a Schools Council report in 1975 were disagreed about the aims of primary education.[9] Older, experienced and married teachers emphasized the traditional role: equipping the child with skills and attitudes enabling him to conform to socially acceptable norms. These teachers directed children closely, controlling what was learned when and how. Younger, progressive, less experienced and single teachers, especially those with higher qualifications, stressed more the aesthetic, emotional and personal development of children and rated intellectual attainment as less important. The report suggested that there was 'a real and important cleavage of opinion between teachers who may well be working successively with the same group of children.'

Remarkably little practical guidance was given to the many young teachers training in the expanded colleges of education. Some students, like Nicholas Otty,[10] documented the futility of the graduate training year at university departments of education. With notable exceptions, lecturers were too distant from the urban classroom. Surveys showed they neglected basic pedagogy; they consistently failed, for example, to teach students how to teach reading. College lecturers were preoccupied with extra student numbers, their curriculum speciality or the committee work of getting courses academically validated. As a body they made little intellectual contribution to solving the urban classroom crisis. Only too often college staffs were working with students who regarded the college of education as a finishing school before marriage, or as second best to a university place.

The educational research establishment offered even less help. Educational sociologists, when not lost in metaphysical conundrums of their own making, persisted in the well-worn groove of social mobility research. Occasionally, as in the case of Little and Mabey, researchers avoided the gag put on them by politicians, teetered on the brink of a major discovery, then stepped back from the revolutionary implications of their research.[11] When significant educational research was attempted, it was often resisted. As we saw, attempts to research the qualities of 'good schools' were blocked by the teachers and their unions. Unacceptable research findings were consistently ignored. For example, teachers rejected out of hand the Stockholm studies which showed that reducing class size did not necessarily lead to improved attainment; and they described as unacceptable the conclusion of the National Child Development survey that children in larger primary classes often had better reading attainment.

The biggest educational research body in the country, the National Foundation for Educational Research, received large amounts of public money. Started in 1946 with 14 people, by 1971 it had 140 staff at its Slough headquarters, including 42 full-time research officers who produced 20 or so publications per year. But for political reasons the NFER was too academic and over-cautious. Only occasionally did it produce a report that had even a slight impact on the classroom, as in the case of its conclusions on teaching French to young children. But even then, a negative caution seemed to be the keynote. 'The weight of evidence has combined with the balance of opinion to tip the scales against possible expansion of teaching French in Primary schools'.

Asked why the NFER was so unadventurous, even conservative, in its research policy, officers and project leaders explained that their sponsors were cautious bodies like the Home Office, the Schools Council and the Social Science Research Council. They gave money for 'measurable research'. Nevertheless, despite its privileged position in sharing with the Schools Council a right to public funding, the NFER constantly lost its better staff to the universities. As a body it certainly gave urban teachers little help in resolving the crises of authority or even curriculum that they faced each day.

Many LEAs set up research units, a promising initiative at first sight. But all too often researchers, like Marten Shipman, complained that their most treasured work was selectively used to justify policies which overall were anathema to them.[12]

The DES was remarkably ill-served for research, as the OECD investigating team noted; besides, no one knew what happened to research findings because of the secrecy which dominated decision making. But in a sense, research did not matter. For research itself had shown that when teachers were asked to rank well-known people in the educational world according to their credibility, they ranked university professors and researchers lowest. Perhaps one of the real difficulties was that researchers did not get into situations fast enough to come up with prescriptions before the educational scene had once more changed. There was in particular a lack of relevant classroom observation, which could have been especially helpful to teachers.

The local politicians who ran education committees, as the Tyndale enquiry showed, played down their controlling role in relation to the urban school, vaguely leaving responsibility to the administrators and professional advisers. The comprehensive school campaigner and London local politician, Caroline Benn, kept a full diary of all her ILEA education committee meetings.[13] She did not record agendas or the way voting went, but how the education committee running a big city school system spent its time. She recorded occasions on which 'genuine educational discussion' took place. Discussion had to last at least five minutes, the length of time it took for a speech to go beyond routine chatter and allow politicians to explore an issue in such a way that shifts of opinion could occur or new ideas gain currency. From her records she concluded that such discussion rarely took place. Various pressures subordinated policy making to administration.[14] Most committees were run by the administrators rather than by the elected members. Only 16 per cent of the committee meetings she attended were devoted to policy discussion; half the time was spent on day-to-day routine, rubberstamping policy decisions; and a third of the time was taken up with the party's own affairs. Although extremely large sums of public money were authorized for educational spending, discussion of educational accountability or school cost-effectiveness rarely took place. Most policy decisions of any importance were made in a caucus meeting of the full majority party held before each education committee meeting.

Not surprisingly, interdisciplinary and corporate planning issues gained little attention. Urban politicians specializing in local housing, education or other policy committees actually took pride in a tradition of etiquette which discouraged interference with the work of other committees. The relationship between urban schools curriculum, social control, and demographic and urban trends was thus never debated by politicians in the major British cities.

The advisory or inspectorate bodies of urban authorities could also have given some guidance. They grew particularly fast following the local government reorganization of 1964–74.[15] Commonly, the adviser or inspector had some general responsibility for a territorial patch of schools as well as providing expertise in a specialist subject and visiting schools all over a city. The adviser's or inspector's function had been described in a sub-section of the 1944 Education Act: 'any local education authority may cause an inspection to be made of any education establishment maintained by (i.e. in respect of grants from) the authority, and such inspection shall be made by officers appointed by the local education authority.' Despite this they suffered much uncertainty and role conflict in the period after 1960. During these years of classroom stress, the old-style local inspector demanding registers, suspicious of classroom noise, closeted over sherry with the head while tremors ran round the staffroom finally disappeared. He was replaced by the harassed, avuncular adviser, who as part of an expanded team commanded less prestige. The best features of the advisory approach were admirable. Advisers became donors of extra equipment or money; patronage was substituted for punitive inspection. But the title 'adviser' disguised a crude, simple fact: schools could not possibly be inspected in a traditional way during such a staffing crisis. The first task of the adviser during these critical years was to visit colleges and entice young teachers to enter the urban classroom. The next job was to hold their hands through the traumatic switchback of the probationary year. But so far as inspecting classrooms or pushing a strong line on curriculum were concerned, the hands of the adviser were tied. They were warned against 'upsetting the heads, the teachers or the union.' Criticism of a young teacher for not wearing a bra or relying wholly on 'look and say' in reading was ill-advised. She might turn round, complain to the union, resign, shift to the school down the road, or take a better-paid job as a secretary. The role of the school inspector was of necessity, as the Tyndale tribunal was so poignantly to reveal, 'to advise and support'. Inspectors could have led head teachers and teachers in calling a general alarm over the urban classroom crisis, but the chance was passed up in the fatalistic assumption that nothing could be done about the ground rules of the game.

Their specialized role and insulated life-style made local advisers ill-informed and apathetic to the major urban educational policy questions which shaped their daily task. Members of Her Majesty's Inspectorate were even more aloof. They had suffered a crisis of low morale and recruitment in the 1960s, when their salary levels had fallen below those of local advisers.[16] Traditionally, schools inspection had been thought suitable for retired colonial administrators, poets needing an income and unsuccessful literary intellectuals. Only civil service skills plus common sense were thought to be needed for the job; recruitment was done on the old-boy network, posts being canvassed by word of mouth. Some critics complained that HM Inspectorate was a secret society, a mixture of masonic lodge and dilettante spy ring.

HM Inspectorate reports on schools were cavilling or wishy-washy documents. HMIs were masters of cliché. Morning assembly was always 'reverently presented': teachers were advised to 'discover' the interests of their children: or make the curriculum 'child centred':

schools should be 'happy communities' – the bland phrases flowed
effortlessly. In the 1960s HM Inspectorate complained that its curriculum function was being threatened by the emerging Schools
Council. Yet it was they who were to leap suddenly and self-
assertively to prominence after 1975 (see p. 169).

10 Cargo-cult and innovation

Curriculum exploration brought back some bounty, but generated even more cargo-cult – teachers desperate to achieve social control and a more flexible curriculum turned to novel techniques and innovations,[1] like the Pacific Islanders who built effigies of American air force planes in their efforts to encourage the sky gods to rain down more food and trinkets.

They were faced with a variety of alternative ideologies. The stress on curriculum pluralism meant that any teacher seeking authoritative advice was likely to find it contradicted elsewhere. Primary teachers, for example, found the Plowden Report and recommendations attacked by left-wing academics as well as traditionalists who opposed the informal classroom.[2] There was also a clear clash over how social order was to be achieved in schools, between those who favoured a traditional curriculum on the one hand, and those who urged curriculum innovation on the other. Innocent young teachers, emerging barely trained into the urban classrooms, caught the contagions of apathy, flight, dissidence or curriculum fantasy. Teachers who stayed tended to resist innovation but accepted the neologisms for traditional teaching methods which were fashionably re-invented by the curriculum developers. The antinomians, the *avant-garde* among curriculum developers, fervently believed that the crisis in classroom control could be overcome by dynamic curriculum reform. Such tactics, a calculated gamble for high stakes, sometimes resulted in successful experimental primary or secondary schools which stayed in the public eye. An innovating comprehensive school might begin mixed ability, subject integration, martial arts, a steel band and a parent-teacher association all at once. Next year the introduction of a competition hovercraft or parachute jumping by sixth formers for charity and the abandonment of school uniform might take place. Primary head teachers, likewise, aiming to attract parents or staff by innovatory zeal, introduced the integrated day, vertical grouping, or the miniature Babel of team teaching in a converted hall called a resource centre.[3] The best innovating schools were undoubtedly superb. But it was little wonder that many suffered from what John Nisbet called 'innovation fatigue'.[4] The nerves of children and staff were frayed by the stress and tempo of novelty. Morale might be high, but battle fatigue was a constant danger. In secondary schools, teachers working on individualized learning could burn themselves out with exhaustion, working until midnight to feed the endless conveyor belt with work cards. The head teacher/publicist and his energetic staff, running to stand still, sometimes won high praise. Indeed, in some of the best known of these schools it was the international visitors and fame that afforded protection against local sentiment. Many teachers went on to headships or other senior appointments, but a good progressive school either retained many excellent teachers or attracted individuals of similarly high calibre.

In many schools the staffing stability needed for team teaching or personal continuity in informal pastoral care was lacking because of high teacher loss. The additional stress on staff sometimes meant that social control crumbled, curriculum innovation collapsed or came to a halt; everything that had been gained could be suddenly lost. Sometimes innovation moved too fast for the children: in one Melbourne school I visited, the children smuggled in traditional textbooks borrowed from friends because they could not cope with the rapid introduction of new teaching styles and curriculum.

The much documented history of Countesthorpe, a secondary school for pupils of 14+ in the outskirts of Leicester, highlighted these tensions.[5] An early assessment by Bernbaum suggested that galloping innovation had its incidental costs. In 1974 a further HMI inspection in response to local petitioning produced the verdict that Countesthorpe was like the curate's egg – good in parts. The HMI report, never published, suggested that too much simultaneous innovation had put the aims of the school in jeopardy. The inspectors did not criticize the radical organization of the school, whereby the principal was bound by decisions taken by a moot of non-teaching staff and older students. Indeed, they found considerable promise in Countesthorpe, and remarked on the warmth and trust in the relationships between staff and students. But they also agreed with local petitioners who had complained of indiscipline, low academic standards and political bias in the teaching. The HMIs condemned the minor vandalism and the lack of social self-control among pupils, although they pointed out there was little vicious behaviour. They remarked on the substantial loss of library books.

Countesthorpe was a distinctive and valuable experiment, a school serving a socially and economically balanced community. The school was uniquely publicized and selective in its staffing. Many much less favoured urban secondary schools attempted similar goals and struck complete disaster. Younger teachers, close in sympathy to their older pupils, were sometimes both unwilling and unable to impose social control in schools which were disintegrating. Only too often the view that a breakthrough in curriculum would solve all problems was eagerly seized upon. There were effective teaching approaches – the phrase 'never smile till Christmas' summarized one of these. Once firm social control and rapport had been established, more classroom materials and smiles could be given out; the over-stimulation of disturbed children was a great weakness of young teachers. However, the curriculum researchers notably failed in not making it clear to teachers that urban classrooms needed differential teaching styles, and possibly differential curriculum, however anti-democratic that might seem. The real challenge was whether you moved on from there.

The specific example of the Humanities Curriculum Project of the Schools Council exemplified the antinomian panacea in extreme.[6] Lawrence Stenhouse, the project director, wished to withdraw the teacher's authority entirely from the classroom, relying on the students and the curriculum to provide social control. This genuinely innovative approach, which had considerable merit, unfortunately proved destructive and untimely, as it undermined social control in classrooms at a time of crisis. Stenhouse was concerned with the relationship of children both to authority and to controversial discussion topics. He argued that the traditional authority of the teacher in the classroom inhibited pupil discussion. The teacher should be a neutral chairman, treating the views of pupils with respect. He should not impose his own viewpoint but instead gently encourage discussion. But neutral chairmanship did not always work. Evaluation officers reported that 'successful teachers' in the HCP felt they were failing; or that a teacher abdicated control of the classroom and behaviour spilled over into indiscipline. Indeed, teachers and their unions were not prepared to accept the philosophy or pedagogic technique. They were particularly concerned over race discussion, asking how a teacher should react if a few demagogic pupils swung their classmates in the direction of prejudice because the teacher was unwilling to assume leadership in discussion. At a time when the authority of the school was already under attack, the adoption of this curriculum reform was often ill-judged. Young teachers who bought the expensive HCP packs were engaging in hopeless cargo-cult. Stenhouse himself admitted that this work imposed great difficulties and personal strain on the teachers, and that there had been many failures.[7]

Primary teachers made similar mistakes.[8] Neville Bennett's research suggested that young urban teachers in primary schools serving council estates rationalized their classroom chaos as 'informal teaching'. Nevertheless, infant and junior teachers, often more intuitive, non-intellectual, and unscathed by professional reading, made fewer disastrous mistakes than their secondary colleagues.

A second, highly-publicized and equally mistaken response was found in those urban schools which renewed emphasis on traditional curriculum, ritual and social control. These schools deliberately adopted the separate culture, strong moral leadership, honours boards, prefects and monitors, streaming and all the accoutrements of the traditional grammar school. Innovations like subject integration or mixed ability were eschewed in such schools. As Colin Lacey and others had shown, such a regime could permanently alienate many pupils.[9] Yet many parents of working class and immigrant children sought out such schools in London and other cities because of their structured social control and curriculum. Schools led by strong personalities, like the charismatic Rhodes Boyson at Highbury Grove, were run with verve, rhetoric and success.[10] When other schools were in disorder these strict, conventional secondary schools were able to improve on their intakes because so many children applied for enrolment. The trend was international. In the US, 'traditional' alternative schools, or an approach which revived regimented learning with black children, were similarly popular. In Chicago, formal Catholic secondary schools were much sought after by aspiring black inner city parents. Church schools in British cities continued to pursue such policies. No one openly stated the obvious conclusion. A decade before, such city schools had been considered reactionary and were unwelcome; now, in circumstances of playground violence and curriculum ferment, they could make a welcome contribution. A well-run authoritarian school could also achieve the social control which was an essential preliminary to curriculum innovation.[11]

The real challenge that illiberal head teachers and their staffs did not often positively meet was the need, having obtained social control, inculcated basic work habits and guaranteed physical safety for children in the playground, for moving towards a more liberal curriculum and organization. Too many schools, having initially pursued a strategy of repression, found it difficult to reap their reward and move on to curriculum reform and improved school democracy. There were no case studies or research reports to help them. During the whole of its early years the Schools Council did not promote a single investigation into the relationship between social control and curriculum in schools.

Meanwhile, running parallel to the trends so far described were the radical activism of the 'school-kids liberation' movement and the experiments with 'free schools'.[12]

The Schools Action Union, active in 1969, committed itself to the reform of schools and society through revolution.[13] The SAU programme called for completely unstreamed comprehensive schools organized to satisfy the needs of people and not just to feed big business with young employees. 'The only authority that pupils should respect is not that of the capitalists, but that of the state of the working class'. The SAU was not popular with teachers: in Birmingham student members found themselves suspended.

The National Union of School Students was launched in 1972 by schoolchildren from all over the country, who travelled to London to support a 25 point policy statement of reforms and changes. They called for greater democracy, the abolition of the head, control of schools by committees of teachers, students, parents and non-teaching staff. The prefect system and school uniforms should be scrapped, together with censorship of school magazines, clubs and societies. The NUSS soon claimed to have 4,000 members.

Even the socialist Workers Revolutionary Party became active in the field of 'kids lib' by 1976. Known for its extreme left-wing politics and through its actor-family members, the Redgraves, the WRP did not impress fifty or so young people who attended one of its little-publicized weekend courses. Everyone was thoroughly searched on their arrival, when combs, nail files and other possessions were taken away. A film of the Jarrow hunger march was shown as evening entertainment; guards were posted in the country house to prevent any larking about at bedtime. The disgruntled children came back with a hazy notion of the need to 'smash capitalism'.[14]

The extremist fringe, however, reflected a growing demand for devolution of control in secondary schools, with more say for teachers and pupils. Countesthorpe College had mixed success in its experiments with democratic participation among pupils. Early in 1972 considerable apathy was reported at school meetings which were dominated by a small, unrepresentative group of students and vocal teachers.

A spate of books on children's rights appeared after 1971. The message was 'school is dead' and the appeal was especially to younger teachers and older pupils in urban schools.[15] The *Little Red School Book* (originally a Danish publication), which urged the destruction of the school as an institution, gained particular notoriety. In 1971 there was a [125] failed attempt to ban it for 'incitement to commit offences in breach of the sexual offences acts'.[16] It suggested that boredom in class might be alleviated by reading pornographic magazines; light-heartedly advised the installation of contraceptive machines in school playgrounds; listed methods of contraception and organizations providing sexual advice; and described drugs as 'poisons which could have a pleasant effect'. More seriously, it opposed corporal punishment and explained how to make formal complaints against teachers or education authorities, or set up a school council. The urban free school and deschooling won enthusiastic followings. Ten commandments suggested in an educational weekly for setting up a free school or deschooling the system satirized the intellectual naïvety of its advocates.[17]

(1) I am the informal non-system of education. Thou shalt have no schools at all.

(2) Thou shalt have any form of education that thou likest: or any likeness of education that can be plucked out of the Third World or out of the underground: thou shalt follow any idea that comes up: for the deschoolers have no set pattern of organisation except in being determined not to visit the education of the parents on the children in any generation: and despising all those who put their trust in schools and examinations.

(3) Thou shalt take any organised system in vain, for the deschooler will not hold him guiltless that does not take all systems in vain.

(4) Remember not to keep any holidays. Every day of the year shalt thou learn something from somebody and pass on something to somebody, either thy sons and thy daughters, or their friends or their teachers who have only been formally educated, or the carpenter down the road.

(5) Do not honour anybody, that thy days may be long in the informal learning situation which the deschooler has given thee.

(6) Thou shalt kill off all forms of organized learning.

(7) Thou shalt not come to adulthood.

(8) Thou shalt steal ideas from anywhere.

(9) Thou shalt bear false witness against all recognised philosophies of education.

(10) Thou shalt despise the middle class man's house, his acquisitions, his children's exam successes, their higher education, their job opportunities, the elaborated code and everything that is theirs.

The influence of Ivan Illich, one of the principal deschoolers, was strongly felt.[18] Illich, a non-practising Catholic priest who had worked with rural and urban poverty in Latin America, had a large following in North America, Europe and Australia. He taught that school instruction produced attitudes towards learning which discredited the self-taught man and rendered suspect all non-professional activity. School learning was seen as the result of regular attendance, the assumption being that the value of what was learnt would increase with the amount of input.

For Illich education had been subverted from an activity into a commodity, for which schools monopolized the market. Education therefore defined class structure in a society where the largest consumers of knowledge claimed to be of superior value. The more education an individual consumed the more knowledge stock he acquired and the higher he rose in the hierarchy of knowledge capitalists.

Schools had created and endorsed this social myth through their role in structuring ritual and grading educational promotion. School timetables even ritualized children's conception of time, with 'filling in your timetable' an initiation rite for pupils at the start of each school term. Subject divisions were imposed in secondary schools. Discipline emphasized social roles and distinctions. According to Illich, Paolo Freire and others, education had become the new world religion; the new world church was the knowledge industry itself.[19] Teachers were purveyors both of opium and the workbench during an increasing number of years of a man's life. Deschooling was therefore at the root of any movement for human liberation and men must free themselves from compulsory school.

Much exciting work occurred in various parts of the world in the deschooling and free school domain. Mini-schools, the division of the leviathan US high schools, store-front academies and the 'school without walls' experiments were all impressive ventures. In Australia, as in the US, the deschooling movement was frequently linked with middle class parental choice. British deschoolers, notably Ian Lister at York University, attempted to provide a theoretical basis for nationwide activity. They were encouraged by a strange assortment of supporters, including those who disapproved of conventional school education for the working class on elitest grounds, the multiracial lobbyists, and the publishing *avant-garde*.[20] A scattering of progressive urban free schools was flourishing in Britain by 1972, catering largely for working class children. The first well-planned free school in Britain was White Lion free school in Islington, run by two former educational journalists. They were backed by an impressive list of patrons including A. H. Halsey. Similar ventures were reported in various British cities.[21]

Inevitably, these charismatic free schools nearly always sought to become institutionalized after some years, if only to ensure their continued existence through guaranteed funding. To function legally as an independent school, any free school had to be registered by the DES, and this could not happen until the school had been inspected and approved by HM Inspectorate. That meant preparing an educational programme, obtaining suitable furniture, having adequate handwashing and lavatory arrangements and acceptable school meals and curriculum. Following the 1944 Education Act children could legally be educated 'by regular attendance at school or otherwise'. Temporarily, the free school could be covered by the 'otherwise' category, often used by local authorities themselves to allow home tuition for children in special need. But all children over 8 years old had to have full-time education, that is at least four hours daily secular instruction.

The Liverpool free school was fairly typical.[22] It had no set programme or regular lessons, and its two teachers and children worked as a voluntary democracy. The school was allowed to continue. But eventually it ran into financial difficulties. In 1974 it folded and more than sixty children were left without schools. Because they had gone to a free school, defying the Roman Catholic Diocesan authorities whose schools they had formerly attended, they found themselves unable to get back into secondary education. The boys had been warned that if they attended the free school the diocesan authorities would not have them back until they had been 'rehabilitated' by special teachers whom, it was insisted, the local authority should provide.

Many difficulties were encountered at the White Lion free school in Islington which, despite becoming fully registered with the DES two years after its opening in 1971, faced imminent closure in 1977 through lack of funds and was barely reprieved. All the children except those in the nursery were expected to do some basic work each morning; 'they are chased and nagged by their allocated adult if they do not!' The work fell into four topics: projects, which among the girls were depressingly often about pop stars and animals; the basic skills; visits from craft and other helpers such as a photographer or potter; and educational visits. The children went out driving, riding, swimming and dancing, as well as staying in cottages and houses lent to them in the country.

The official attitude towards free schools was mixed; often pejorative, sometimes patronizing, occasionally encouraging. Local councillors did not know what stance to adopt.[23] To welcome free schools might be to admit that state schools had failed. Helping free schools could mean that priority funds for a state school might be threatened. Critics like Midwinter argued fiercely against the contradictory logic of free schools, avowedly private ventures, asking for public support.

Others pointed out that such progressive educational experiment seldom survived transfer to the state sector, as the failure of Duane and Mackenzie had shown. While some radicals attacked free schools simply as another form of private education, a view borne out by experience in the US and Australia, the White Lion School notably failed to attract the middle class of Islington. Moderate critics therefore argued that by providing second-rate facilities, drop-out teachers and inferior curriculum the free school enthusiasts ran the risk of adding to the accumulated deprivation of their pupils.

Free schools did, however, demonstrate the attraction for children of being a known individual in a small non-authoritarian setting. They took the problem children out of the ordinary classroom and kept them off the streets. They satisfied the obscure feelings of parents and children that small, 'personal' schools might be better than the large anonymous ones, and encouraged a mood of public sympathy towards smaller comprehensive schools.

The greatest contribution of the free schools was the initiative they stimulated in the state sector. Local authorities began to steal the emperor's clothes, upstaging the free schoolers by themselves providing alternative schools or units within the LEA system.[24] Unwilling as they were to assist the private sector, and progressively less able to afford the £700 or more a year fees which by 1976 were required to send maladjusted children to any available places at boarding schools, local authorities set up free schools of their own; these were variously known as truancy projects, guidance centres or intermediate treatment units. Second language teaching units also took the troublesome children with a multiracial background who needed special help with English.

11 Teaching English: a curriculum case study

Nowhere was the general complexity and confusion over curriculum more clearly seen than in the disagreement over the teaching of reading and language development among urban children. Throughout the 1960s and 1970s, in Britain, the US and Australia, there was continuous controversy about reported static or declining reading achievement. Surveys by Morris in 1964 or ILEA in 1968 showed that one in six of 8-year-olds fell into the category of non-readers, and just as with patterns of examination success, proportionately too many of these children attended urban schools.[1] Many children needed infant methods of teaching reading at the junior stage or even beyond, yet few junior teachers and virtually no secondary teachers were adequately trained to teach children to read. Experts differed over the trend in reading standards when comparing tests from different decades. Many disagreed with the NFER investigators, Start and Wells, who in 1972 concluded that reading standards had declined.[2] But everyone agreed that reading standards were static at a time when advanced technological societies, according to UNESCO, needed ever higher levels of functional literacy.

Folk-lore had it that the teaching profession was split over teaching methods and that teachers chose a phonics, Look and Say, ITA or some specific scheme which excluded all others. The truth was more complicated. Successive investigations over a twenty-year period showed that published reading schemes were invariably the basis of the initial teaching of reading.[3] But even amateur statisticians admitted that research showed that most schools used more than one scheme. And those who were familiar with the schemes knew that meant most teachers were using more than one method.

'My Grandad's so old he can remember when every child could read and write by the time they left the infants.'

Goodacre's survey of reading schemes in schools in 1968, for instance, showed that 81 per cent of primary schools used *Janet and John*, while another five main schemes were used by 30 to 40 per cent of schools. *Janet and John* enjoyed phenomenal success in the late 1950s, following American publication of the scheme. The carefully graded vocabulary and constant repetitions appealed to teachers, although many older classroom professionals clung to the Beacon scheme, introduced originally in 1922, for its systematic phonics work and the quality of its stories. The Bullock Report showed that by 1973 teachers had increasingly turned to the Ladybird Scheme, which had the virtue of being available for parents to purchase themselves. By 1978 the 'Breakthrough' approach had gained classroom popularity in 46 per cent of schools. This was a rare success for the Schools Council. Significantly, far from being an *avant-garde* innovatory scheme, 'Breakthrough' produced in packaged form the practice of many ordinary classroom teachers over the years. Teachers had often encouraged children to learn to read and write simultaneously by making up their own sentences. Now the approach was commercially marketed,

with an accompanying psycholinguistic handbook, a shrewd ploy
which gave 'Breakthrough' appeal for the innovatory and the traditional teacher.

The national preoccupation with reading standards grew yearly.
The difficulty, as Neville Bennett's research was to show, was in
identifying how much time teachers spent on the teaching of reading
in the informal classroom. Less time was given to the formal teaching
of reading as craft, music and other creative subjects were increasingly introduced into the primary school day. Reading and writing
activities were woven into the pattern of the integrated day and were
not easily measured.

Urban conditions of staffing confusion and classroom stress made it
impossible to assess the best reading approach except according to the
circumstances of each school. This was best illustrated in the bewildering story of the Initial Teaching Alphabet. ITA, devised by James Pitman
in 1961 and propagated through bequest money, aroused opponents
and allies in the educational world to almost unrivalled emotional fervour. Pitman produced an alphabet of 44 written characters each of
which represented only one spoken sound. ITA changed the appearance of some 50 per cent of words in simplifying spelling. Startling
claims were made for the new alphabet after experiments started by
John Downing and others in 1961. An evaluation by the Schools Council
in 1965 led Warburton and Southgate to assert: 'ITA is a superior
medium to traditional orthography in teaching young children to read'.[4]
But whatever the merits of ITA, it was never given a proper chance
and therefore could not genuinely be found wanting. Professional
enthusiasm cooled rapidly even in the experimental schools. It was not
just that parents complained they could no longer read with their
children because of the dearth of published ITA material available from
bookshops, or even that the transfer from ITA to traditional spelling
was sometimes difficult, as teachers pointed out. The main reason for
ITA's failure in urban primary schools was that head teachers found
their high staff turnover meant constant retraining. There were never
enough teachers experienced in ITA's use. Despite its varying success
in Papua, New Guinea, and parts of the US, ITA never really caught on
in Britain.

Middle class parents approached their children's reading problems
with demands for structured teaching. The dyslexia myth, (from the
Greek *dus* or 'bad': and *lexia*, i.e. 'word') simply meant word difficulty
or blindness. Curiously enough it did not occur below a certain level of
intelligence, although exactly what the condition was fourteen experts
labouring for five years did not succeed in explaining. But the blanket
term was just the right blend of scientific jargon and vague conceptualization. Assiduous pressure compelled the DES to advise special pro-

vision for the dyslexic child, who was defined as a pupil whose disorder was 'manifested by difficulty in learning to read, despite conventional instruction, adequate intelligence and socio-cultural opportunity'.[5] The Bullock report, however, concluded in 1973 that the esti-

Colin Wheeler

'Well, Wayne, it's to stamp out the advantage of those who can read before they come to school.'

mated 90,000 'dyslexic' schoolchildren in Britain were not helped by the label: 'We believe that this term serves little purpose other than to draw attention to the fact that the problem of these children can be chronic and severe'.

Innovations and changes in children's reading habits were highly publicized but less dramatic than sometimes claimed.[6] The many brightly-illustrated children's books which appeared were often more popular with librarians than with children themselves. Children's [133] bookshops were sometimes successfully sponsored within schools: and the cheap paperbacks available in the primary classroom stimulated book-buying among the most disadvantaged children. Small publishing enterprises in London's East End and elsewhere issued 'working class' biographies and other writing by local people which were popular with school children. But efforts made by Leila Berg, author of the Nippers books, and others in attempting to replace the trivial appeal of Enid Blyton or the chauvinism of Biggles by writing authentic working class stories were not contagiously successful. Working class children did identify themselves and their parents with the people in these books who quarrelled on holiday and ate fish and chips. But research suggested that 9- to 10-year-old working class and middle class children still preferred Biggles, Blyton, or in school, the insipid Ladybird books with their chocolate-box artwork, tame children, expensive consumer objects and middle class life-style. National surveys of children's reading habits showed that, stimulated by television serialization, old favourites like *Black Beauty* or *The Silver Sword* continued their popularity, while in 1974 Ian Fleming and Enid Blyton were the most popular authors among the older adolescents.[7] The Thompson company's *Beano* and *Dandy*, with their horrendous stereotyping, were still the most popular comics for boys up to the age of 14 years. And despite the emphasis by primary and secondary teachers on reading poetry, and encouraging children to write it, the percentage of children reporting that they read poetry at home had halved since a survey in 1940. On the other hand, the massive growth of information books, particularly classroom 'resource' texts like the Macdonald Starters, had enormous impact.

Teachers were not seriously distracted by much of the new material for teaching reading and writing. Ronald Ridout or R. J. Unstead, long regarded as sacred monsters by progressive teachers in primary or secondary schools, continued prolific writing lives which reputedly made them millionaires. From 1952 onwards some 54 million copies of Ridout's books for average and remedial children were sold, with over 300 titles in print in 1976. Ridout's royalties exceeded all the Schools Council projects put together.[8]

Psycholinguistics and children's language development, rather than the broad sweep of urban policy, became fashionable among teachers concerned about literacy. The intellectual history of that trend throws important light on the whole curriculum movement.

Without doubt the most significant figure influencing teachers and teachers in training towards a new emphasis on the relationship between language acquisition and classroom attainment was Basil Bernstein.[9] Not since Bergson lectured on laughter in the Sorbonne in the

1920s had such admiring, spell-bound audiences gathered round a university guru. But it was Bernstein's misfortune to be gloriously, linguistically misunderstood, the victim of mangled exegesis. A sensitive, philosophical mind in the European tradition, much influenced by the sociologist Durkheim, Bernstein brought some of his difficulties upon himself through the frugality and the abstruseness of his publications. Yet for the cognoscenti he was a sharply lucid, amusing writer and thinker.

Bernstein was popularly interpreted as enunciating a dichotomy between the restricted speech code of working class children and the elaborated code of middle class children which was also the language of higher education. His researches suggested that children from the lower working class used language which was deeply embedded, or context-bound, in the situations where it arose. Those children and their families used language as if everyone shared their knowledge and preconceptions. They conveyed meaning not explicitly but implicitly, so that outsiders who had not shared the experience found the working class talk 'restricted' and difficult to follow. The working class child might therefore be at a disadvantage in school tasks where the elaborated speech code dominated classroom communication. Working class children might be handicapped by their restricted code, for unlike the middle class children who could operate in restricted codes, for instance, using slang for special situations, the working class child was not able to switch codes. Bernstein and his associates bore out the child development research of the Newsons in confirming that middle class children took up a wider range of linguistic options.[10] Middle class mothers communicated more fully with their children, particularly in giving explanations. Bernstein also suggested that working class children could be puzzled and slowed down by the teaching style and implicit assumptions of the informal classroom. As time went on, Bernstein interested himself less in psycholinguistics than in the sociology of the school curriculum.

As he himself complained, Basil Bernstein became a dangerously misunderstood cult figure. He was misinterpreted as asserting that working class children needed to be helped to escape from the narrowness of their restricted code. Some argued that he presented a 'deficit' view of the working class child and his culture, thereby advocating compensatory education and undervaluing working class culture. In fact, as we have seen, he argued in at least one major article that 'education could not compensate for society'. Nevertheless, interpreters like Denis Lawton, who worked with Bernstein for a time, suggested that working class children might need a differential language programme and curriculum in order to benefit from school.[11]

Every student in a college of education by 1970 and thousands of newly trained teachers knew all about Bernstein's theories. Then came the debunking. Bernstein was attacked by the 'new English' teachers in the University of London where he worked, and principally by his colleague Harold Rosen, who savagely criticized a lack of precision in Bernstein's theories of 'language and class'.[12] 'Whereas in the 1950s

'I keep telling you! You only paint it. She says what it is.'

TODAY WE ARE GOING TO DISCOVER GRAVITY

children had their IQs branded on their foreheads, in the 1960s more of them had the brand changed to "restricted or elaborated", as the result of Bernstein's influence', asserted Rosen. Had not Labov in the US shown that lower class Philadelphian blacks could talk with more vigour and clarity than their middle class counterparts, provided they were sufficiently relaxed and confident with their interviewer?[13] Rosen argued for a similar recognition of the vitality, precision, and logic of British working class speech and personal writing.[14] His argument, although given a new twist, was far from original. Richard Hoggart in his book on the *Uses of Literacy*,[15] and a whole school of romantic anthropologists, Marxists and literary sociologists – Raymond Williams, Brian Jackson, Peter Willmott, Michael Townsend, Eric Midwinter – had argued from the 1950s that the urban working class culture of pigeons, brass bands and racy narrative should be treasured more highly.

But Rosen spoke out of a new tradition of secondary English teaching which had dramatically reformed the curriculum and political strategy of English teachers after the early 1960s.[16] Largely graduate, invariably secondary teachers, members of the 'new English' movement through their organization the National Association of the Teachers of English (NATE), shared the black romanticism of the anthropologists in admiring working-class culture, especially the seedier side of life. Sometimes, perhaps, it was the contrast between their own background and the working class milieu which appealed. Often it was because teachers lived similar lives. Housing stress and low salaries had pushed inner city teachers into a life-style identical in many respects with their pupils and the parents. Often they lived in the same neighbourhoods, used the same shops, pubs, launderettes and street markets.

These young teachers created an English teaching revolution in the classroom. They set great store by personal, creative writing arising from children's own experience. Fluent discussion and writing, and relatively little attention to accurate spelling, formal grammar, or systematic teaching of reading skills was their classroom emphasis. Young English teachers in the 1960s revived the romantic nineteenth-century notion of 'enthusiasm', encouraging the working class child to remain a literary primitive.[17] This was a splendid reforming movement in the hidebound grammar schools where Rosen and others had spent most of their teaching careers, but it was often untimely, subversive and even destructive in the comprehensive classroom.

The 'new English' teaching tradition was at first politically radical, although it was later criticized as revisionist by the extreme left. Many of the new English teachers indoctrinated themselves and their classes in attitudes critical of the police, local government bureaucracy, indus-

try and employers. They did not hesitate to encourage this ideology
in the children's writing, or classroom discussion. Christopher Searle
was an extreme example of this trend.[18]

The 'sociological English', as it was called, was disseminated in
important new English teaching textbooks like *Reflections*. This was an
English course from a South London comprehensive school published
in 1965, offering controversial extracts for pupil discussion on urgent
social themes such as housing, war, old people, relations between the
sexes – topics which had not traditionally been considered proper
matter for English classes. It was the precursor of many similar
anthologies.

The new wave of English teachers was committed to the comprehensive school, to unstreaming, subject integration and team
teaching. They were enthusiastic curriculum imperialists. They
wished to see policies for 'language across the curriculum' which
involved their collaboration with other subject departments. Through
their influence creative writers were invited to be resident in secondary
schools;[19] school bookshops were opened; children began to produce
poetry of very high quality; excellent CSE Mode 3 and other examination syllabuses were devised. Their achievement was considerable. In
less than a decade a coterie of a hundred or so influential figures in the
London Association of the Teachers of English, and later its national
body, NATE, working with the BBC and a few publishers, and infiltrat-
ing the Schools Council, achieved international impact.

By the mid-1970s the charismatic fervour curdled and institutionalized; bureaucratic consolidation, political wrangling and collective
self-doubt overtook the movement. Through their control of the
Schools Council English panel the elder statesmen of NATE had
launched curriculum development projects which looked at the writing of 11- to 18-year-olds between 1966 and 1971.[20] A new taxonomy
and theory of children's writing emerged. Using a technique of
analysis more reminiscent of Aristotle's *Rhetoric* than of any curriculum thinking in the twentieth century, they defined with scholastic
zeal types of 'audience' and categories of children's writing. They
expounded an aridly analytical system, their writings turgidly con-
tradicting their own advice that child or adult writing should exhibit
freshness and originality.

Many of the original revolutionaries were by now establishment
figures playing for higher political stakes. Those few who stayed in
teaching jobs, like Michael Marland, had throughout pursued a more
moderate stance – and sometimes been lampooned for it. Their influence, together with the best of the new English tradition, was evident
in the recommendations of the important Bullock Report. The Bullock
Committee, set up in response to public concern over reading stan-

dards, recommended a greater emphasis on the teaching of reading and the need for a designated member of staff responsible for the reading and language curriculum in each school.

But the Bullock Report also argued for stronger central intervention in the curriculum policies of schools and local authorities. It might not have been surprising to find leaders of the 'new English' dissociating themselves from anything which might interfere with the individual freedom of the English teacher in his classroom. Yet, on the contrary, when the Assessment of Performance Unit was set up in 1976 by the DES to devise reading and language tests in order to tighten up on the British classroom, leading figures of the 'new English' movement hurried to support that body. Casuistically, they argued that they should take control in case the APU took off in the wrong direction. Not unexpectedly, these gamekeepers of the English teaching establishment came under attack by the next generation of English teachers. Younger English teachers suspected that their senior colleagues were mistaken in collaborating with a government, DES and HM Inspectorate clearly intent on imposing rigid schools inspection, testing and possibly a common core curriculum on urban schools. The 'new English' establishment had attempted to swallow up other subjects through policies of integrated studies, team teaching and 'language across the curriculum'. There had been in many schools what looked suspiciously like a take-over of history, geography, and the weakest subject of all, religious education. Now a central language policy for schools or whole LEAs might usher in a centralized curriculum. The 'new English' teaching revolution, objected the younger teachers, had not been fought for that.[21]

Left-wing teachers among the rank and file of NATE began to question the romantic emphasis on personal writing and sociological talk in the classroom. The extreme left, politically militant and articulate, did not get any nearer to identifying the background urban crisis, but the English teachers who were members of Rank and File, or readers of *Teaching London Kids*, began to attack their complaisant seniors.[22] Promoting classroom discussion of controversial topics, argued the politically active younger teachers, had turned the older generation into tools of the establishment. By channelling political feelings into stories or classroom talk they had distracted children from political action. Children should spill out of the classroom and begin to attack politically a system which provided poor housing, encouraged war, racist attitudes and unemployment. NATE had lost its conscience and sense of purpose.

Younger English teachers saw that the issues were more complex than some people made out. It was not simply a battle between 'goodies', led by Rosen, Britton or Labov, and the 'baddies', the *Black*

Paper critics who upheld traditional parsing, grammar and spelling.
The criticism of the sociologists of knowledge or structuralist critics like Lawton had to be answered: they argued that without carefully planned teaching, especially of reading, many less able working class children could become yet more disadvantaged. The English teachers, in their enthusiasm, while achieving much, had in many urban schools destructured departments, integrated curriculum and innovated trends which they did not stay to follow through. Sometimes those teachers who did stay were driven to exhaustion, when the standards they had set themselves were so high, and everything they had fought to establish collapsed about their ears.

Secondary English teachers were also finally compelled to take a more serious approach to the teaching of reading and the problems of the multiracial classroom.[23] Even as late as 1977, it was still very rare to find an English Head of Department who believed that he should teach or know how to teach reading. NATE had serious discussions about whether this was a matter which concerned them. Some enthusiasts still argued publicly in the educational press that spelling did not particularly matter. But pushed along by the Bullock Report, the Open University, the United Kingdom Reading Association and all those who were anxious about the multi-ethnic classroom, the 'new English' movement adopted a more sensible line. They became interested in neo-structural views of the reading process, as advanced by Frank Smith or Kenneth Goodman,[24] systematic new attempts to explain the reading process in more complexity.

Under the umbrella of working class cultural pluralism, Rosen and others had dodged the difficult problem of the linguistically disadvantaged child from a multi-ethnic background, evading the question that teachers were increasingly asking: what could be done to improve the lagging attainment of immigrant children or the British born children of immigrants?[25] Multi-ethnic experts now began to show that all children needed structured language, reading and comprehension activity – and not just children in the multi-ethnic classroom. Nowhere was the curious interplay between politics, curriculum neo-structuralism, cargo-cult and the growing national obsession with literacy better illustrated than in the case of English as a second language project materials. An early attempt by the Schools Council, the 'Scope' project, produced materials for Pakistani and West Indian immigrant children.[26] However, having initiated this useful curriculum development with a small team, the Schools Council was unable, under its terms of reference, to disseminate it through inservice education. 'Scope' was stock-piled in educational premises and relatively little sold or used. The under-achievement of West Indian and other immigrant children in British schools continued to arouse bitterness and disillusion among teachers and the immigrant communities.

Anyone putting forward a project proposal to solve this politically sensitive problem continued to obtain generous funding. A later Schools Council project, 'Concept 7–9', investigated whether West Indian primary children suffered from 'dialect interference' in their language and reading efforts.[27] Its conclusions were perhaps predictable: West Indian children in Britain were bi-dialectical, speaking one dialect with their family and other West Indians, another with their white friends and perhaps a third with their teachers. In the jargon of Bernstein, they had developed the ability for code switching; by the age of 7 or 8 years most West Indian children achieved considerable mastery of the English spoken in Britain, as well as talking the West Indian dialect of their home. In their formal speech or writing in school tasks, West Indian children used conventional grammar rather than Creole, indicating a reasonable control over standard English. That demolished any argument that Creole grammar interfered seriously with reading comprehension. The team found that the children often had poor attainment because their early reading experience had emphasized accuracy at the expense of comprehension skills. Their difficulties in this respect were similar to those experienced by children from Birmingham, Liverpool or London who spoke non-standard English but who were not of immigrant origin. Teachers corrected children not only when they got the meaning wrong, but when they got the meaning right and the teacher regarded their grammar or pronunciation as wrong.[28] Consequently, when the 'Concept 7–9' team produced four boxes of highly structured teaching material and techniques they were as suitable for the backward Cockney as they were for the Bradford Pakistani or the North Kensington West Indian child. In 'Concept 7–9' formal syntax and oracy were taught by repetition through structured games and similar approaches. There was an obvious lesson here. Large numbers of urban children would benefit from a structured approach to the teaching of one language, comprehension and probably reading skills. A recommendation unacceptable when it came from the *Black Paper* adherent, urging more structured teaching in language, comprehension and early reading skills, was uncontrovertible coming from the leftish-inclined second language specialists.

Curriculum distortion occurred, then, not just because of the staffing crisis, managerial dilemmas, EPA projects or unrealistic timetabling, but because teachers and others left out of account the varying impact on the urban school of curriculum reform. In many schools energetic innovation was valuable and timely, but the progressives, whether 'informal' primary classroom teachers or the new wave of

secondary English teachers were often, in a phrase of Sartre's, 'right,
but wrong for being right.' In ignoring the need for differential curriculum and teaching style their enthusiasm often destructured and
sometimes destroyed schools. Their lack of judgement and narrow
vision hastened the arrival of a counter-reformation; and they unwittingly fed ammunition to those who wished to wind the clock back by
years.

12 Electric, plastic classrooms

The urban school curriculum was ceaselessly distorted. There were innumerable causes. If it was not that the teachers were pursuing some grand design of total curriculum renewal, it might be the cancellation of sports day because mob violence was threatened from truant members of another school. Curriculum planning was often hit and miss. The examination system was still a demanding task-master. Widespread discrimination against girls was reported in 1976.[1] There was often a shortage of subject teachers. A whole comprehensive school of 2,000 pupils might be timetabled next year for one weekly lesson of music for each pupil, although the senior staff knew perfectly well that in September there would only be one music teacher in the entire school. One large urban authority introduced a special mathematics curriculum that non-specialist teachers could teach, based on mathematics work cards in the style of 'do-it-yourself' cookery cards. The aim was to provide children with at least some mathematics at a time of teacher shortage; the result was, as so often, second-rate curriculum and teaching for the already disadvantaged child.[2]

The hidden curriculum was equally intractable. The invisible message from staffrooms was sexist: 60 per cent of primary and secondary teachers were women, 62 per cent of head teachers men. Attempts were made to correct racial bias through teacher recruitment and by using reading materials which recognized the presence of immigrant children. But the schools had to compete with television and the half million comics bought weekly in Britain. *Jack and Jill, Lion, Buster,*

Princess, *Tina* and *June* all encouraged sexist or racial stereotypes.[3] [143]
Children observed from them that non-whites were evil, treacherous,
violent or stupid. Africans were stereotyped as 'natives', American
Indians were 'injuns' whose chief activity was the war dance. Teachers

'Mr Henshaw is in charge of curriculum planning.'

could be equally at fault in trying to redress bias. Some teachers used
the traditional West Indian Anancy folk stories in the multi-ethnic
classroom: just as often that brought censure from West Indian parents
who complained they sent their children to school to learn formal
English and not West Indian dialect. Black Studies courses were temporarily fashionable in urban secondary schools in appealing to the
alienated black Birmingham or London adolescent. But such an option
could easily divide the school community with black children opting
for their curriculum and other children opting out. When they already
sat at separate tables in the dining room what good was that? Black
studies did successfully teach the history of the Berbers, Christianity in
north Africa, the growth of the kingdom of Ghana or the spread of
Islam. Calypso records were played and West Indian meals were
cooked, but as a curriculum it never gained substantial impetus.

But the trend towards importing cargo-cult into the contemporary
classroom proved the biggest distorting influence of all. This policy of
cargo-cult was not questioned until the pressure of the debate was
deflated by the sober critics of the middle ground, economic stringency, the parental lobby, increased inspection, and the return of

staffing stability. But meanwhile many schools, particularly in the deprived cities, used their new-found prosperity to purchase the materials and equipment of the new technology rather than pursue genuine innovation. With the desperation born of a sense of imminent catastrophe, schools bought everything they were offered. If you had no children's work to display on open evenings, at least you could put out all the lavish goodies you had bought with your EPA allowances. A spate of curriculum projects – schemes, equipment, books and multi-media kits – poured forth from the Schools Council, on the hypothesis that if you unleash enough projectiles some of them will hit the target. The English school system was an ideal test bed for Schools Council wares, with its traditional independence, especially the *laissez-faire* right of the head teacher to choose the curriculum.

Just as school dinners were transformed by textured vegetable proteins and artificial ingredients, the growth of the plastics industry and technology made an enormous difference to primary and secondary teachers. Vast quantities of cheap apparatus, like Unifix, Lego or constructional kits turned the infant classroom into an astonishing Aladdin's cave. Improved adhesives and magic markers, or clay that did not require firing, transformed art and craft. The plastics revolution and the supermarket provided schools with cheap junk materials. Lighthouses were made out of detergent bottles, primary maths and art flourished with egg boxes, bird-seed, yoghurt cartons and domestic detritus. 'Learning by discovery' was only possible with consumable materials which could be economically used and destroyed by children.

In the secondary schools, particularly the urban comprehensives, superb science and craft workshops were created.[4] There the exciting curriculum was taught using the new technology: infra-red ray photography, sculpture with resins, pebble polishing, film making, go-kart or hovercraft construction – these all demanded first-rate teachers, equipment, workshop facilities and contemporary materials.

In craft, design or Nuffield applied science, a new technology rendered traditional skills of less importance. It became possible to build a hydrogen filled balloon for the A level physical science course or to use a radio-controlled camera for aerial photography.

These developments raised the hazards of fire or poison.[5] Adhesives were now available which gave off an inflammable vapour or formed glue which was impossible to remove from the fingers without the use of solvent – of great appeal to the unruly or disruptive urban adolescent. Polystyrene used in model making, could, when cut with a hot wire or sculpting tool, irritate the eyes or cause dizziness. The hydrogen peroxide used to add to plastic resins for craft and artwork could explode.

An expansion in the educational school equipment industry went
hand in hand during this period with innovatory trends in building,
architectural design and curriculum. The largest suppliers of educational equipment, Arnold's of Leeds, opened vast new warehouses
and computerized their ordering system. Lightweight expanded polystyrene, vinyl-covered cubes and other shapes were developed for
school use. Inflatable play equipment for indoors, miniature tram-
polines, and other new PE equipment were introduced. Drama boxes
in the smaller schools were built to double as platforms and apparatus
in PE. One of the biggest improvements in secondary school gym-
nasiums was the introduction of a dense foam rubber mat known as a
crash or safety mattress (giving the gymnast added confidence because
he was unlikely to hurt himself on landing).

In all schools cardboard machinery abounded: reading laboratories
or information kits, carefully packaged and designed. Publishers
embarked on multi-media packaging: by the mid-1970s even the pro-
saic Ladybird Reading Scheme included cards for the Language Master
tape machine, charts and other mixed materials. BBC Radiovision, a
tape slide approach based on radio programme material, was enormously successful, as was its home grown equivalent – photo plays
made by children themselves in school with Instamatic cameras and
portable tape recorders.

Audio-visual aids cargo-cult was not invariably successful. 'Whatever happened to teaching machines' was a cry often heard at educational conferences by the 1970s. The learned exponents of linear and
branching programme techniques had often been seen with their metal
boxes at educational conferences in the 1960s. But by the 1970s the
main contribution of the teaching machine was in the Fire Service, the
army or the prison rather than with schoolchildren. A major project,
trumpeted by its manufacturers as solving the reading crisis, the Talking Page, quietly disappeared from sight.[6]

Nevertheless, new audio-visual aids machinery, such as the over-
head projector, Language Master, Synchrofax, videotape recorder,
induction loop or talking typewriter all had an important part to play.[7]
The cassette tape recorder became an essential and versatile aid for
teachers engaged in speech and oracy activities, following new
emphasis on classroom talk as the key to later attainment. Two variations of the tape recorder, the Language Master and the Synchrofax,
which used sound-sensitized cardboard records, were widely used by
reading specialists, or even in general curriculum, and were a great
help to many children. The recording of school broadcasts, on radio or
on videotape recorders, became common and influenced curriculum
and timetabling. Pupils became familiar with a range of new audio-
visual aids in school, quite apart from possessing their own transistor

radios and tape recorders. More exotic was the talking typewriter, a large-face electric typewriter used in reading clinics and some schools for children who were 'dyslexic' or had severe reading problems. The induction loop system (also used by many museums) allowed the

'I like him. By the time he's got everything set up, the lesson's over.'

listener with ear-phones to pick up information by walking round the room – an innovation particularly helpful for the partially-hearing child as well as in the primary school classroom. Many schools improved their 'reprographic' facilities by buying an electronic stencil cutter which gave unlimited copies of drawings, or an offset lithographic press to print the school magazine or curriculum worksheets.

'Resources', a compendium noun which could include people, money, building and curriculum, became the fashionable catchword.[8] Serving large comprehensives in London, and sometimes elsewhere, was a new professional, the media resource officer. The large school, running a small publishing unit to produce curriculum materials, could no longer rely on a harassed head of department or an ancillary worker lacking in sophisticated audio-visual aids skills. Knowing what was available, where it could be ordered, and how to manage print, photography and reprographics, the media resource officers acted as curriculum gatekeepers. Together with the school librarian they often influenced the curriculum as much as the heads of departments themselves, and were sometimes found determining the curriculum with the willing acquiescence of their busy teaching colleagues.

Accompanying this trend was a move towards the establishment of a resource centre in each school;[9] the library as such became obsolete, and the new setting included books and other forms of printed or audio-visual resources. In some authorities teachers' centres acted as

resource centres; sophisticated attempts in the US and Canada to
harness educational technology had created, in Ottawa, for example, a
central resource centre linked by co-axial cable to every educational
institution.

But the most important technological contribution to curriculum
change was made by television and radio. Despite the suspicion with
which teachers regarded television, it became their chief curriculum
competitor.

Local radio made a valuable minor contribution to the school curriculum. The first stations were set up during this period in the hope
that local radio would revive and support the sense of urban community which had so faded under the impact of industrial society and the
national media. Teachers were seconded to work as producers, and by
1973 about eighty of them were working in local radio stations on
educational broadcasts.

Educational television services were not a success. The follies of the
eighteenth century were built by autocrats with private wealth. Those
of the twentieth century were built by highly paid bureaucrats in
central or national government. Local authority educational television
services were the twentieth-century education officer's equivalent of
the folly. With the desperate shortage of teachers in Glasgow, London
and other cities, it was argued that television could project talented
teachers into the classroom at a time of acute staffing shortage. It was a
way of sharing the good teachers round. At 1967 prices, the job could
be done in London for about £150 each year per school, less than
one-tenth the cost of a teacher. The economic argument was tempting.[10] By 1972 London, Glasgow and Plymouth all produced their own
education programmes for schools. In London in 1972, seventy-eight
programme series were broadcast (BBC and ITV together produced
only the same number of series for the national audience). London
alone employed one hundred full-time staff and thirty-two seconded
teachers. In Hull, which already had its own telephone service, the
existence of a cable system which could carry the television signal
capitalized on existing provision. But despite the wide range of programmes, including a few excellent series, urban teachers proved
indifferent. There were a number of advantages to local educational
television, but there were endless criticisms. Teachers and pupils alike
felt that the high standards of BBC and ITV were not matched by local
ETV. Children complained about the poor acting, stagey sets, boring
monochrome and the slow pace of programmes. Although ETV services had been established by Glasgow (1965), Plymouth (1966) London (1968) and Hull (1969), there was a question mark over the future
of many services by the mid-1970s.[11] By 1976 London had decided
virtually to close down its educational television service. Against a

background of a no-growth educational economy and severe cuts in public spending the expensive white elephant had to be jettisoned. Closed circuit education television had failed everywhere, from Hawaii to London.

Yet there was no question but that British national television, admired the world over, was a real alternative school for the urban child, who was able to obtain home tutoring of a very high quality.[12] 'Blue Peter', 'Magpie' or even the current affairs programmes, the dramatization of classics, nature and animal programmes, offered an interesting, varied and well-presented curriculum.

Research showed that children concentrated even on 'difficult subjects' when these were presented by people they trusted. Television personalities, from the pre-school programme presenters of 'Playschool' or 'Rainbow' up to the actor heroes of serialized classics, became the new urban teachers. The highly informed truant and autodidact became a familiar phenomenon, especially following the advent of colour television.

Children formed the largest and most important minority in any television audience. In 1973 eight million children between 5 and 15 years old, comprising 16 per cent of the total population, watched an average of 25 hours television per week, while adults watched an average of 17 hours. There was a phenomenal demand for information among children (also reflected in the information book revolution in school publishing). In 1973 John Craven's 'Newsround' was watched by 50 per cent of 5- to 7-year-olds, 59 per cent of 8- to 11-year-olds and 53 per cent of 12 to 14s. Eight million people watched 'Blue Peter', perhaps the most highly educational programme, including 50 per cent of 5 to 7s, 81 per cent of 8 to 11s, and 61 per cent of 12- to 14-year-olds.[13] 'Vision On', a series for deaf children, created a teaching revolution single-handed and enjoyed world success.

Television provided the core curriculum. It taught children to read. Despite the sociolinguistic derision, a very large amount of television used complex syntax, as any brief examination of 'Superman', 'The Avengers', 'Dr Who' or many crime and space serials would show. In schools, if teachers would not sort out their own curriculum radio and television did it for them. The proportion of schools taking music programmes or reading series provided a national core curriculum by default.

Despite this teachers were suspicious of the mass media. Hoggart and others had pointed out that mass media artefacts were potentially valid forms of cultural expression. But one survey showed that though large numbers of teachers thought that the mass media had great influence on pupils' work, not more than one in five was willing to incorporate it in classroom teaching in any positive way. Often, their

expressed aim was to innoculate pupils against the deleterious effects
of imitative violence and pop culture. Urban teachers, who tended to
see their pupils as zombies controlled by the media,[14] sometimes

'For a change, sir, couldn't we do something that hasn't been on Blue Peter?'

pretended enthusiasm for the 'youth culture', but the children were
not easily deceived. Older teachers' habits in life-style, consumerism
and culture made it difficult for them to display any sympathy for
popular culture and the mass media. Some teachers of urban children
made it clear that they were out of touch with their pupils' concerns in
proudly asserting that they would not have television in the house. In
such attitudes not only were the present benefits of the media ignored,
but the opportunities for closing the cultural gap and for using versatile
resources were rejected.

Alongside the introduction of new resources, much valuable curriculum progress and exploration took place. The variety of new ideas
and innovations was bewildering and applied throughout the curriculum. A new syllabus, including communism as well as the world
religions, was advocated as a replacement for the old approach to
religion in schools. Anthropology, though still recognized as a school
or examination subject, was increasingly considered as a part of other
subjects. Interest in astronomy, stimulated by the moon landings and
discoveries of quasars and pulsars, led to school projects; one London

'It all started when we set out to find out how the Egyptians measured.'

comprehensive had its own planetarium. The first centre for educational puppetry was set up following the enormous popularity of television puppets. Photography flourished as a school subject. 'Thinking' was reintroduced into the curriculum after a gap of several hundred years, and was enthusiastically accepted by children and teachers. Children enjoyed being asked to think up a design for a postman's bicycle or a dog-exercising machine. Moral indoctrination on the lines of traditional Christianity having been abandoned, a Donatist revival, led by Peter McPhail and his moral education project, assisted by the humanities curriculum and the exponents of the 'new English' resumed examination of moral issues in the classroom. Individualized games were increasingly offered by PE departments, with competitive team games increasingly less in favour.[15]

Games approaches swept the schools from the infant classroom to the sixth form.[16] Monopoly, chess, dressing up, 'Cowboys and Indians' and the Wendy house were no longer the prerogative of the primary classroom. The older pupils played games all day as well. Elaborate games taught sixth formers the Stock Exchange system, United States geography, the Soviet economy or the provisions of the Industrial Relations Act. Pupils played their roles as Prime Minister, social security officer, King James II, blackleg striker or company chairman.

A more flexible and realistic musical culture in a growing number of

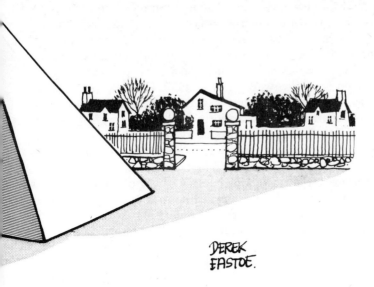

DEREK
EASTOE.

schools reflected the children's own interests. Multiracial steel bands, swing bands and pop groups were introduced; jazz orchestras were formed in many urban schools, and a national youth jazz organization flourished in the main cities. Mathematical activity also became more audacious. Dull civic arithmetic, income tax, hire purchase and gas meters, was replaced by popular maths projects, and sometimes several departments would co-operate in team teaching. Experiments with real relevance for the classroom were undertaken, such as the Nuffield team attempt to identify a hierarchy of concepts in the form of a concept tree which could be adapted by the practical teacher for classroom use. Geographers made journeys of discovery into 'qualitative' subject matter. They found, for instance, that pupils had inside their heads 'mental maps', an idiosyncratic perception of geographical space often shared by adults and of great importance to planners.[17]

There were implications in this curriculum style for school democracy, pupil choice and other aspects of the hidden curriculum. There was an increasing selection of subjects children could study. Choice itself became a school subject; consumer-packs like 'Suzy meets the super-shopper', presented older students with problems like: 'What can a consumer do when her jeans split the first time she wears them?'[18]

In the multi-ethnic school there was encouraging progress. A review of multiracial education in 1973 showed that 60 to 80 per cent of teachers saw the preparation of pupils for a multiracial society as one of their aims.[19] More teachers were dealing with racial prejudice and its associated problems in debating topics for fifth and sixth forms, or including in their syllabuses literature about the countries of origin of immigrant children, and short stories, poetry and novels by African, Caribbean or Asian writers. Humanities teachers, particularly geographers, looked with renewed interest at the Third World. Radical changes occurred in history syllabuses, with world history approaches to the fore. Art departments used art forms and techniques from a wide range of cultures including batik, puppetry, mask making and calligraphy. The home economists in the housecraft flat diversified their menus and there were fewer schools where Hindu girls were producing beef casseroles and Muslim girls bacon and egg pies which would never be eaten by them or their families. But much needed to be done. No amount of curriculum innovation could keep pupils from the trauma of black adolescent unemployment, for instance.

If the immigrant urban child had a new curriculum, so did children at the other end of the spectrum of privilege, the 6 per cent educated in the private sector and in the misleadingly named 'public' schools.[20] The public schools were influentially involved in the Schools Mathematics Project, an innovatory syllabus which proved too sophisticated for teachers in many urban schools.[21] Independent schools experimented early with resource centres, and offered urban children sixth form places or set up urban centres, like the Dartington Hall link with Manchester.[22]

The teachers who emphasized personal writing, children's own experience and investigation, found that the immediate locality had much to offer.[23] A community school curriculum, which asked children only to write about football pools, brass bands, and canals, might be naïve. Many children preferred witches, pirates, chess or ancient Greeks. But the nearby environment became increasingly important to most teachers. Children interviewed their parents about memories of the Blitz and VE day; or their grandparents about life before the first world war or the Depression. The fire engine drove into the playground and was inspected by the juniors.

Nowhere was the local curriculum emphasis more marked than in English and social studies.[24] In its early days social studies emphasized civics, with such titles as 'visual citizenship', or 'our community at work'. Early textbooks looked like schoolbooks, unmistakably educational. But especially after ROSLA the characteristic format of a social studies or English anthology closely resembled the quality Sunday newspaper colour magazine. The brand leader, Penguin Education, in its topic books on drugs, family life, or aggression, used a format involving many photographs, a minimum of words, basic information, and plenty of suggestions for follow-up work. Foundations for this approach were inventively laid in the primary school with the flood of information books for younger children. Project and enquiry work flourished in secondary and primary schools.[25] Published resource packs were now the basic stock-in-trade of all English and social studies teachers, and were more than simply cargo-cult. Regional and local curriculum materials were produced for local studies, sometimes by LEA publishing teams concerned with an urban curriculum for the school leaver age-group, as happened in north-west England. Many organizations such as Shelter, community service volunteers, Help the Aged or the Town and Country Planning Association produced teaching packs on housing, old age and other topics.

'It's the walking wounded from the history project up at the castle.'

If the adult participation in planning recommended by the Skeffington Report of 1969[26] was ever to happen, some insight into environmental decision-making needed to be part of any urban child's normal schooling. Study of the urban environment, scheduled buildings, tower blocks, play provision, graffiti or vandalism – in a way that engaged the imagination and emotions – was extremely rare in the secondary schools of the 1960s. But especially after ROSLA, study of the urban environment was seized upon in a desperate search for 'relevance' in courses for the non-academic majority in their final year.[27] When this was badly managed, it meant introducing teenagers to a local community with which they might already be more familiar than their teachers. But some schools increasingly emphasized not only bringing the community into the school but also taking the school out to the community. School lessons began to focus on planning decisions, and other issues taken up by community action groups and the local press. Following a proliferation of field study centres in the countryside, teachers recognized the need in an overwhelmingly urban society for placing a similar emphasis on urban studies. US students in the 'school without walls', where attendance was not necessarily compulsory, learnt in the outside urban setting; spinning, soldering, music, photography and motor mechanics were all studied with qualified people in their own studios or workshops. This was a pattern not often seen in Britain; but a curriculum interest in the local environment was evident in all major cities in the world where urban educational experiment took place, producing a generation of children whose education has led them to scrutinize the urban environment.

After 1972, following their importation from the US, British town studies and urban nature trails became increasingly popular.[28] Teachers who had always undertaken some local study were now supported by videotape, film, photo slides and work sheets they had prepared on the school offset press, or at the local teachers' centre. By 1976 about two hundred urban and nature trails were available in Britain, produced by colleges of education, museums and teachers centres, and encouraged by many bodies including the Council for Urban Studies Centres.

'Street work' was the most positive feature of the community school curriculum.[29] Children moved round the neighbourhood using Instamatic cameras, recording their experiences on clipboards or tape recorders. They might compile a 'worst buildings guide', make consumer assessments of small cafes or of shop prices, or conduct a campaign for a play-space, returning to the classroom to order findings and complete the work. Such work required a considerable amount of curriculum planning by the teacher, if local people were not to be persistently pestered or public amenities invaded. Nature trails within city parks, which guided or signposted schoolchildren round points of interest gained in popularity. But school parties could not go on endlessly pulling leaves off trees; it became necessary to arrange for the park keeper to provide a sack of fallen leaves or cones rather than let children collect them.

There was phenomenal growth in educational visits and school journeys.[30] Working class parents especially were, if anything, over-generous to their children, saying: 'I want her to do what I never had the chance to do'. Sailing, skiing, sea cruises, Land Rover safaris, and other ambitious school journeys flourished, and there was always a free place for the teacher travelling with ten or so children. Some of the [155] best, and worst, teaching went on in school journeys. Unfortunately, some teachers, already exhausted, took the view that a school journey with demanding urban children was a joy ride and let them run around, without curriculum objectives and with little control. On the contrary, teachers needed to be as meticulously organized on school journeys as in the informal classrooms. They had to cope not only with planning, and with excitable children, but also with the emotional changes that many children showed even on the shortest residential trip. The classroom extrovert might collapse overnight with homesickness, or the withdrawn child would turn out to be the one to discover the dead seagull, or who knew where birds had laid their eggs in the hedges round the youth hostel. Some of the tougher outdoor pursuits offered hazards to the inexperienced teacher; mountain walking, in particular, brought one or two catastrophes. There was no national requirement that any teacher taking a school party should possess even the simplest first aid qualification, and teachers were often ignorant of the terrain and unused to conditions.

There was a wide range of opportunities now open to the urban child. In 1961 834 pupils went on an inaugural school cruise. In the next twenty years hundreds of thousands of children and their escorting teachers visited Europe, the Mediterranean, West Africa and the West Indies.[31] The cruises even began to cater for primary children. Teachers liked the cruises because they offered classroom facilities with adventure as well as practical geography, history and language lessons.

With the increasing popularity of the continental package holiday Butlins, after much internal debate, decided that their seaside towns, standing empty for something like thirty weeks of the year, should be developed for 'adventure in education'.[32] In the first experiment at the Minehead camp children visited farms on Exmoor, combed beaches for fossils, undertook map reading and field studies. Army youth teams worked with the children in the camp on adventure playgrounds, commando courses, trampolining, fencing, archery and other activities. Eventually the holiday camps were integrated with the urban schools system. Many schools and local authorities bought their own residential centres, older country houses purchased cheaply at a time when private owners could no longer afford the heavy costs of maintenance. It seemed a pity that boarding and public schools could not be used for the same purpose – as *colonies de vacance* centres for urban children.

Urban children were also provided with opportunities to visit farms.[33] Farmers, impressed by examination courses, at first gave priority to middle and secondary schools; but gradually they catered more for younger children, giving them a chance to see farm animals and where food came from or what life in the country really meant.

Museums began to change their attitude, making deliberate efforts to attract and interest school parties.[34] Children were allowed to handle exhibits; projects and exhibitions were designed specially for them.[35] Sometimes teachers were attached to museums to undertake educational work, teaching or producing curriculum materials. A new type of museum professional appeared, the 'school organizer'. The busy urban teacher shepherding a lively group, including the inevitable handful of disturbed children, welcomed informed and stimulating assistance from experienced colleagues.

Unfortunately all this imaginative work was not matched by any growth in educational work experience. Professional attitudes over the raising of the school leaving age, trade union obstructionism and Dickensian fantasies of child exploitation among teachers all prevented a positive approach. Not until the Holland Report and the full impact of youth unemployment in 1976 were new schemes mounted in an area with great possibilities.

13 Counter-reformation with Inquisition

Despite promising innovations and lively ideas for change in many individual schools, curriculum thinking both nationally and locally was still drifting and uncertain. But increasingly vociferous public opinion and an emphatic shift of stance among politicians, civil servants and curriculum researchers brought inquisition and counter-reformation by 1975. The most unfortunate victims of the clamour for improved classrooms were the children whose schools were publicly investigated, exposed as shoddy, violent or incompetently staffed. But the first casualty, the Schools Council, attracted little sympathy.[1]

The curriculum theocracy, arcane priesthood and gothic profusion of Schools Council projects flourished for a decade before the whistle was blown. Admittedly the Council was hamstrung by its constitution; but its disastrous policies were largely of its own making. Showering teachers with curriculum edicts from on high did not work. Project teams, as the directors retrospectively reported, had not involved teachers sufficiently, except for rare exceptions like the 'Middle School' or 'Mathematics for the Majority' projects.[2] Relatively few teachers had been involved in writing materials. Dissemination and inservice promotion had been conspicuously lacking.

The Schools Council found that its curriculum proposals disappeared without trace a few years after any given project team had disbanded. Occasional successes, like the 'Breakthrough to Literacy' scheme, were remarkable for their rarity. A researcher tracing the English footprints of the Nuffield science project some years after the project team had dispersed, reported: 'Nuffield Science is alive and flourishing – in Canada!'[3]

Shipman and his colleagues studied the history of a Schools Council integrated studies project.[4] A weighty teachers' guide and five boxes of curriculum material for the first four years of secondary schooling had offered teachers an attractive menu. But, returning to the pilot schools, Shipman found that there could be no guarantee that curriculum innovation had taken hold. Even a head teacher's interest provided no certainty. Original project paricipants had varying motives, and personal conflicts or political intrigue made nothing safely predictable. More curriculum development in integrated studies was occurring not in the pilot schools but in schools where individual teachers from the original project now taught.

The Schools Council now came under savage attack. Critics complained that it had even failed in those areas where easy success might have been expected. Most projects emphasized the 8- to 13-year-olds; yet the Council's impact on the growth of middle schools had been disappointing. But the trouble was that the real power was concentrated in the teachers' unions and the LEAs, who had made it impossible for the teachers' centres to be used as local dissemination points for national curriculum projects. It was they who, perhaps understandably during a staffing crisis, had agreed on the spending of rate support money intended for the inservice training of teachers on other priorities. Together they had made it impossible for the Council to have any real power over the classroom teacher.

The public began to demand scapegoats for the country's poor educational and economic performance. Parents complained that they were not represented. The Council was rebuffed by the DES over its examination proposals for secondary pupils. In 1976, in a pre-emptive strike designed to divert attention from their own dismal record, HM Inspectorate (many of whose members had served on secondment at the Schools Council and helped shape its policies) brought out a *Yellow Paper* which criticized the poor performance and quality of the Council and its projects.[6]

Finally, confessing the disastrous mess into which it had blundered, the Schools Council announced plans for improving curriculum research and dissemination. Teachers would more often be drawn into preparing curriculum. Project compilers were advised for the first time to sell their ideas and materials through policies of positive promotion.[5] Representation on the Council was expanded to weaken teacher control.

The implementation of the progressive curriculum, especially the 'informal' classroom and teaching style, came under criticism. An Australian visitor, for instance, concluded after four months of school

'We want him taken off common core and put on nitty-gritty.'

visiting in six counties in 1974 that the 'informal' approaches recommended by the Plowden Report had not failed: they had never got off
the ground.[7] A research team at Lancaster, led by Neville Bennett,

reported in 1975 that only 17 per cent of teachers ran open classrooms according to the Plowden definition. Most teachers still sat children separately, in pairs or in the same seats for most activities. Most teachers closely supervised physical movement, and more than half admitted to smacking, even if they normally found verbal reproof sufficient. Class teaching was favoured, and a subject-centred curriculum still predominated in junior classrooms.

When Bennett published his full findings in 1976 they provoked public controversy, and received heavy television and press coverage.[8] He and his collaborators, strongly sympathetic to the informal classroom viewpoint, were saying, reasonably, what *Black Paper* advocates had shouted: there was often less progress in basic skills in the informal classroom. Bennett found no evidence even to support the progressive argument that creative writing was always superior in the informal classroom. Only in one of the thirty-seven classrooms closely studied did informally taught pupils show higher attainment than nearly all the other children in the survey; in this class an experienced teacher spent most of her time teaching basic skills by informal methods.

Received ideas about teaching style in the informal classroom were criticized by Bernstein and other sociologists, who suspected an invisible pedagogy. Sharp and Green found that an infant school serving a largely working class housing estate reinforced middle class academic and cultural attitudes through its informal style.[9] Informal teachers did not make explicit their expectations of the children and many working class children were mystified by the teachers. Joan Tough, in a Schools Council project, produced recommendations and materials for a renewed emphasis on structured language experience for all children.[10] Already, as we saw, teachers concerned with the immigrant child had come to the same conclusion. The progressive establishment was on the retreat. Alec Clegg, formerly education officer of the West Riding of Yorkshire, a passionate and veteran advocate of the progressive movement, remained unrepentant.[11] But recantations were made by Bruner and by other curriculum reformers. The Nuffield mathematics specialists began to say: 'We never told you don't teach tables, we just said if you do makr it enjoyable'. Piaget had been venerated, and the obscurity of his theories left unquestioned by English primary teacher educators for over thirty years. Now, for the first time, Piaget's classic experimental conclusions began to be questioned. An experimental psychologist, Peter Bryant, claimed that children could reason abstractedly if they learned items of information properly beforehand.[12] Jerome Kagan asserted for cognitive learning what the child care theorists were saying about emotional response: the effects of early deprivation could be reversed.

Educationists, psychiatrists and child development workers were all reappraising traditional research and analysis based on middle class continental children of the 1920s and 1930s.[13] Indeed, like the social workers, teachers were beginning once more to risk emphasizing the importance of self-discipline and social control. Didactic pedagogy, which would have aroused hoots of derision ten years before, re-emerged. Michael Marland's *The Craft of the Classroom*, marked by its brevity and simple common sense, was an educational bestseller during 1976.[14]

The most emphatic attack on curriculum pluralism came from influential moderates who proposed simply that 'teachers act as teachers'. They demanded support for a common curriculum, in comprehensive or progressive primary schools, and called for the resumption of traditional criteria in choosing such a curriculum. Gabriel Chanan, for example, rejected the community school curriculum where 'in every subject of learning there has to be a demonstrable connection between the pupil's experience and the knowledge being introduced'. For that ignored two fundamental educational objectives: the attainment of a reasonably broad and complex world view, and the appreciation of other people's points of view. To rely simply on the child's sense of relevance was not good enough. Any responsible curriculum must offer the child access to a reality beyond his immediate experience. What was crucial was the relationship between subjects and the priority of material within subjects. Academic knowledge still offered immense resources, though it did not have a monopoly of concentrated thinking, as the work of Labov and others had shown.[15]

If this sounded suspiciously like the re-invention of the grammar schools and the academic curriculum by counter-reformers, doubts were easily quietened.[16] After all, these were prophets of the left calling for radicalism, rather than high priests of the right. It was not what was argued, but who argued it, that seemed to make the difference. The general tide of opinion had turned. John Nisbet's warning of 'innovation fatigue', Bennett and the debunking researchers, Chanan's neo-orthodox curriculum proposals, the noises being made by a few philosophers of education and the educational sociologists all combined in the same refrain of counter-reformation in discipline and curriculum. Educational theories, practice and expenditure were beginning to be called to account.

The public storm and inquest over the urban school was symbolically enacted in a courtroom drama set in London's County Hall. For several months the death of a small junior school in a multi-ethnic neighbourhood was subjected to inquest. Educational disruption had finally reached the point where legal catharsis was as necessary as it had been in the social work tragedies of Tina Wilson, Stephen Meurs and Maria Colwell.

The William Tyndale School in Islington combined most of the explosive ingredients already identified in our housing and classroom analysis. It contained very disturbed inner city children including many of immigrant origin, and manifested an epidemic of classroom maladjustment and poor attainment. It contained politically active teachers and also attracted the attention and involvement of 'committed' gentrifying parents. It aroused a storm of first local, then national controversy over the disadvantages and strengths of the informal classroom, compensatory education and the political ideologies surrounding them. It revealed fundamental faults in the administrative, political and inspectorate workings of the largest urban education authority, which had inevitably arisen from the years of public neglect.

In 1973, the school was thriving, yet by January 1974, two terms after the new head had taken over, it was in turmoil. On the floor below the head teacher of an infant school and her staff were constantly upset by the disorder and misbehaviour of the junior children. Poor teaching, staff quarrels and backbiting alarmed managers, teachers and many parents who had first supported the new head. Collective decision making in the staffroom, introduced by the new headmaster, had broken down, along with school discipline. Many of the staff had strong political leanings, either to the left or to the right.

Realizing that the situation had deteriorated beyond recall, the ILEA appointed an independent lawyer to conduct a tribunal. But although they dodged out of the ring at this point, their strategem was to rebound on those politicians and officers who hoped to avoid censure or responsibility. The tribunal became a sensational running story in the press, lasting several months and finally costing more than £100,000. The final report by Robin Auld, QC was an obituary for the urban classroom, a lucid, judicial summing up of the consequences of two decades of educational stress.[17]

Auld judged that excessive freedom had been given to the children. He noted disagreements among the staff and inadequate curriculum planning, and condemned the irresponsible politicking of individual managers. He criticized most severely the Chairman of the Schools Sub-Committee, who was later to resign, and ruled that the headmaster had been an able teacher but not a successful leader. The District Inspector, other officers of the ILEA and teachers had not provided 'efficient education' or 'education sufficient to the requirement of its pupils'. He also criticized the Inspectorate. Their role was to advise and support teachers, to act as a warning system to the ILEA of any potential trouble or difficulties; yet neither inspectors nor politicians had risen to their responsibilities.

The Auld Report did not identify the historical circumstances of the previous twenty years which had caused such deterioration in urban classrooms. But the same could have happened in other cities and in other schools. Politicians, inspectors and teachers had played according to the rules of the game as they saw it. Urban confusion and difficulties in staffing schools had meant that urban teachers had been left to get on with it.

Auld criticized the senior ILEA politicians and officials for letting the school drift into anarchy. But little disciplinary action was taken against them, and there was only one political resignation; all of the censured officers and inspectorate were left in post. Some years previously a failing London comprehensive school, Rising Hill, had been closed and its head teacher, Michael Duane, appointed a senior lecturer in a college of education of the same authority. Harsher measures were applied in the case of the Tyndale teachers, who were finally sacked, not for incompetence but for striking unofficially.[18] Everyone knew there were many large as well as small schools also heading for disaster. Teachers and government officials looked around them with foreboding, wondering whether deterioration had gone too far. Large comprehensives were especially prone to disaster; like ocean tankers, they needed prolonged notice if they were to alter course to avoid catastrophe.

Discreet DES silence during the Tyndale debacle suggested that individual LEAs would be left to get their own houses in order. But it was equally clear that the climate of opinion had changed. It might be fair after the years of neglect and ridiculously low salaries and status among teachers for LEAs to be given time to tighten up on their schools. Nevertheless, public opinion dictated the policy; there would have to be rapid improvement in urban schools.

The public was aware that the financial condition of the teacher had been transformed, and expected a consequent improvement of schools. An economic recession, a teacher surplus, the sweeping cuts in LEA budgets, and government limits on educational expenditure, had meant a closer look at the classroom.[19] Large sums of public money were involved – and teachers were no longer cheap labour. Tightening up had not been possible during staffing shortages, but teachers were now classroom captives who could not easily move for promotion. With very few newcomers entering teaching from the colleges, except in secondary 'shortage' subjects, improvements in the classroom could be affected only by strengthening inspection or inservice training. As the politicians learned daily from their postbags, the public wanted a stern line to be taken over teacher performance and classroom standards.[20]

During the struggle for economic revival, industrial leaders claimed that teachers were feather-bedding young people and disinclining them to industrial careers.[21] Industrialists and employers were right in complaining that many younger teachers were ideologically antagonistic towards commerce, business or even careers in the police, considering them aspects of corrupt capitalism. Teachers responded that Britain's poor economic performance could be blamed partly at least on the low level of training for employment offered to most school leavers.[22] Attempts to improve transfer from school to work, especially through work experience, were often frustrated by workers themselves through trade unions.

The balance of opinion among the public and employers was critical of the schools, and the standard of education they provided. During a time of high unemployment, especially among immigrant school leavers in the cities, the general public became more aware of the economic and political importance of education. During 1976 and 1977 they saw on their television sets a heavily-publicized attempt to improve adult literacy, particularly among younger adults, which was implicit criticism of schools. The Manpower Services Commission was sternly critical of the literacy and numeracy of school leavers and the use of the last year at school.[23]

The Confederation of British Industry complained that teacher control of examinations had lowered standards. Teachers, in deciding who would pass examinations and devising their own syllabuses, were evading accountability and resisting the needs of employers. The CSE examination, which aimed at giving pupils of middle and less than average ability school leaving qualifications, was especially at fault. CSE could be taken in three forms: Mode 1, an exam set by a board and marked outside the school; Mode 2, an externally marked exam set on a syllabus devised by teachers within their school; Mode 3, in which syllabus, exam and marking were all in the hands of teachers in the individual school. External moderation was in name only, employers complained, being provided by boards of local teachers. Continuous assessment, updated syllabuses and emphasis on oral examination in the CSE might be educationally progressive, but was not reflected in the educational attainment of potential young workers. The employers were joined in their censure of CSE strangely enough by the sociologists of education, who complained that teachers making continuous assessment without real objective standards were showing bias against working class children.

The GCE examination system was also under fire. Alan Willmott, in 1977, showed that poor quality GCE candidates were being given better grades than they would have received in 1968. His work was controversial.[24]

Conventional educators claimed that at least the existing examination system produced better attainment than and avoided the excesses of continual standardized testing, as practised in US school systems. But the vast, unwieldy examinations system certainly gave cause for concern. As the Minister of Education pointed out, there was a widening gap in examination performance between suburban and rural school children, and those living in the conurbations. There was a strong lobby for a common system of examining at 16+ which might replace both GCE O level and CSE. Some wanted to see an innovatory examination, a Certificate of Extended Education, for sixth formers who could not cope with the full GCE A level. The comprehensive schools movement seemed to have abandoned its early opposition to examinations and accepted them as a necessary evil. When the ginger group PRISE* was inaugurated in 1975 it was left to a speaker from the floor to ask, amid minority applause only, whether the comprehensive school movement was not still committed to the total abolition of examinations. The neo-structural moderates of the comprehensive movement were not at all sure that they were.

'I don't like it. You don't like. Nobody likes it. The external examiner likes it. That's *why we make it.*'

What did seem clear was that social mobility was no longer solely achieved through academic success in school. Many pupils turned

*Programme for Reform In Secondary Education

aside from the sixth form towards practical or technological careers which required fewer academic qualifications: their time might be better spent in further education or at the polytechnic than among the university elite. The dual grip of schools and the universities, relying heavily upon inflexible curriculum and examinations, had been broken. Nevertheless, education authorities still used examinations to select or allocate children to comprehensive schools (or, as we saw, to compose mixed ability class groups within them). The unreliability of examiners had been proved by Hartog and Rhodes as far back as 1936, who when analysing marks in traditional written exams over a wide range of subjects had found amazing variations. Forty years later teachers still continued the endless cycle of examinations with their sometimes barbaric rituals. Each year, for instance, hundreds of paintings in oil and water colour, prepared by GCE A level pupils, were burned immediately they had been marked.[25] What more telling illustration could there be of the educational philistinism of the examination system and the teachers who taught to it?

Nevertheless, it was apparent that by a variety of means, including the examination system, the government would shortly launch major strategies for tightening up on the urban teacher and the classroom. As a first step, the stranglehold of the teachers unions over the Schools Council was broken by the Labour Secretary for Education, Mrs Shirley Williams, who instructed a committee to consider how representation could be enlarged to include parents and others. Ignoring HM Inspectorate and the Schools Council, the government through the DES set up the Assessment of Performance and Educational Disadvantage Units. By 1976 the APU was well advanced in preparing national testing and assessment procedures.[26] In reading, language development and mathematics it was claimed, the APU would monitor standards nationally. It would give guidance to the minister, not prescribing the curriculum, but 'testing its impact'. Many asked privately whether, once the political mechanism had been created, there was anything to prevent the government of the day dictating a central curriculum. In 1973 the Bullock Report had recommended that each school should have a reading curriculum written and available for view; this had had considerable impact on schools and LEAs. The straws had been in the wind for several years.

No one was therefore very surprised when in 1977 a Great Education Debate, initiated by the Prime Minister, was held at regional centres up and down the country. A large number of people addressed themselves to the question of how to improve the performance of the schools system.[27]

A Green Paper published later that year bore the heavy influence of a Prime Minister sensitive to the current anxieties of his electorate.[28] It

urged that each LEA should produce a common core curriculum, although individual schools could interpret that curriculum as they wished, and proposed compulsory retirement of selected teachers over the age of 50 'because of redundancy or in the interests of the efficient exercise of their function'. It made it quite clear that idle or negligent teachers and heads must increasingly be removed or given early retirement.

Immediately after the publication of the Green Paper a key House of Commons expenditure subcommittee chairman, Janet Fookes, announced:

> At present there is virtually no way in which a head teacher can be replaced other than on grounds of appalling misconduct. But misconduct is not the problem. We are more concerned with the head teacher who does not measure up to the new responsibilities of a big school, or who starts well but who runs out of steam.

The subcommittee urged fixed-term renewable contracts for heads.[29]

Only teacher shortage and economic crisis had prevented

implementation of the 1972 James Report and a subsequent White Paper. That had called for 35 days release for first year teachers, and would have given experienced teachers inservice release in their employers' time. In the new circumstances of 1977 the Education Minister hinted at a possible revival of that strategy. If the LEAs could not be relied on to spend the £7 million rate support grant annually awarded for inservice education the department might have to intervene. The unions, concerned about teacher unemployment, expressed their support for programmes of inservice release, although they had not apparently considered that this might further the imposition of a standard LEA curriculum.

One conclusion was already incontrovertible. Head teachers were not infallible. They had shown their unreliability in ignominious squabbles over comprehensive intakes, and their short-sightedness in accepting the EPA and compensatory education myths. Yet the Tyndale affair showed that the head teacher was still the key figure in the running of the school, and that it was extremely difficult or embarrassing to arrange his removal. If the schools system was to be tightened up, it would no longer do to horse-trade ineffective teachers and heads between schools, or promote them to become college lecturers or inspectors.[30]

It was not only *Black Paper* advocates, but also moderate critics of the Labour Party establishment who began to argue for more severe limits on the power of head teachers. Both Maurice Kogan, a left-wing professor, and Rhodes Boyson, a right-wing shadow minister of education advised a re-examination of the head teachers contract. A five- or seven-year renewable contract would do no harm to the vast majority of heads, or teachers, and would certainly strengthen educational accountability. Others on the Right argued for payment by results through a voucher system.[31] Parents should be given vouchers for each child, which they would then use to buy places at the school of their choice. According to the individual scheme, the value of the voucher could be fixed or varied. The voucher system had enjoyed varying success in the US, though it had not been proved that it provided increased parental choice. But there was a basic problem of the degree of access enjoyed by parents offered such choice. The relative freedom of owner-occupier parents to improve their choice by moving house was not also enjoyed by the public housing tenant. A system of choice by default already operated in city primary schools where declining school rolls had caused head teachers to compete in offering curriculum or teaching styles which appealed to local parents. It had not improved the less popular schools, and it made favoured schools even more selective. Some American cities, like Philadelphia, had allowed a large sector of the public school system to cater for parental choice,

with different schools offering alternatives of traditional and informal
classrooms, packaged with evocative titles like 'the little red school-
house' or 'the learning odyssey'. Official anxiety to retain middle
income families in the inner city had resulted in them being given their
own schools. The consumer role of parents and pupils was stressed. In
Britain too, middle class parents would have a stronger voice. The
Taylor Committee, on the government and management of schools,
recommended in 1977 that parents should become the most influential
group on school governing bodies, taking a greater interest in the
curriculum.[32] Pupils too would not just be discussing whether vinegar
should be provided with the chips, times of access to the classroom, or
rules about wearing jewellery or homework times. The informal
primary and the comprehensive school consulting with pupils over
their curriculum choices as consumers would have to consult with
parents if they were to be consistent with their educational philosophy.

The Tyndale Report elegantly censured the inspectors of one local
education authority for not doing enough inspecting (as a survey
conducted by ILEA itself revealed, inspectors had been spending only
five per cent of their time inspecting schools because of an excessive
burden of administrative work). The urban LEAs, already concerned
about local elections, became anxious to pre-empt central intervention
by the DES, HM Inspectorate or interference in curriculum by a reformed Schools Council. Events had moved very fast. Inspectors and
head teachers had regained professional control over teachers for the
first time in two decades. The labour market after 1974 had favoured
the employer, with growing competition for nearly any teaching post
advertised. In 1976, 20,000 mostly young teachers were unemployed.[33]
Politicians were talking of compulsory retirement for incompetent
teachers. In the cities, the inspectors had the new task of transferring
teachers or making them redundant because of both education cuts
and declining rolls. Inspection could once again replace 'advice and
support'; and if the government insisted that each LEA have its own
common core curriculum the authority of the inspector or adviser
would be automatically strengthened.[34]

What was the role of HM Inspectorate to be? By 1976 local advisory
teams were 2,000 strong, while the HM Inspectorate numbered only
442 staff. But morale had recovered. Great efforts had been made to
appoint a higher-quality staff. Inspectors had formerly complained
that the curriculum monopoly of the Schools Council and the virtual
abandonment of formal school inspection had denied them any real
role. Now definite moves towards central intervention by HM Inspectorate in curriculum and schools inspection were proposed.[35] A Yellow
Paper prepared by the Inspectorate itself, the government Green

[170] Paper, the Great Debate and a series of newspaper stories leaked from DES sources signalled the watershed. In particular, the Inspectorate planned formal visits to ten per cent of all British schools in what amounted to a reintroduction of the traditional inspection.

Sheila Browne, the new Senior Chief Inspector, was behind the *élan*, drive and rejuvenation of HM Inspectorate.[36] She had no direct experience of ordinary state schools; indeed, like Fred Jarvis, General Secretary of the NUT and chief spokesman for 250,000 teachers, she had never taught in a classroom; it was hard to believe that the teaching

profession could not produce leaders for highest responsibility.
Nevertheless, despite her lack of experience, Sheila Browne proved exceptionally good at her job. As the new Senior Chief Inspector she talked of encouraging inspectors to take a broader interest in social provision such as health, housing and social services in their relationship to the schools. It was an encouraging sign, for HM Inspectorate, in recognizing the benefits of corporate management, was half way to looking at total urban policy. Some doubts remained, however. Any re-investment of power in an Inspectorate which had collected so many second-rate professionals in its ranks over previous decades was bound to cause misgivings.

Meanwhile Maurice Kogan argued that there was an urgent need for the more open government which had been promised in election manifestos. The DES should be made more accountable, its posts opened to public advertisement and its research base improved. John Vaizey, having seen the Department at close quarters, urged its dismemberment and replacement by a small secretariat which would serve the LEAs. All any minister really needed was a small staff of senior officials who could find out what other departments were doing and help the minister read his cabinet papers. The Swedish system, with a highly centralized curriculum and school administration, worked very effectively with such a pattern.

Above all, a more co-ordinated approach was needed within central government, so that national education policy and corporate management strategy within LEAs would fit in with overall urban social policy. A Central Policy Review Staff ('think tank') paper in 1975 recommended 'a joint approach to social policy (JASP),[37] improvement and co-ordination of central policy government across departments such as Education and Science, Health and Social Security, Environment, Employment and the Home Office. Individual departments should adjust their priorities in the light of joint decisions, for there has been too little systematic thinking, inadequate information and few inter-departmental initiatives in most social problems.' The relationship between central and local government was especially unsatisfactory. The need for politicians in Whitehall and elsewhere to think harder about long-term urban strategy was being firmly spelled out.

14 Children's rights and counsellors

A counter-reformation occurred in educational social work as it did in school curriculum. In the early 1970s the expectations of teachers, social workers and parents concerned with the urban child began to alter. Like the move to middle ground in the curriculum debate, the social work counter-reformation had visible impact on life in schools. Teachers and public became alarmed about child-battering, neglect, and teenage suicide arising from unhappiness at school. Several child deaths prompted soul-searching and widely-publicized legal enquiries. The names of three children in particular, Stephen Meurs, Maria Colwell and Tina Wilson, were to become engraved on the public conscience. These children were the tip of the iceberg of endemic maladjustment and unhappiness in the urban setting; they were the victims of human fallibility and failure of the professional system. Local government reorganization, new social work training following the Seebohm Report,[1] changing children's legislation and pastoral care systems in school had all proved remarkably ineffective in providing help where it was needed.

The urban child was becoming increasingly deprived, victimized, indisciplined and disturbed. Younger children featured as prominently in the statistics as older children. When the records of 1,000 young offenders who came into the hands of the police in three London boroughs between 1972 and 1975 were analyzed a steady rise in the number of 10-year-olds committing crime was observed.[2] The most common offences were shoplifting and smashing or setting fire to

things. They also frequently stole from vehicles and attempted to drive
them away. In damaging property, younger children could often be
more destructive and ingenious than their older brothers and sisters.
Police reported that most of the trouble happened after school but
before mothers got home from work; the offenders were the familiar
'latch key' children. But even then, when most children were in their
homes by 6 p.m., there was always a minority whose parents let them
play late in the evening, or even at night, when darkness acted as a
cover for their misdeeds. Housing estates, as we have seen, were
particularly prone to this sort of misbehaviour. The Metropolitan
Police reported that 80 per cent of infant offences were committed in
the company of older brothers and sisters who were usually about 10
years old. Black children and the immigrant community, police
reported, did not produce a disproportionate number of infant and
juvenile offenders. Nor was criminal misbehaviour by children occurring on the horrifying scale or with the appalling stereotypes observed
in Ulster. There, as Morris Fraser showed, children were often fighting
their parent's war, experiencing psychiatric breakdown from anxiety
or fear of urban violence.[3] Urban 8-year-olds in Ulster were being
taught to count three before they threw their lighted petrol bombs so
that the victim had no chance of escape.

During most of the 1960s little was done about the increasing child
neglect and lack of parental control. In Britain, the child under ten
years could not be prosecuted, and was usually taken to a police station
and given a lecture while his parents were called. For 70 per cent of
offenders that was the end of the matter, but the remaining 30 per cent
continued to get into trouble; the social services department was then
contacted. The theory was that the social worker would see all the
adults involved with the child – parents, educational welfare officer
and schools, offering practical help like encouraging the family to
obtain benefits to allow mother to give up her job, arranging a child-
minder or assigning a male social worker where the father was missing. But the system did not work; and dissatisfaction with the social
worker's role and the legal supervision of young children began to
grow. The voice of the teacher in the urban classroom was often
loudest, next to that of the parent, in complaining.

Following the reorganization of local government and social work
training between 1964 and 1974 social workers who had formerly
specialized in a particular branch of their profession became 'generic'
social workers.[4] The case-load of those who had worked only with the
elderly would now include the disabled, the truant, the juvenile delinquent, the unsupported mother and the child below school age
(although they did not usually take over educational social work).
Simultaneous reorganization of social work and local government

[174] were extremely unsettling. The social workers emerging from the new broader training recommended by the Seebohm Report were mostly young and new to the job. There was high staff turnover; a youthful, expanding social work profession was subject to the same personal and housing stresses, generation gap and presence of political dissidents as the ranks of the teachers. Social workers, who were not educational welfare officers, found professional difficulty in carrying heavy case loads of varying problems. Often there was a conflict of loyalties: they were committed to family support rather than making sure children attended schools. They often condoned truancy because of their loyalty to the larger family unit; as when, for instance, older girls stayed away to help mother with the younger children. Newly qualified social workers still wearing their polytechnic scarves found it difficult to be authoritative with urban children and their families, partly because they had been trained to emphasize permissive, or non-directive social work techniques. The Seebohm orthodoxy argued for a minimum of moralizing by social workers in a society whose values were pluralistic and where it was difficult to arrive at agreement about moral behaviour. Had social work training attempted to pursue a strong line, it would anyway have been frustrated by the legislative blandness of the Children and Young Persons Act of 1969.

Many children suffered from the currently approved doctrines of relaxed social control in the home and in the classroom. Too often freedom became lack of direction or neglect. Academics and researchers influencing social workers and teachers were not helpful. Dr Spock and his British counterparts, widely read by parents, inadvertently encouraged the abdication of parental control during a period when it was badly needed.[5] Child psychologists and psychiatrists, together with educational experts, enjoyed a field day. The influence of Klein, Freud, Winnicott and Bowlby was paramount. Teacher training mystiques arising from the work of Froebel and Piaget discouraged young teachers from attempting firm social control or formal classroom activity; during urban crisis these ideas destructured classroom life in a damaging way.

John Bowlby, a British psychiatrist whose views became international folklore, was perhaps responsible for much of the muddled thinking. In his book on *Child Care and the Growth of Love*, which after 1952 brought him an international reputation, Bowlby examined the effects of war separation which had split up families and orphaned or despatched thousands of children to hostels or the countryside.[6] His concluding hypothesis had been that up to the age of three the mental health of young children noticeably deteriorated if they were deprived of a 'continuous, secure and warm relationship with their mothers'. Psychologists, case workers and teachers accepted Bowlby's ideas as

sacrosanct over twenty years. Any mother, the theory ran, was better
than no mother. It was not until the 1970s that orthodox researchers (as
opposed to the reactionary right) began to question this view of 'maternal deprivation' which held that early experience inevitably exer-
cized a persisting influence over later development. Studies by Rutter,
the Clarkes and others, as we have seen, began to suggest instead that
children who experienced early adversity did not suffer the permanent
damage that had been suspected.[7] Reviewing the literature in *Early
Experience: Myth and Evidence*, the Clarkes concluded that the unfortunate effects of early deprivation could be successfully reversed by a
good home and schooling. The urban school catering for the child with
deprived or damaged personality could be influential in helping that
child to grow back into a balanced adult.[8] There was now, too, professional support for more positive intervention in families where children were being rejected, especially by their mothers, to counteract the
idea which had somehow arisen that any home was better than residential care in an institution.[9] Bowlby now modified his position.
Nevertheless, the high-quality fostering, residential care or support
that was needed to back up such intervention was still a long way from
being provided.

Several nationally publicized cases of the death, battering, or severe
neglect of young children also led people to question the accepted
ideas of when social workers, especially when asked by the school,
should intervene. Stephen Meurs, a neglected 3-year-old in Norwich,
died in 1973 from starvation and pneumonia, even though the family
was known by a variety of agencies to be failing the child.[10] Social
workers had not co-ordinated their efforts or even managed between
them to make one effective visit to see the child. Even more significant
for teachers was the tragedy of Maria Colwell, a 7-year-old living in a
housing estate in Brighton, who in 1973 was battered to death by her
stepfather.[11] She was officially under the supervision of a local authority social worker; her teacher had repeatedly expressed concern, as had
neighbours and others who knew the family. The report of the ensuing
legal committee of inquiry dwelt on the questions of parents' and
teachers' rights and responsibilities. Were parents to regard their children up to the age of sixteen as chattels, their natural and legal property? The enquiry report expressed a fear that the social workers,
talking the language of their clients, had accepted their cultural values,
thereby alienating the other professionals such as teachers, doctors,
education welfare officers, health visitors and the police, all of whom at
one time or another were involved in the Maria Colwell case.

What was the role of her teacher?[12] Maria Colwell's teacher expressed her anxieties to the educational hierarchy but she never met
the educational welfare officer who had consistently tried to visit

Maria, nor did she meet the social worker. Indeed, the educational welfare officer did not know that the social services department was involved. Trust and communication in the deeper sense between teachers, educational social workers and social workers did not seem to exist. The committee of enquiry reported that the weaknesses of the new social work service set up following the Seebohm Report and subsequent local government reorganization had nowhere been more glaringly demonstrated. In the mid-1960s professional social workers had begun to guarantee, taking salaries for the purpose, that children would not be cruelly neglected. And yet they were.

Press coverage of the Colwell case, the legal report and public wringing of hands by the local authority administrators prompted action by central government ministers and civil servants. Within days of the publication of the Maria Colwell report both the DES and the DHSS issued circulars urging their respective services to work together in this sensitive field.

Doctors, influenced by evidence from the USA, had identified an increasing problem of urban child-battering from 1961 onwards.[13] By 1976 British doctors estimated that 4,400 children were being treated annually in hospital casualty departments for what was neutrally called 'non-accidental injuries'. Although the average age of the battered child was 18 months, young children of school age were frequent victims, and the long-term emotional damage was often evident in the urban primary classroom. Most mothers of battered children were of sub-normal intelligence or emotionally immature and dependent, while over a third of the fathers displayed gross personality defect and often had a criminal record. Unlikely explanations were typically given by parents for their children's injuries: 'he walked backwards into a door handle' or 'an electric fire'. Too often no action had been taken, however, because of lack of evidence.

The NSPCC constantly criticized local authorities for failing in their statutory role of protecting the child in their reluctance to institute care proceedings or court action. But in 1976, there was a move forward. A 'red alert' system was introduced by the new large hospital districts to ensure action on any suspected battered child observed in school on the same day. The assaulted child could be examined, photographed and legal or residential placement be immediately provided. This kind of incisive intervention was new, and teachers had an important role to play in such an 'early warning' system of vigilance.

Evidence now began to stress the importance of the parental attitude to social control. The work of Bernstein in sociolinguistics or the Newsons working in Nottingham over two decades, showed that the way in which parents controlled or talked to their children was extremely important for general discipline.[14] The Child Poverty Action

Group, in a three year study of high risk families living in public housing in a Midlands town, found that children supervised strictly by their
parents even in a poor neighbourhood were much less likely to become
juvenile delinquents. Such research coming from a radical organization changed the professional climate in attacking the idea of maternal
deprivation, arguing, as it were, 'bring back dad', for the revival of
discipline.[15] The danger was, of course, that the evidence would be
used for a full-scale resurgence of authoritarian discipline in schools.

Urban children particularly at risk were also identified by the Finer
Report (1971), which made teachers and educationists much more
aware of the problems of one parent families.[16] The report found that
five-sixths of single parents were mothers, and that paternal deprivation, whether caused by death, divorce or separation, clearly had bad
effects. Teachers were also familiar with the problem of 'ghost fathers',
men whom their wives and children saw little of and who contributed
only a pay packet, having emotionally deserted the family. This con-
cealed or spiritual desertion was reported as frequently in middle class
as in working families.

From all sides came demands for more firmness and intervention in
child care, which had a ripple effect on the urban classroom. The Court
Report (1976)[17] asked for better urban hospital and health facilities for
children. The vast child-minding problem, amounting to a massive
evasion of the law concerning day-care of young children of working
mothers by unregistered minders was at last tackled.[18] Child-battering
cases were urged into court by the NSPCC and social workers in the
interests of relieving parental anxiety if not of protecting the child.
There was an exciting range of experiments from the toy library to the
multi-purpose pre-school centre. The nursery classroom curriculum
and social management of the younger children in the classroom
became more structured. Teachers began to talk and read about discipline in the classroom, as they had never done in the years of non-
directive emphasis. Sonia Jackson, Mia Kellmer Pringle and others
began to demand a ministry for children.[19] A children's crusade had
arisen. The debate had moved onto the middle ground so far as
younger children were concerned. Would the same thing happen with
children in the secondary school?

The management of 'out of control' secondary pupils gave increasing difficulty. The juvenile courts were especially criticized after the
Children and Young Persons Act of 1969, the last major piece of
legislation affecting young offenders. That Act aimed at dealing with
children in trouble outside the court and in the community rather than
using institutions. The responsibilities of social workers were
expanded and the powers of juvenile court magistrates correspond-
ingly restricted. But the timing of local government reorganization and

the immense and growing scale of the task made it difficult, if not impossible, for social workers to respond to the job they had been given. No child under the age of 10 could now be found guilty of a criminal offence, and it was extremely rare for the police, unless nudged by the Home Office, to prosecute children under 12, the age of criminal responsibility (the case of the child murderess Mary Bell was one rare exception).[20]

The 1969 Act looked at child care and delinquency from an altered viewpoint. It blurred the distinction between children in need of care and those in need of control and punishment, leading to confusion, not least in the minds of children themselves. The child victim of a drunken father, or girl living in a house of prostitution, came under the same accusatorial gaze as a hardened young criminal. The Act also reduced the power of the courts. It denied them the power to impose sanctions on young people for non-payment of fines or compensation orders, leading to repeated complaints that the law had been flouted and the authority of courts undermined. Violent juveniles on remand who could not be sent home, but for whom a local authority residential place was not available, frequently had to be returned to the court as 'unruly' before being despatched to a remand centre or prison. The supervision orders which replaced probation were most unsatisfactory, and there was an enormous increase in custody orders, which was just what the legislators had been trying to avoid. A large number of young people were placed in custody who would have been on probation and at liberty a few years previously.

Two contrasting solutions were proposed. Magistrates, police, probation and social workers who accepted the thinking behind the Act, demanded more community homes for juveniles, and more power for the courts, especially extra powers over persistent offenders. Other, more radical reformers said that punishment should not be mixed with welfare. They wanted to get rid of the informal atmosphere of a 'care court' and to provide for offenders the full rigours of the law, raising the age of criminal responsibility to twelve and providing secure units for children under fourteen years who were a public menace.[21] Others suggested reviving probation, with officers integrating their work with moves towards school counselling.

Child psychiatry, the psychologist and the child guidance clinic fell into particular discredit at this time in the minds of urban school teachers.[22] These experts were sought in desperation in the final resort, but had little to offer. The medical bias and time-consuming treatment of individual children meant that child guidance as an advisory service to teachers was almost entirely ineffective. Bernstein and others also argued that it was only the articulate middle class child and concerned parent who could benefit.

Psychologists nevertheless began to urge that the medical concept of the psychiatrically 'ill' child who went to the clinic as a 'patient' requiring 'treatment' should be replaced by an emphasis on the schools psychological service, seeing the child as a 'client' in relation to school and home. They argued that the psychologist, working with the social workers, parents and teachers had a key role to play. Nonetheless, educational psychologists were still regarded with suspicion. They were recruited from among teachers, but were better-paid, surrounded with medical mystique, and identified themselves with doctors rather than with teachers. During the flourishing years of the tripartite schools system, psychologists had been the educational witch doctors who mixed up the spells of the 11+ test, enjoying enormous power over children, teachers and parents. Having lost their power base in the control of 11+ procedures, they had begun to climb on the bandwagons of school counselling, autism, dyslexia, or the teaching of reading. They even offered themselves as psychiatric confidants to teachers under stress, moving into such controversial techniques as encounter and group therapy.

'If you're a boy, get your hair cut. If you're a girl, trousers aren't allowed.'

Teachers claimed that the 1969 Act weakened the authority of the school as well as that of the police and magistracy. A teachers' union in 1972 collected 52 case histories which suggested that head teachers and local authorities were not giving support to teachers who were handling difficult children.[23] There was a rising tide of school violence, including more cases of assault by girls. Experts explained the increase in violence among secondary school girls by pointing to the changing attitudes towards women and the more independent, less specifically 'feminine' lifestyle which girls were adopting. Trevor Gibbons, Professor of Forensic Psychiatry at the Maudsley Hospital in London, observed that girls were not being protected by their parents as they had once been.[24] They went around with boys at a much earlier age, often in gangs. West Indian girls, bigger and better developed at an earlier age, were reported as 'accepting beatings at home as a form of discipline', and when fighting did not pull hair or punch but used broken bottles or knives. Headmistresses reported more playground fights between girls in general. Even so the figures for violence of girls of school age was only one-tenth that of boys.

The apparent increase in violence in the urban secondary school classroom and playground was supported by the self-reported assessments of adolescent London boys aged between 12 and 17 years.[25] In interviews with Belson in 1973 they reported violent acts covering a range of behaviour. Those who saw themselves as a 'bit violent' had hit a boy with bare fists in a fight, deliberately smashed a window, shouted at some meths drinkers or told their teacher to 'get stuffed'. 'Extremely violent' boys had deliberately hit a boy on the face with a broken bottle, forced a girl to have sexual intercourse, fired an airgun at a boy passing in the street outside, loosened the screws on the handlebars of bicycles, taken a hammer to a car or broken into a house and smashed the interior. Half the violent boys went uncaught. Those most prone to serious violence had less-skilled parents, came from large households, didn't enjoy school and played truant. Coloured boys were not represented among those who had committed a great deal of violence. One of the best predictors of violent behaviour was the number of violent boys living in the neighbourhood.[26]

But perhaps the most serious weakness of the Children and Young Persons Act (1969) was in its treatment of truancy. Such was the view of the House of Commons expenditure committee which reviewed the working Act in 1976. Between 70 and 80 per cent of all children who came into conflict with the law began by absenting themselves from school, observed the committee members. Yet the 1969 Act not only made it necessary for education authorities to prove that truancy had taken place, but they also had to persuade social workers that the child was in need of care. Teachers complained that their efforts were being frustrated by legislation, by the raising of the age of criminal responsibility and by too much reliance on social workers who were more concerned with the whole family than with the individual child who might be truanting.

Compulsory attendance at the urban school had just over a century of tradition (see Table). Professional manoeuvring over the 1972 rais-

1870* Attendance 5 to 13 (local option)
1876* School attendance committees set up
1880* Compulsory attendance 5 to 10; employers of under 13s without local education certificate penalised
1893* Minimum leaving age raised to 11
1899* Minimum leaving age raised to 12
1900* No employment under 14 without certificate
1918* Compulsory full-time from 5 to 14
1926 Hadow report recommends raising age to 15
1929 Legislation for raising to 15 defeated
1936* Age to be raised to 15 in 1939 (war postpones)
1938 Spens report says raising to 16 "inevitable"
1944* Age raised to 15 (delayed by war). Provision for raising to 16 "as soon as practicable"
1947* School leaving age raised to 15
1959 Crowther report recommends raising to 16
1963 Newson report recommends raising to 16
1964 Decision taken to raise age to 16 in 1971–72
1968 Rise postponed a year in economising package
1971 Decision that rise should take place from Sept 1972
1972 February: Order in Council to raise age from Sept 1972

---

* Act of parliament   (*New Society*, 17 May 1973)

ing of the school leaving age was not an admirable story.[27] The lobbying by teachers determined to see the school leaving age raised was followed almost immediately by their confession that it had been a terrible mistake. Professional vested interest (salaries were linked with the size of schools) encouraged secondary heads controlling the professional associations to press for the raising of the school leaving age. In addition many teachers saw the outside world of employment as soul-destroying and exploitative; adolescents should therefore be protected from it for as long as possible. Yet at the time of the Russell Report, which argued for adult and community education throughout life, many asked whether it would not have been better to have let those children leave who wanted to at 15 and offer them further free education later on.

Large numbers of dissatisfied sixth formers who had had enough of school work and school ritual escaped into further education colleges, where at least they had a personal timetable, and could dress, smoke, eat as they wished and chat in an informal cafeteria; and they could belong to a Students' Union. They might even be taught more effectively because of the better staff–student ratio. Those who remained in the schools often had a poorer deal. ROSLA was unfortunately introduced during a desperate teacher shortage when, in London, for instance, many children were on part-time schooling in secondary schools. Not surprisingly, many older pupils truanted. Those who

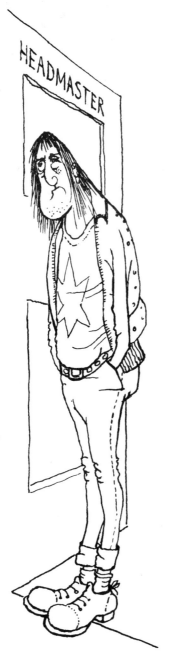

'Can I go to play now, Sir?'

remained, often disturbed, unruly, or just bored and unco-operative,
added to the teachers' difficulties.

Scotland Yard reported in 1974 that truants continued to push up London's crime rate.[28] Between 1969 and 1973 metropolitan juvenile crime arrests rose by 40 per cent. Juveniles were now responsible for more than half the recorded number of cases of burglary in the capital, two-fifths of the robberies and motor vehicle crimes and more than a third of all shoplifting and personal theft. In Lambeth, a neighbourhood heavily populated by West Indian immigrants, the juvenile crime rate rose in 1973–4 by some 65 per cent. Police estimated that one-third of all secondary children in that locality played truant; in twelve days in one truancy sweep by the police 734 children, most of them between 13 and 14 years of age, were returned to thirty schools. During this period the underground stations in south London were the scenes of frequent mugging incidents by West Indian youths, which seemed to occur coincidentally between one and two in the afternoon, the time of the dinner hour for schools.

But why could schools not just impose severe discipline on difficult pupils? A survey carried out in 1972 by *The Times Educational Supplement* showed that out of 127 responding LEAs only a small number had banned corporal punishment, and then only for certain categories of children – usually physically and mentally handicapped children in special schools, primary and infant children.[29] Education officers stressed that corporal punishment was undoubtedly declining, and two large urban authorities, Inner London and Edinburgh, had recently banned physical punishment from their primary schools. Problems of definition arose: what was the situation, for instance, of the London teacher of infants who occasionally slapped the leg of a very naughty child? Was that corporal punishment?

Most local authorities issued regulations to teachers, in addition to the DES requirement that every school must keep a punishment book in which all instances of corporal punishment were recorded. In most schools a special point was made forbidding punishment on the head or boxing the ears, and it was emphasized that instruments of punishment should never be in the hands of a teacher engaged in teaching. Nevertheless, there were many contradictory practices. Norwich stipulated that corporal punishment should never be inflicted immediately, while Cheshire advised teachers that punishment should be instant and quickly forgotten. Not surprisingly, the educational lobby for the abolition of physical punishment (STOPP) was extremely active and achieved sporadic bursts of press and public interest. In 1977, for instance, lobbyists attacked the GLC for obtaining their canes from a sex-shop proprietor.[30]

Some of the most disturbed children did eventually go off to board-

[184]

'You play empathy with me and I'll play empathy with you!'

ing schools or special schools. For, despite criticisms, much successful work was done with children sent to ESN schools.[31] But most of those who gave trouble had to be coped with in the large, complex secondary school. Such schools therefore often had a hostile, edgy and tense atmosphere – or at best were genially chaotic. In many schools the approach to what had been traditionally called the 'sin bin', often now labelled 'the sanctuary', was the most telling indicator of disciplinary style.[32] The progressive secondary school, democratic and non-directive in teaching and curriculum, might set up a sanctuary where a popular member of staff or even a parent was stationed.[33] Pupils were encouraged to take themselves there if they felt likely to misbehave or dodge lessons. It was a preventive sanctuary. Many teachers favoured the sanctuary unit, since it avoided the trauma of split loyalties, thus making it easier to persuade the boy or girl back into the classroom. In the more authoritarian school a punitive line was taken. Pupils would be sent to a special room only after misbehaviour, and then made to work hard under strict supervision.

A common sanction against the violent, disruptive or maladjusted pupil was suspension. Despite increasing public and parental disquiet over suspension procedures, following the Children's Act (1969), which made it much harder to get a child into court or residential care,

excluding a child from school became virtually the only method of
self-protection for teachers. In 1967 166 London children were suspended from school; by 1972 the number had doubled; a similar pattern was reported in other British cities. The National Association of
Governors and Managers and the National Council for Civil Liberties
expressed alarm that children were being suspended for long periods
without school governors and parents being properly consulted.
Heads reported that most of the children suspended were 'violently
disruptive pupils' who after two weeks' or less suspension were
allowed to return to school: unfortunately, in half the cases there was
no reported improvement in behaviour. It was clear that truanting or
suspended pupils tended to become even more anti-social in their
activities outside school, and a variety of alternative, free school and
special units began to be provided by both LEAs and voluntary bodies.

Demands for firmer authority and more effective counselling support for secondary school children gathered strength after the suicide
of Tina Wilson, a 15-year-old Southampton schoolgirl, in 1973. Tina
took an overdose of aspirin, having written a suicide note which
blamed incessant school bullying for her death. A legal enquiry conducted at the request of the Southampton Education Committee found
that she had truanted 64 times that year. The enquiry criticized the
school for not notifying the parents, for not investigating her truancy,
and for insufficient co-operation with the educational welfare service.
Neal Rutter, QC concluded by recommending that a full-time school
counsellor should be appointed to the Redbridge Secondary School
where the tragedy occurred.

Within secondary schools, in addition to the provision of sanctuary
units, specialists were appointed to undertake social work or counselling. Any teacher could be paid a special responsibility allowance, and
during the 1960s and 1970s it was increasingly a source of resentment
among subject teachers that these allowances were being awarded for
pastoral work to tutors, year mistresses, house masters or home-
liaison officers.[34] A school-based social worker was sometimes
appointed, to work with children up to the age of 13 years and their
parents.[35] A growing number of school counsellors, their training
influenced by American practice, worked with older pupils in the
secondary school, the emphasis being on the relationship with the
individual pupil rather than the parents or adolescent group.[36] Often
the counsellor, trained to take a 'non-directive' stance, resisted taking
on a teaching timetable in case the authoritative style of the teacher
interfered with the counselling task. This often marred the relationship
of counsellors with their colleagues; bad feeling also arose from the
refusal of some counsellors to break confidentiality by telling colleagues or even the head teacher what they had learned about the

criminal, sexual or disturbed emotional life of individual pupils. Should not the counsellor report that she had learnt from a pupil that a serious crime was about to be committed; or that a drug network was flourishing in the school? Some teachers felt aggrievedly that they were being gossiped about by counsellor and interviewees in the small room down the corridor. Nevertheless counselling grew in importance and influence. Some colleges of education began to offer a joint course in teaching and social work, and by 1972 there were 4,000 trained counsellors working in schools, most of whom were not counselling full-time but had taken up senior posts involving other duties.

Comprehensive counselling services also grew up outside schools, since social work help was sometimes only accepted by adolescents when unconnected with the school. Doctors, the local authority social workers, youth club workers and independent clinics all offered counselling.

The role of the educational welfare officer in the urban school was reshaped. Following the Seebohm Report and local government reorganization, the ex-servicemen and policemen who knocked at the doors of truants had begun to work with the new young social workers. Tensions arose when official policy was more sympathetic towards contemporary social work theory than the authoritarian tradition of the 'school board man'. In London the educational welfare service was unique in remaining unsatisfactorily a service in its own right. Elsewhere educational social work was often integrated into the new local authority structure, but officers did work in an educational setting, and could assert the rights of the individual school child rather than being simply concerned to hold families together.

Social workers employed as community workers and teachers employed as community education workers combined on joint projects. Hybrid teaching appointments became increasingly common, especially in the campus community schools. Teachers were appointed with both a social work, counselling or youth club role and a part-time teaching timetable. In many secondary schools, teachers were paid to operate a 'third-session' day, often a sports club or homework session. They were the equivalent for older boys and girls of the after-school play centre for younger 'latch key' children.

It was not only the education service which expanded its range of provision for difficult secondary school pupils. The new social services departments with responsibility for community social work contributed original approaches. Young professional social workers undertook community work, ran adventure playgrounds, youth clubs and play schemes. Many ventures were also sponsored by voluntary organizations. Helped by urban aid, charitable money, and social services grants, adventure playgrounds, an idea imported from Scan-

dinavia, appeared on many run-down sites in the major cities in the
1960s.[37] Built with the intelligent use of spare materials, they attempted to channel children's vigorous play and destructive impulses; rope
swings, wooden frameworks, earthwork mounds, a shed where
equipment could be stored or wet day activities carried on and, in
charge of it all, talented leaders sometimes professionally trained for
the purpose, attracted children to the playgrounds. Successful adventure playgrounds were soon running all the year round, attracting
large numbers of children who in term and holiday times would
otherwise have become delinquent. The adventure playground team,
sometimes as many as five or six people, nevertheless had an isolated
job and were under pressure. There were the dangers of getting into
conflict with the employer, whether it was the social services or the
education department, or antagonizing local colleagues such as police,
headmasters or teachers. It was tempting for the inexperienced adventure playground leader to help the truant escape through the back
fence as the educational welfare officer entered the main gate. There
was always a risk that informal leadership would turn into demagogy,
nihilism or complicity with the adolescent underworld. That risk was
especially great when success was based on emotional rapport with the
problem teenager.

Holiday play schemes, another innovation, sprang up increasingly
in the deprived inner cities, particularly on housing estates.[38] They
catered for children of all ages, providing coach trips, street theatre,
sports activities, discos and camping. Sometimes play schemes linked
with play centres, school premises open during the holidays with
professional staff. Occasionally, special reading projects were built
into play schemes or play centre provision so that children could work
during the holiday to improve their attainment. A completely new
idea, the 'urban farm', in dockland or a run-down neighbourhood, or
on vacant acres of railway property, provided a gentler environment
for other city children.

The urban state 'free school' also had its part to play. Until the 1960s
the free school movement had mainly flourished in country residential
schools largely catering for the working class, maladjusted child or the
children of the affluent middle class. Homer Lane's Little Commonwealth, an approved school run as a therapeutic community during
the first world war, had initiated the tradition which A. S. Neill
popularized.[39] Lane had come to England in 1912 after successfully
running a 'junior republic' in the US for difficult boys. He himself had
been much influenced by the work of Makarenko with unsettled adolescents in the USSR just after the Revolution.[40] The inhabitants of
Lane's school had been over school-leaving age: but his co-
educational, self-governing and informal educational approach had

been extemely successful with them. Unfortunately, his belief in the value of love as a therapeutic influence was injudiciously applied to the young girls in his care. This resulted in unpleasant court proceedings, his exile and early death. But a large literature of subsequent experiments testified to his influence.[41] Over the next fifty years similar ideas were supported by local education authorities buying places for maladjusted children in the numerous country residential schools which were set up. Although the theoretical approaches of Montessori, Froebel, Winnicott, Bruner and many other progressives had supported the logic of a free school with informal classrooms in the city, no really successful experiment had ever got off the ground. Now in desperation, and stimulated by the urban free school evangelists, local education authorities had started to experiment in that direction. The new Jerusalem was to be built in the city; a note of welcome realism.

Nevertheless, such schools could not provide a final answer. It was still the ordinary secondary school which had to cope with the bulk of the problems of truancy, delinquency, and the mildly maladjusted child.

15 Social mix for urban classrooms

In Great Britain, the US, Australia and New Zealand urban schools policy was by 1977 on the edge of momentous reappraisal.

It was clear that the increased social and educational justice sought through education had not arrived.[1] Left-wing educationists no longer argued that equality through the schools or income could only be financed out of economic growth or surplus. Egalitarians had traditionally argued that while the poor could be given the benefits of economic growth and expansion, income redistribution which took from the better-off would never be accepted. Yet the experience of the US, with its wealthy economy, had shown that despite affluence and an economic boom, surplus resources were more likely to be diverted to foreign policy than to the inner city school. Influential voices were therefore raised to demand the solution which had been clear all along. Planners, lawyers and housing experts began to reappraise the situation. Decisions were made in Britain, and the understanding grew in the US and Australia, that policies for a socially and economically varied community were the educational solution.

In the US the pursuit of desegregation in schools led educational thinkers into scrutiny of housing and planning. In Britain, practical trends and legislation in the spheres of public housing and city planning carried implications for socially mixed schools. In Australia, problems of multi-ethnic education and housing led Wendy Sarkissian and others towards the question of social mix. Positive planning began to replace old-fashioned urban sociology, with its transitional zones and assumptions about the inevitable deterioration of cities.[2]

The picture changed most rapidly in Britain where a 34 per cent public housing sector allowed considerable legislative control over the future of cities. In the US there was only a 4 per cent public housing stock, but there was growing understanding of the impact of ethnic, housing and social class patterns on schools. The unsatisfactory attempts at school desegregation led US educationists to pinpoint the relationship between housing patterns, parental choice and big city schools. Independently of the British experience, US investigators concluded that social mix policy was the only answer to the phenomenon of white flight or the exodus of black middle income families from large cities, which often accompanied the desegregation of schools. Having identified as a culprit the massive social class drift from their cities, experts began to assert the need for rebuilding urban social class structure rather than relying on compensatory education or networks of alternative schools.

The relationship between school desegregation and white flight in the US had at first seemed easy to explain. Differences between white enrolment in city schools before and after desegregation were attributed, quite simply, to the resistance of white parents. But there was more to it than that.

During three post-war decades, the inner core of most US cities had acquired low socio-economic status. Remaining black or white middle class families worried increasingly over where to educate their children; and school systems which were increasingly segregated, socio-economically and racially, had emerged. By the early 1970s it was apparent that school desegregation all too often succeeded only in weakening the commitment of middle class families to the central city.

The appalling problems of the US cities during the late 1960s and early 1970s, for instance the bankruptcy of New York, were well-known. But what was perhaps less well understood was that the growth of the 'ghetto' areas was actually encouraged by federal housing legislation, which in the 1960s openly favoured segregated suburban developments in granting mortgage and insurance for new housing and its purchase. Families were also helped at the other end of the transaction when they bought their house in the suburbs.[3] Housing subsidies increased opportunities for lower income whites, and young families in particular, to move out. Record levels of housing construction were concentrated in the suburbs. Thousands of housing units were eliminated from central city housing stock in the process of urban renewal. City families now experienced high income tax, the highest homicide and violent crime rates, cutbacks in their police force, the massive abandonment of housing in the city, and the loss of more than a fifth of the city's job and revenue base. Only in the mid-1970s did

housing administrators begin to support the purchase of suburban
housing for blacks. Even then, housing policy was a sustained incitement to urban exodus, constantly destroying the chances of successful
school desegregation. Now 'minority' communities began to flee from
the central cities whenever they were able to buy suburban housing. 54
per cent of black residents of Chicago in one survey indicated a strong
wish to escape from the central city. Many cities witnessed 'black
flight' as well as white, and in all cases it was higher income families
who moved first. The concern of the blacks was not that the public
schools had become black institutions, but that they were becoming
low status institutions. Black middle income parents who continued to
live in central city areas increasingly bought private education for their
children.

US researchers vigorously disputed the issues of 'white flight' and
'tipping': whether and how desegregation of schools accelerated the
decline of white enrolment in central districts.[4] Research in Florida and
elsewhere showed that white withdrawal to private schools reached a
maximum point when the proportion of black students went beyond
30 per cent. Cities which began with large minority populations before
school desegregation suffered especially from white withdrawal. An
analysis of white flight by J. S. Coleman and his colleagues led them to
observe: 'The effect of desegregation on white loss is dramatically
different for a city that has largely black schools and largely white
suburbs, and for a city that has a small proportion of blacks and no
sharp racial differences between city and suburbs'.[5] Accelerated white
flight was more likely in the former. The conflict over bussing in Boston
reached the international press; in Memphis white enrolment in the
public schools fell by 20,000 after a bussing order, and the number of
children in private schools rose by 14,000. The New York Times reported
that Memphis lost 46 per cent of its white public school students
between 1970 and 1973, while it ranked second among the major cities
of the nation in poverty.[6] Attempts to introduce bussing were generally unpopular. International experience suggested that even parents
who were sympathetic to school integration did not accept bussing.
They complained of children exhausted or occasionally lost in the
endless bus rides which persisted year after year. Unless the integrated
school had markedly better classrooms, teachers and discipline together with less racial hostility the parents would still buy out.

But the picture was even more complex. The 'tipping' of US schools
resulted in resegregation in transitional neighbourhoods which might
be in the inner city or the suburbs, but towards which a growing black
population had been steered through the housing market. These
'transitional' neighbourhoods were especially avoided by white
buyers, and a vicious circle was thus completed.

However, it became apparent that issues of race and class in the US, as in Britain, had been confounded. The ethnic enclave could break up and yet the schools could grow worse as a deprived lower class community, possibly ethnically mixed, assembled itself. Schools where the poor and disadvantaged congregated were no more attractive to 'minority' middle income Greeks, West Indians or Hispanics than they were to 'respectable' white parents. US schools desegregation was often characterized not so much by an influx of black children into a white children's environment as by an influx of lower class black children into a middle class environment which might be black- or white-dominated.

The biggest obstacle to developing desegregated schools in multi-ethnic urban neighbourhoods in the US, however, was the extraordinary strength of the historical tradition of housing segregation in cities. The few stable inter-racial or even socially mixed neighbourhoods in cities had arisen in peculiar circumstances. There was little chance for municipal intervention, with only 4 per cent of the housing stock belonging to the public sector.[7] Many companies gave housing loans, as in Britain, but using a 'red-lining' policy by which they refused to lend on properties in inner city districts. Black estate brokers in a Detroit school desegregation case spoke of rebuff, subterfuge and humiliation endured when they attempted to obtain property in white districts.[8] When Washington DC desegregated its schools, real estate brokers were constantly telephoning the school board to find out which schools would serve given neighbourhoods.

A complex picture could be built up. In Philadelphia, a large proportion of white families in racially mixed areas were Catholics. There were numerous parochial schools in the area and few blacks were Catholic. It was safe to choose a parochial school. In Chicago the middle class black parent avidly sought places in the Catholic high schools for their children. It was the same elsewhere. In Australia, following a change of immigration policy in the mid-1960s, a wave of 'new Australians', Mediterranean Catholics, arrived to swell attendances at schools formerly monopolized by Catholic families of Irish origin. US appeal judges concerned with desegregation in a city like Detroit or St Louis, where only 30 per cent of whites remained, gradually began to realize that their verdicts could be counter-productive. All too often court orders could cause the withdrawal of white students from schools which until then had been well balanced racially. The 'judicial numbers game' simply did not work. How could you desegregate schools in Kansas City where two-thirds of the school pupils were 'minority' students and 80 to 90 per cent of them were already attending inner city schools? Such circumstances made it impossible to achieve anything but a simple-minded legal definition of desegrega-

tion. Yet the court orders demanded by activists continued in a steady
stream.

In Philadelphia, Cincinnati and many other cities, just as in middle class Melbourne or Sydney, a different response was to offer parents a network of 'alternative' schools to which the board either gave grudging support or 'bootleg' supplies, or turned a blind eye. Philadelphia had a 'school without walls'; Cincinnati offered a variety of alternative options ranging from work on inland waterways to working alongside a member of the city council.[9] Some cities, like Cincinnati, also provided schools for the performing and creative arts or, as in Australia, schools offered bilingual programmes. 'Alternative' elementary schools catered for progressive parents wanting a Montessori approach as well as the black parent wanting a traditional classroom with a special emphasis on reading. In many cities, empty classrooms were used to provide free schools for drop-outs, and store front schools or street academies were also encouraged.

Magnet schools, offering a special emphasis on some aspect of curriculum, flourished in many big cities. The magnet school programme in Houston, for instance, began following the failure of a 1970 court order mandating major action to promote integration. Eleven pairs of schools had been desegregated, but the level of integration within them deteriorated between 1970 and 1974. A magnet scheme was therefore inaugurated in 1975. Students worked in a 'cluster' programme in particular schools, joining others from a different background for one week or less at a time. This plan, copied in other cities, was not aimed at complete racial integration but at moving towards it.

Magnet schools offered an alternative to parents wishing to send their children to desegregated schools. Experiments such as that on New York's Upper West Side, where in 1977 elementary schools were joined together in a 'mini magnet' system designed to encourage middle income parents to remain in the neighbourhood, had a positive social purpose. Magnet schools could certainly play a part in creating or retaining socially mixed classrooms. But, as some critics warned, as long as little systematic information was gathered about the socio-economic composition of the enrolment of magnet schools, there could be hazards. The dangers of creaming off or elitism needed careful monitoring. Only the severity of the US educational crisis could justify what seemed to be a selective trend. For surely what the Americans were reinventing, unless social and housing class factors were sensitively considered, was the grammar or selectively technical school which the British had been so busy abolishing.

The US picture was not entirely depressing. Where school systems started off with the right balance, school desegregation had been successful. Charlotte, in North Carolina, promoted a widely admired 'integrated' schools' system. Parents could not easily work in Charlotte and live outside the school district because the desegregation plan involved the entire county. Obviously, where white flight was difficult, there were inbuilt safeguards against residential instability. In St Louis, the city administrators who had insisted a hundred years earlier on shedding their hinterland attempted to reclaim it so as to have a large enough school district to prevent white flight. In Kansas City urban lawyers successfully attacked in the courts the mortgage companies and banks who made it difficult for blacks to buy into the suburbs.

Havighurst and others came to the conclusion that socio-economic balance might be more important than the mere desegregation of the schools, but the US courts had seldom been willing to consider this in drawing up plans for desegregation: 'The courts have not considered socio-economic factors because the constitution does not address itself directly to prohibiting discrimination on the grounds of social class. The constitution has been satisfied by a legalistic effort to reassign and transport pupils with a small and frequently temporary reduction in the proportion of minority students'.[10] It was the same story again as in Britain, where failure to talk in terms of social or housing class had damaged the comprehensives and the urban informal school movement.

In the US Havighurst argued the need for 'a change in the legal theories used to decide major school desegregation cases'. He concluded that: 'Bold efforts are needed to achieve the kind of desegregation policies outlined, but the success of these efforts could make possible the survival of big cities and improve the quality of life.' Emphasis would need to be laid on the establishment of middle income housing in inner cities. Many families were willing to live in neighbourhoods that were integrated socio-economically and racially and to send their children to schools in those neighbourhoods if they had the confidence that a good balance could be maintained in open institutions. Socio-economic balance would be a prerequisite for the revival of that confidence and of the public schools.

An articulate minority had long advocated social mix in town planning, both in the US and in Britain.[11] Many arguments were advanced. Socially mixed neighbourhoods promoted intellectual and cultural cross-fertilization, in ideas, food habits or fashion. Socially mixed communities increased equality of opportunity, making people freer to move up occupational or social ladders or participate in economic or political life. When people lived together, the rich might see the problems of poverty more clearly. Neighbourliness with a sense of community might be regained. Mixed communities were more likely to throw up effective leaders. A high degree of residential and educational social mobility which encouraged people to leave the district threatened kinship, neighbourhood, family and community networks and loyalties, while a range of housing types and tenures in one area would allow upwardly mobile residents to stay. Any residential area of the city should reflect the diversity of the urban world and those who lived in suburbs or slums therefore experienced a loss of quality of life. The cities depended on a range of people to run services, and for this socially mixed community was essential. Social mix in housing was needed so that workers could afford to live in the cities, otherwise railways, hospitals and schools would be short of staff.[12]

Ideas of social mix in the ideal community had sprung up in various forms in Britain from the nineteenth century.[13] The most influential, prolific writer on social mix among contemporary urban planners was Lewis Mumford, whose early work, a blueprint for British town planners, urged that town planning provided a physical basis for better community life.[14] Arguing strongly against segregation of any sort, Mumford wrote on the benefits of residential mix in Sunnyside Gardens, New York, where over eleven years he recorded the neighbourhood success in *Making the Institution of Democracy Work*. He effectively popularized the neighbourhood concept in the inter-war years and urged British planners on after the second world war.

International interest in social mix revived after the second world war in the debate about a new society. The experience of the electorate in the armed services had led to an approval for social mix. The socially balanced neighbourhood was an honoured place in planning texts: although neither the degree of mix nor the means of achieving it were ever spelled out clearly. In the 1960s the myth of suburbia was rigorously attacked in the US, where a new interest in down-town neighbourhoods like Greenwich Village, containing vibrant diversity which the suburbs lacked, was stimulated. Jane Jacobs, in *The Death and Life of Great American Cities*, celebrated the inner urban neighbourhood with its special chemistry of people and architecture.[15] In Britain the architect and local government politician Nicholas Taylor argued with others for a revival of the urban village, a return to small-scale community planning and the abandonment of tower blocks schemes.[16]

The occasional British planning expert asserted that the battle for comprehensive schools in Britain had been anticipated in the battles over desegregation across the Atlantic. For *en route* to the supreme court ruling in 1954 that segregation was unconstitutional, US civil libertarians championed social mix as promoting equality of opportunity, though sadly, as we saw, their efforts were ineffectual. The concept of social mix had its opponents – in both Britain and the US black militants argued against integration in housing or schools because it threatened the solidarity of the black community.[17] British Marxists like Brian Simon or the sentimental anthropologists of the Bethnal Green school seemed to believe that social mix weakened working class community.

In England there was little drive from the academics like David Donnison and his colleagues, who confessed themselves quite unable to decide upon the pros and cons of social mix. Community experts like Peter Willmott commendably revived the social mix debate in specialist seminars or journals.[18] But, perhaps quite rightly, the academics only ended up asking for more research to disprove or prove the case. Did living next to people actually lead to greater tolerance of social difference? Did middle class leadership in socially mixed areas produce positive benefits for residents? Did people in mixed neighbourhoods engage more often in common social or political pursuits? Were the underprivileged helped – were services more efficient, less costly and more accessible to them? And there were the educational questions. What was the impact of gentrification on schools? To what extent could

'. . . and furthermore, headmaster, I don't like the imposition by your staff of middle-class values on my children.'

a racially mixed school be truly integrated? Anyone who had spent much time in the ethnically mixed school had observed that black children could sit in one part of the cafeteria, while whites or Cypriots sat in another; the same was true of classrooms, assemblies and athletic events. More research was needed to examine the links between inter-racial friendship, socially mixed classrooms and self esteem, academic organization or even curriculum choice. Nevertheless, if its advocates were right, social mix might be a key to the survival of public commitment to the urban classrooms.

The debunking by Jack Barnes of the EPA strategy had its effect in Britain.[19] From 1974 government spokesmen began to announce that geographical priority areas rather than educational priority schools were needed to combat deprivation. 'We need to designate areas to which all the social services give priority', declared Roy Hattersley, a Labour minister. 'Today we have a whole range of unco-ordinated policies. There is a great deal of wasteful duplication and a notable absence of concentrated effort.'[20] The upper hierarchy of government finally began to reappraise the strategy for inner cities and the conurbations. While teachers and educationists remained oblivious to the new trends and did little to promote social mix, many others acted. The British public housing sector was not as heavily loaded as its American counterpart with problem families, despite the general decline in standards. Neighbourhood stabilization policies could be attempted quickly and effectively through the legislative controls available in town planning and public housing. Such initiatives became excitingly frequent after 1970.[21] Positive moves towards economic revival in cities and the diversification of housing tenure were most encouraging. A 1973 GLC document on planning strategy reflected a growing international mood: it declared that 'if it is thought desirable that the present exodus of firms and people must be stopped, the only way to bring that about is to ensure that housing, employment, travel, environmental and manufacturing conditions taken together are no less attractive in London than elsewhere. Ideally, people should live near or have access to their place of work and feel themselves to be an integral part of the socially and economically balanced community.'[22] London planning experts and local people themselves began to argue for a socially mixed community in the rebuilding of dockland for 150,000 people, the greatest town planning project since the Great Fire of London. The dockland plans contained the most advanced formulation for social mix yet seen in Britain, the US or Australia.[23]

Other factors helped considerably. The Department of the Environment gave more help to local authorities concerned to restore employment or socially varied community life in the cities. Early in the 1970s the British property market collapsed suddenly after some years of boom. Private speculators suddenly ceased to compete with the public housing officials in buying urban land or houses, and the arena was left free for the housing experts and planners. Furthermore, between 1974 and 1978 the economic recession redistributed income involuntarily in British society. The difference between the standard of living of the worker and that of the middle class professional narrowed. Even the post-Houghton prosperity of the British teacher did not raise his standard of living substantially above the skilled working class, although it did remove him from nearness to the poorer families. The erosion of income differentials made possible, even encouraged, the co-existence of different urban lifestyles in the same neighbourhood.

The specific strategies adopted by the national housing and planning strategists passed unnoticed by professional educationists, but had great importance for the urban classroom. It would be essential for any teacher or parent seeking understanding of the urban school to understand the technical housing mechanisms which had begun to operate. No single device could guarantee the revival of urban life and classrooms, but taken as a whole the housing strategies were powerful and sophisticated.[24]

The international pattern of gentrifrication by middle income parents offered another potentially hopeful prospect.[25] As we have seen, middle class parents who had moved back to the inner city could become vigorous, if troublesome, activists on behalf of public education. However, the invasion of largely working class districts by highly organized middle class parents able to manipulate the housing market and the local authority grants system had diverted help intended for the younger, poorer families and ousted poorer residents. To meet this problem a category of 'priority neighbourhood' for housing rehabilitation was introduced under the Housing Act of 1974. Where local authorities, often working with housing associations, wanted to create housing confidence or slow down the decline in rented property they could do so. In designated Housing Action Areas (HAAs) the housing department had special powers. Anyone selling a house which contained tenanted accommodation had to notify the local authority who had the first right to purchase. Housing departments now had a mechanism for controlling the social composition of a neighbourhood or even a street. Through a five year plan of municipal purchase, rehabilitation and re-letting of individual houses, each local authority could disperse concentration of problem families and generate social mix. However, massive infusions of government money available from 1972 for the 'municipalization' of housing stock in British cities were controversial in their impact. Local authority housing departments bought private housing as it came onto the market, not just in housing action areas, but in neighbourhoods which formerly had no public housing at all. The London Borough of Camden municipalized housing in Barnet, the most middle class of the outer London boroughs. Middle income residents in a commuter village forty miles from London battled with the GLC who had acquired newly completed houses for their waiting list. They complained: 'It is not that we do not want council tenants as neighbours, it is that our prospective buyers do not want them'.[26] Clearly the introduction of social mix had to be sensitively undertaken, whether in middle class districts or slum neighbourhoods.

The Housing Corporation, an independently working body set up in 1971, but aided by the government to the tune of several hundred million pounds each year, began to act as a think tank and financial sponsor for housing experiment. The Corporation lent money to the housing associations to buy and convert older housing, in an effort to encourage their further expansion. It also set up a Housing Co-operative body which after 1975 encouraged co-ownership schemes and housing co-operatives involving tenants' self-management.[27]

After a decade of largely successful development the housing associations were changing their own policies, and by implication their attitude to social mix.[28] Early in the 1960s they had concentrated on the homeless problem family, buying dwellings which they could purchase and convert cheaply. By the 1970s they virtually owned whole streets in difficult neighbourhoods, like North Kensington in London. They discovered that they themselves were causing serious social dislocation. The lack of neighbourhood balance in a community dominated by problem families put explosive pressure on teachers, social workers and medical services. The increasing shortage of bus drivers and hospital ancillaries put the associations under pressure to give a quota to such workers, and they began to do so. In the public sector local authorities, also aware that essential services were undermanned, did the same. The housing waiting-list rules, which demanded that candidates had lived in the locality for years or had been born locally, were waived. In London housing was provided for teachers from 1969 onwards. Introduced during the worst period of staffing shortage, the quota soon ran at 315 dwellings a year.

Management policy in public housing slowly began to change.[29] Existing residents in public housing were more often given the opportunity of taking new or rehabilitated dwellings near their old address. Married children could live nearer to parents. The rehabilitation of old houses was emphasized, tower blocks were no longer built and there was a new emphasis on low-rise, high-density houses with gardens. Public housing managers introduced more schemes for local tenants' participation. If only because of the inflation of management costs it was felt that the tenants would have to be more involved in self-management and participation. It was actually cheaper not to treat the public housing tenant like a serf or second-rate citizen. Tenants should have a major say in estate design, management, caretaking, tenancy rules and the adjudication of disputes.

Housing managers had become more sensitive to the criticism that problem minorities were being concentrated on certain municipal housing estates or blocks.[30] The policy of putting large numbers of unsupported mothers or West Indian families together was questioned. By 1976 the changing of opinion led to suggestions that the records of ethnic origins of public housing tenants and occupants could be kept, in order to ensure that minorities were not unfairly relegated to poor quality accommodation. Large cities like Birmingham, or boroughs like Camden, started recording ethnic origin and telling tenants why.

But this did not tackle the central barrier dividing British people in their housing. The invisible Cutteslowe Wall still dominated and separated public housing tenants and owner occupiers. The amount of subsidy given to the public housing tenant had in no way made public housing more popular. By 1976 only 45 per cent of housing costs in the public sector were covered by rents, compared with 73 per cent in 1965. Public housing was anyway getting too costly, quite apart from the unperceived burden on social services and schools which arose from concentrating disturbed children and their families on urban housing estates. Local authorities all over Britain were concerned about the high level of rent arrears and vandalism on show-piece housing estates, such as Thamesmead in London, which had been envisaged as an ideal environment which would attract a socially varied tenantry. A new idea, the sale of council houses to long-term tenants, was supported by moderates of the Left as well as housing policy experts of the Right, although many right-wing Labour politicians went on arguing against it.[31] Council house ownership during a period of house price inflation could benefit the poor family more than any other kind of help. Individual freedom from petty rules and restrictions formerly imposed by the housing bureaucracy would also be a great achievement. The cycle of poverty and low self esteem could be interrupted for the first time in the lives of many families, and the distinction between house ownership and public housing could be eroded before it caused permanent damage to the structure of the cities.

Progressive public housing authorities therefore introduced schemes of rent mortgage, community leasehold or equity sharing on an experimental basis. The GLC and Birmingham, together with others encouraged by the Housing Corporation, allowed tenants to use any of these schemes of paying a mixture of rent and mortgage. After a period of time accumulated rent could be regarded as the mortgage downpayment, and the tenant thus became a potential owner-occupier. The great advantage of such schemes was that they encouraged the more ambitious, socially active tenant to remain in public housing estates, and thus maintained a more lively, varied community. Tenants became house owners without changing their address. That was a tremendous step forward. For nothing had been more threatening to social mix than that social mobility which took tenants out of urban schools and inner city public housing.[32]

All these new housing schemes had long-term effects which had clear consequences for the schools, and not least for community education. Finally, in 1977, the government announced a major policy shift towards a total strategy for the inner city.[33] Now it was up to educationists, especially teachers, to enlarge their vision and actively campaign for the urban strategy which was proposed. In particular, they would have to consider the role of the school and the teacher in such a society, and be prepared for radically new approaches.

16 Community schools and teachers

A community, consumer voice in the use and management of schools was increasingly demanded from the late 1960s,[1] and educational pressure groups had an important role to play in achieving it.

But pressure groups, whether for broad comprehensive reform or minority provision, were highly vulnerable to the blandishments of fashion and special pleading – middle class parents, for instance, were often found demanding special treatment for their dyslexic, autistic, or talented child, with Labour politicians, head teachers of state schools or university lecturers of left-wing persuasion among the most unabashed lobbyists. Pressure groups also tended to quarrel amongst themselves.[2] Regular palace revolutions occurred at the fountainheads of middle class educational consumerism. The Advisory Centre for Education (ACE) based at Cambridge, for instance, attempted to influence the state school system and promote educational reform.[3] But it never really recovered from fundamental errors which accompanied its origins. It had no membership organization. More of its time was spent answering queries about private schools rather than state classrooms; and despite attempts to reach a working class public through education shops in large department stores or at Butlin's holiday camps it never achieved major influence.[4] The Confederation for the Advancement of State Education (CASE) fared slightly better. Recognizing that giving 'best buys' and acting as a middle class consumer service as ACE had done was not the best way of helping the community in general, CASE emphasized practical action. It conducted surveys of holiday play facilities, provision for handicapped children, how to be a school [203] manager, obtain a maintenance allowance or help in a literacy scheme or lobby for comprehensive school reorganization. But there was embittered debate in CASE over the question of private stance and public commitment. Should officials persist in buying private education for their children while working for CASE, the membership asked itself?[5]

Pressure groups of both the Left and Right began to show increasing interest in accountability through school management and to argue that renewable contracts would improve school leadership. Head teachers should have to justify their decisions at governors' meetings, in order to encourage a general sense of involvement and responsibility. In the period which preceded the Taylor Report of 1977 with its wide ranging recommendations for change, few were satisfied with the government and management of schools. Baron and Howell in a substantial review in 1972, for instance, found that large authorities frequently grouped schools together under a single governing body: but this was very unsatisfactory from the point of view of the individual school.[6] The relationship between governors and the chief education officer was crucial: 'without doubt the authorities in which the governors are most likely to play an active part are those in which the CEO favours their doing so', observed Baron and Howell, echoing Caroline Benn. But their study showed that in most authorities, governors did not dream of taking a close interest in curriculum matters, despite their official responsibility for 'oversight of the school and its curriculum'.

Until the reforms proposed by the Taylor Committee were implemented the role of the school manager or governor was stereotyped in the public imagination. They were local worthies, members of the Rotary Club, whose main concern was a prominent place on the platform on speech day rather than any commitment to education; or perhaps hard-nosed politicians, who owed loyalty to the party more than to the school. How far could governors, and parents, now be partners rather than rivals to the teachers in the urban school? A Schools Council report asserted in 1976 that: 'the majority of parents have little desire to interfere with the way schools are at present organized and controlled, but on the other hand there is firm evidence that many parents would welcome greater information, consultation and involvement in their children's education than is available to them at the moment.'[7] The average preoccupied, busy parent perhaps did not want power. But half those interviewed thought their contact with teachers was insufficient, whereas the teachers by contrast 'tended to be satisfied with the present level of contact between home and school, and more specifically with the opportunities given to the parents to be involved with the life of the school'. In 1973 the National Association for Governors and Managers recorded that at least thirty-two local education authorities had appointed teachers or parents to the managing or governing bodies of schools, elected by other parents or sometimes by parent-teacher associations.[8] A radical move in some authorities (among them Derby, Ealing, Rochdale and Nottingham) had been to include pupils on governing bodies, although legally no one under 18 could be a governor. That problem could be surmounted. The election could be opened to all pupils between 16 and 18: or the elected pupil was officially known as an 'observer'.

There were three possible roles for school government. Governors could be abolished, so that the LEA's schools committee acted as the governing body for all schools. Governors could be directly elected by the parents or local community, running the risk, as in countries like New Zealand, that there would be a small poll and that elected governors might clash with elected education committee members. Or managing bodies could be similar to the Community Health Councils, with a predominance of parents but including professional representation. The Taylor Report recommended new governing bodies: a quadrilateral partnership, composed in equal numbers of representatives of four groups – the LEA, school staff, parents (and possibly pupils), and the local community.

The Taylor Committee found that there was a clear need for the inservice education of governors and managers. But it did not consider the far more important idea of a support service which could respond to what governors saw as their needs. Professional educationists were slow to take up such an idea, but as the Australians had shown, the teachers' or education centre could be important here. Teachers' centres should expand their role to become education shops, media resource agencies, exhibition places and community education forums for managers, parents, governors, teachers and social workers, in fact anyone with an interest in education. The aim was not to interfere with the school as an individual community, but to provide a centre for communication and information. Uninformed controversy, as the Tyndale case had shown, was destructive of public trust. In any case, at a time of public concern and economic stringency in state education, the expertise and resources of the teachers' centre were a community resource which needed to become more widely accessible.

Another move was made in 1971 which would promote the role of the parent: a radical plan for neighbourhood councils was proposed; these would be secular versions of the parish council of the traditional English village which had always worked so successfully. The Skeffington Report had urged greater participation to keep higher authorities informed of public opinion. Neighbourhood councils, it was suggested, should have power to precept from the rates to make local improvements and provide amenities such as nursery schools and playgroups, playing fields and swimming pools, youth clubs, home help services or small yards with car repairing equipment or other services. Local surveys had found that 70 per cent of people were in favour of neighbourhood councils. But except in a few cities where community politics were fashionable, neighbourhood councils did not at first make rapid headway, although they clearly had much to offer.[9]

As we earlier concluded, increased social mix, with public participation in local, environmental and educational management would be tremendously helped by the community school and community education policies. From the 1960s community schools had flourished in the conurbations.[10] During a period of generous educational spending many new schools undertook community provision – the large campus comprehensives as well as the small community primary schools. The Cumberland community school built around a public footpath symbolized the vision of planners and teachers. In London, on the Isle of Dogs, the £2m community campus and school opened in 1976, incorporating an Adult Education Institute, a Youth Centre, a sports and leisure centre, a day centre for the elderly and a day nursery.[11] A community school at Sutton-in-Ashfield, a declining mining town which was given extra economic support as part of government policy for 'grey areas', opened in 1974, sharing the building with an ice-rink, bowls centre, restaurant, theatre and sports hall where mum could drop in from shopping just up the road to join the children. At the new town of Milton Keynes a campus of three schools, with community education facilities, restaurant and bar, swimming pool and media resource centre served several thousand children and the townspeople.

Interest in community schools in industrial neighbourhoods originated with Robert Owen who at New Lanark set up the equivalent of a mid-twentieth-century housing co-operative and community school, using the corporate paternalism found in the twentieth century in Fiat of Milan or Broken Hill, the mining capital of Australia. But for most of its history the movement had a rural emphasis. In the 1930s the aesthete Henry Morris, an officer in the Cambridgeshire education authority, had set up many village colleges. Morris saw the village college as a rural centre containing a secondary school: not as a social centre which used the school after four o'clock.[12] In the 1970s the EPA enthusiasts revived the community school in the urban setting. Halsey, Midwinter and their colleagues were criticized by some for suggesting 'that the community school seeks to obliterate the boundary between school and the community, to turn the community into a school, and the school into a community'.[13] With Illich they saw the

'Please Sir, my dad wants to know if I can stay in school at weekends.'

community school concept as a sweeping, heretical claim for the school as the new saviour of society.[14]

Most people agreed, however, despite the problems of what to charge the public or of caretaking eighteen hours a day, that it was essential during a period of tight public expenditure to make multiple use of school amenities. It was quite wrong that swimming pools and games fields should be closed down during holidays, evenings and weekends in the cities when children had need of them.

There was keen debate over community school size. Should they be hypermarkets of corporate life?[15] Was the giant community school just a part of the fashionable trend towards centralization, like the hyper-market or modern sports complex? A small tenants' hall nearby might be better than an ambitious suite miles away. Did old age pensioners find a shorter journey to their local primary school made up for having to use furniture or lavatories designed for 5-year-olds? Might not an adult interested in improving his French prefer to travel a few miles a week to use a language laboratory? Sportsmen certainly preferred modern facilities to the small ill-equipped church hall, or dimly-lit huts on inadequate ground facilities.

'Run – it's the community service kids – they're worse than the police.'

Some argued against the small community school, stressing the danger that creating such a school in a 'ghetto' neighbourhood would narrow urban life-styles and discourage social mix.[16] Others argued that there was little value in a community campus in an urban setting as a centre of corporate life if it flourished at the expense of the pub, street corner, launderette or even living room. On the other hand the large secondary comprehensive campus, taking up to four or five thousand children and serving as many as eight hundred thousand adults, posed its own problems. Rural secondary schools had already found that a dispersed population did not stay on for after-school activities or attend for community education if they were dependent on rural bus services: the same applied to city dwellers who had to make their way through traffic jams or bad neighbourhoods.

Community education had entered a volatile, creative and informal phase. New expertise increasingly enlivened urban life. Cheap video equipment recorded public opinion, and was replayed in launderettes; community education and theatre teams highlighted local planning issues in pubs, schools and tenants' halls. Bookshops and coffee-bars selling paperbacks of working-class biography written by local people sprang up.[17] The community education teacher travelled out of the classroom, perhaps to help seven or eight Asian women with English lessons in the home of one of them. The diversity of community education initiatives made this one of the most exciting spheres in which to work.

The relatively neglected Russell Report on Adult Education (1973),[18] in the first official review on the subject for fifty years, highlighted some of the current trends. The Committee argued for *éducation permanente*, the concept of continuing life-long education from the cradle to the grave. But its recommendations for second chance educational opportunities were acted upon only in the form of a national literacy campaign.

But what were the teacher's attitudes in the midst of all this change? During this period, as we have seen, teacher morale and salaries improved considerably (though the British teacher was still well behind the average European teacher in both pay and conditions[19]). By

'I feel so good riding this now I can afford not to.'

1977 there was a danger that a retreat into defensiveness over accountability, and the privileged life-style conferred by a major comparative improvement in pay, would distract teachers from urban sympathies. One survey found that 64 per cent of teachers did not see themselves as public servants,[20] although public service was an integral part of any sociological definition of teaching.

The conservatism of the teaching profession should not be underestimated. The declared voting intentions of British teachers in 1974 and again in 1977 showed most intending to vote Conservative.[21] 72 per cent of teachers in 1977 also favoured the retention of grammar schools, which Labour were committed to phasing out. Curiously, teachers with more professional qualifications and enjoying better pay and easier working conditions voted Labour. Some 50 per cent of all teachers, mostly women primary teachers whose pay was low, qualifications minimal and whose hours and conditions were often the toughest, voted Conservative in 1974. Most intending teachers also voted against the then Labour government. But this was perhaps not so surprising. A national survey of probationer teachers in 1972 looked at their social origins.[22] It found that most women teachers (and a majority of teachers were women) came from a middle class background, while most men teachers had working class origins. The vociferous leftish political urban teacher or college student was untypical.

Teachers were also the most conservative occupational group in their housing choices. A 1974 survey of family expenditure reported that teachers were the largest occupational group of owner-occupiers, 80 per cent of teachers being heads of households in houses or flats which they were buying.[23] Teachers spent little on drink or tobacco and below the national average on clothing, footwear and food. They spent above average only on transport, services and housing. The teacher was prepared to spend money to live in and travel from the suburbs. The family expenditure survey noted 'the solid middle class image of teachers which emerges when their spending decisions are examined.'[24]

A picture was thus built up of a largely female teaching profession, politically and economically conservative, committed to social mobility through owner-occupation and educational selection. No wonder the EPA head teachers had placed last and thirteenth in their priorities 'changing the social composition of school intakes'. As the largest professional group working in the cities, teachers had had a better opportunity than any to witness the collapse of urban life, yet they still pursued a personal life-style of suburban owner-occupation and professional paternalism. Few city teachers, unlike their rural colleagues, lived near their pupils; the press and mass media had repeatedly pointed out the paradox of prominent educationists, cabinet ministers, inspectors, politicians and teachers sending their children to selective, fee paying or public schools. Many teachers shared the views expressed by the headmaster of one of the most difficult secondary schools at Kirkby, near Liverpool. While president of the Headmasters' Association in 1974 he said: 'I remain committed to the comprehensive idea but I am not prepared to sacrifice my own son while he and I are living in a society in which the purchase of an educational advantage is possible'.[25] Unhappily, however, too many urban primary and comprehensive schools had deteriorated beyond the point where it was fair to condemn teachers or parents reluctant to enrol children in them.

The teacher as an isolated professional, consumer and commuter, and the administrator needed to come into contact with the social realities outside the school gate. If some multiple attack on problems of housing, education and employment could now break the cycle of deprivation and inner city decline, the teachers could make a special contribution. They were literate and articulate, in daily contact with large numbers of parents and the children who were future parents and workers in the cities. Teachers exemplified more than any other occupational group the social and housing class drift which had opened up a great chasm in the urban community. They had a greater obligation than most to change their ways. But the cherished convictions of the commuting teacher, based on a mixture of genuine middle class values, housing anxiety and a comforting belief in compensatory education had a long history and could be hard to dispel.

Teachers had had a hard time – indeed, the strenuous conditions of their work had often blinded them to wider issues. Many teachers who had subscribed to the EPA myth, believing that massive extra educational resources would put things right, had worked themselves into illness or early retirement. Each day they put themselves at risk, climbing into the EPA boxing ring and propping up the victims. If they had failed to criticize the social policies which made their professional lives more difficult perhaps that was understandable. But it was also clear that they had accepted the much needed additional financial rewards for themselves and schools with ostrich-like unconcern about the need for a total urban strategy. They were willing to break their backs planting roses in the window boxes of the poor – but they weren't prepared to demand schools with adjacent playfields or houses with gardens. It was not their fault that many of them had not been trained for the multiracial classroom; but the performance of black and Asian children in British urban schools could have been much improved if teachers themselves had insisted on having more non-white colleagues working in the classroom. Yet in 1975 a Whitehall ban actually halted direct entry of teachers from the West Indies and Asia; and teacher unemployment meant that even those black or Asian teachers emerging from the British colleges would have a poor chance of getting a job unless the urban education authorities welcomed them particularly. British-born black children anyway sometimes found it difficult to accept black teachers – many had absorbed the white stereotype as the proper norm and did not want black teachers around to remind them that they were black. But such attitudes were obviously negative in the long term, and would have to be skilfully eroded by black teachers. Sadly, many education authorities had no real policy on this aspect of teacher employment.[26] In 1976 the ILEA was unable to say how many black teachers were scattered among the 20,000 teachers in its ten divisions. It was only the rare education authority, like Bradford, which had won high regard for its imaginative community policies, which was able to say precisely at that time 'we have 45 non-white teachers working in our schools'.

The reformed colleges of education, where teachers trained shoulder to shoulder with social workers and others, and thus broadened their outlook, would still have an important role. The colleges of education had been major beneficiaries of the boom in public expenditure on education and people were beginning to call for results. Teacher training could no longer go on in rural and priestly isolation. The few individual experiments initiated before the 1970s by colleges of education which set up urban studies and teaching practice centres in cities needed to be extended.[27] Urban teaching practice put enormous stress on student teachers, but it demonstrably improved their urban understanding and their future chances of professional effectiveness.

For the experienced teacher, implementation of the James Report[28] suggestion of a term's secondment once every five or seven years, with the opportunity to study or work in local offices or factories, might now be possible. Replacement teachers were in good supply and work experience for teachers as well as pupils would help the urban classroom. There was even more talk of interdisciplinary courses with social workers, teachers, housing administrators and others working together. An emerging need was for some training to help teachers to become more willing to take into account the realities of the economy and employment. The recommendations of the Holland Report[29] in tackling school leavers' unemployment had at last sharpened teachers' understanding of what schools could do during an economic recession; but British teachers also needed to look at the collaboration between industry, unions, parents and major employers which in the US had harmonized high school curriculum with the economic pulse of cities.

Above all, teachers would need to look at innovatory moves towards the socially varied community. Perhaps they themselves would need to make some residential commitment, living in the city for a phase of their career, possibly in the general neighbourhood of the school, though no one wanted to compel the teacher to live next door to the school, so that kids were forever hanging over the back gate (ruling out consideration of any scheme for getting teachers living locally had been an extraordinary decision at the outset of the Liverpool EPA project). A neighbourhood commitment might be particularly appropriate for a teacher with pastoral responsibility. Such a prescription might be thought totalitarian or against the spirit of an open society, but it could work – in Chicago, a city which had resisted the full impact of urban devastation through a powerful administration, teachers after 1976 were required to live within three miles of the city centre,[30] and by 1978 New York had made a similar proposal. Such drastic legislation was not necessary, however, in Britain, where many teachers and professionals lived within cities. The problem was often, rather, how to strike the right balance. Although in many ways it was not ideal, the neighbourhood of gentrification provided a good starting point, as many parents within it showed particular commitment to state schools.

Improved teacher training, a less meritocratic view of schools and housing, reduced emphasis on compensatory education, constructive curriculum experiment, financial realism and links with the outside world; all these aims could be pursued by teachers. They would need however, to become more politically capable. They would need to support the revival of inner city economic life now being proposed. They could press for regional inequalities between poor and rich education authorities to be diminished. They would need to enlarge the awareness of urban parents and community, as they had done in their own interests prior to the Houghton salary award. They would need to monitor and pressure social work, housing and child care colleagues even while co-operating more fully with them. They could demand better corporate management in local and central government spheres. The individual teacher could say loud and clear in the staffroom that putting the social composition of school intakes last in the educational priorities of the school was burying professional heads in the sand.

The problems of the urban school were not simply educational ones. It is true that new ideas and theories of education in the 1960s and 1970s had resulted in new kinds of schooling and administration that did not always work as well as had been hoped, in uncertainties due to lack of experience, in enthusiasms and disasters. But teachers and administrators were trying to deal with one corner of a vast problem. Social conditions altered extremely rapidly after the second world war, and changes in schools were only part of those changes. An emphasis in Britain on state provision led people to ask what kind of service the state should supply. New social structures and expectations led them to require something new from schools even while placing an increasing burden on them. In terms simply of numbers, more people were getting more education. What education should or could that be? In concentrating on a purely educational answer, educationists were making the teacher's job far harder. As I have tried to show throughout this book, it was the total urban policy which had to be considered if schools were to have any chance of success. No school is an island, much as some teachers would like to think them so.

The broad view is always the hardest to put into effective action. The ideas must be there, the policy has to be formulated, but co-operation and individual effort are also needed. Even the individual needs a wider grasp of 'cross-departmental' issues. One of the most encouraging things about the British system is its potential for coping with the [213] wider issues, because of its traditions of innovation in housing and town planning spheres, of state involvement and responsibility, and of the considerable freedom of the teacher to respond to the school and the children with whom he works. City classrooms all over the world will continue to change, but the British classroom can perhaps show the way in which other countries might move.

Glossary

Adviser
Previously titled inspectors, advisers were appointed in larger numbers upon local government reorganization in Britain in 1974 when new Local Education Authorities were formed. They support and inspect the quality of classroom work, especially that of teachers in their first professional year. Local advisers and inspectors are quite different from HM Inspectors (*see below*).

ancillary
Sometimes called auxiliary, or helper (generally a woman) – in the US jargon a 'para-professional'. A paid helper who assists teachers in supervising children, preparing classroom materials, etc.

Assessment of Performance Unit (APU)
A 40-strong team of DES (Department of Education and Science) staff which, working with outside experts, centrally monitors curriculum and children's attainment in the British schools system.

AUR
Alternative Use of Resources. A scheme allowing heads and teachers greater flexibility in the use of the school budget (*see also* virement).

Autism
A psychiatric affliction: a state of withdrawal or non-communication in young children, sometimes mistaken for retardation.

Bennett Report
This highly publicized piece of educational research published in 1976 showed that informal education was less widely practised than had been imagined, and showed no superiority over traditional teaching style.

bilingualism
A word with two meanings in the British school system: (1) teaching children a

foreign language, e.g. French or Spanish; (2) teaching children in their mother tongue, or the dominant language of their home background.

Black Papers
A series of periodic publications, and a right-wing movement which while containing some truth has unhelpfully polarized educational debate.

block banding
Sometimes known as 'coarse' streaming: roughly grouping children according to ability in several similar classes for the same age group. Used by schools for teaching, and by LEAs as a form of disguised selection in allocating children to secondary schools.

Bullock Report
An influential report subtitled 'Language for Life', published by the government in 1975; deals with language and the teaching of reading.

capitation
The school budget 'per head' given for books, paper, 'consumable' or other resources.

CASE
The Campaign for the Advancement of State Education; a consumer movement particularly involving parents who have chosen to put their children in state schools – much more common in Britain than Australia or the US.

catchment
The geographical neighbourhood or zone from which a school is allowed to recruit (*see also* wedge catchment).

CEE
Certificate of Extended Education. An examination and curriculum for the less able sixth former, received with varying degrees of enthusiasm by teachers.

collegial staffroom
A school where power is shared between the staff and the head.

community education
The name given to the branch of an education authority which deals with adults.

community school, community curriculum
The linking of the school with the neighbourhood, in particular by developing a curriculum which reflects those links.

comprehensive school
Usually a largish, sometimes co-educational, secondary school, where children start at 11 or sometimes later. Often more selective in social or housing class, sexual or religious factors, than the name would suggest.

consortium building
Where a group of LEAs combined to build schools by prefabrication methods, usually for cheapness but sometimes on educational grounds.

corporate management
An idea, mooted upon local government reorganization, but strenuously resisted by LEA administrators, that LEAs should work as a team with other departments under a Chief Executive.

counsellor
Variously a psychiatric or educational social worker, careers adviser or personal problems consultant working with secondary students, especially in the larger comprehensive school.

Countesthorpe
The best-documented experimental state school; in the county of Leicestershire.

CSE
Certificate of Secondary Education. An examination and syllabus for children not clever enough to do the GCE (General Certificate of Education) but now put forward in a revised form as an examination for all to take.

cycle of disadvantage
The vicious circle of poverty, in which one problem leads to another, making it impossible for the poor and disadvantaged to break out of their circumstances unless some dramatic intervention is made.

Department of Education and Science (DES)
The government department (formerly the Ministry of Education) controlling schools, and increasingly the curriculum.

Department of the Environment (DOE)
The government department responsible for housing and planning.

Department of Health and Social Security (DHSS)
Government department responsible for running the Welfare State.

dinner lady
One of the many new faces in the school, not a school meals cook, but a woman who supervises the children at lunchtime while the teachers rest.

dyslexia
'Word blindness', a condition which has not yet been fully explained.

educational disadvantage
A more fashionable phrase than 'educational deprivation', it is applied to 'black' or 'poor' children – and is a euphemism for those who live in inner city slums or public housing projects.

educational psychologist
A highly paid professional, formerly an educational tester, but now with a more significant role in the assessment of disturbed children or the provision of alternative education.

educational welfare officer
A social worker in the schools system, usually not based in a school, who has a commitment to children rather than the broader social work responsibilities.

EPA
Educational Priority Area. Part of a city or disadvantaged district where schools can obtain extra resources, 'positive discrimination' and extra money for staffing.

EPA index
A sociological measure, used principally in Liverpool and London, listing

schools in order of educational priority in order to allocate extra help pro- portionate to need.

equity sharing
A method of allowing public housing tenants part-ownership while still renting their dwelling.

ESN
Educationally subnormal. Describes children with low IQ and attainment who need special educational provision, usually in special schools.

free school
An independent or alternative school, usually small, run in improvised accommodation in the inner city by drop-out, young and enthusiastic teachers. Although proliferating in the US, and sometimes in Australia, free schools have been upstaged in Britain by LEA equivalents.

General Improvement Area (GIA)
A city neighbourhood where generous grants have been made available for improving older property and the immediate landscape of the local streets.

Green Paper
A discussion paper put out by a government department (*see* White Paper).

Her Majesty's Inspectorate (HMI)
The central government team of inspectors of schools.

Houghton Award
A substantial salary award made to teachers in 1975 in specific recognition of their contribution to society.

Housing Action Area (HAA)
An inner city street or neighbourhood, similar to the General Improvement Area (GIA) but with more sophisticated safeguards, at least in principle, against 'gentrification'.

housing co-operative
A collection of not more than 100 houses or flats managed by the tenants themselves and legally registered.

induction
Also known as the probationary year, the equivalent of US internship; the first year of teaching, at the end of which the teacher becomes fully qualified.

informal or open classrooms
The phrase Americans and other visitors to British primary schools use to describe what they find so difficult to track down. A progressive classroom where the teacher proceeds by spontaneity and intuition, rather than the flexible lock-step approach of a prescribed curriculum.

Inner London Education Authority (ILEA)
Formerly one of the world's largest, now fast-shrinking, urban schools systems, noted for its experimental vigour and its wealth. Formed in 1964 from the equally famous LCC (London County Council).

inspector
There are two kinds (*see* adviser, Her Majesty's Inspectorate).

integrated day
A classroom or curriculum regimen when the whole day is indivisible and there is no timetabling for individual subjects.

JASP
The Joint Approach to Social Policy: 'a framework for assessing systematically the use of educational resources which crosses the boundaries of traditional institutions, thus illuminating policy choices which otherwise might be masked.' Links up Departments of Education and Science, Health and Social security, Environment and the Home Office.

LATE
London Association of Teachers of English (*see also* NATE).

Local Education Authority (LEA)
There are 100 of these (similar to the US School Boards) in England and Wales, each covering between them 150,000 and 3½ million of the population.

magnet school
A city school in the US where the curriculum or catchment is designed to attract parents and therefore pupils.

media resource officer
Sometimes known as a Learning Resource Officer: a specially trained non-teaching professional who makes curriculum resources and runs the audio-visual aids in a secondary school.

middle school
In the US and New Zealand an Intermediate, in Britain sometimes called a Junior High School, the middle school system usually caters for children between 8–12 or 9–13 years. Less popular than was expected – they have not really caught on.

mixed ability
Unstreaming in the secondary school, the teaching of a common curriculum according to individual ability.

multi-ethnic, multiracial
'Black'. British schools do not recognize their 'white' ethnics like the Irish, Welsh, or Scottish.

municipalization
Government financial assistance to local housing departments enabling them to buy up private housing as it comes on to the market in order to extend the public housing sector.

NAME
National Association for Multiracial Education. A pressure group of teachers in cities like Birmingham or London, largely concerned with West Indian and Asian students.

NARE
National Association for Remedial Education.

NAS/UWT
National Association of Schoolmasters/Union of Women Teachers. The second most powerful teachers' union.

NATE
National Association of Teachers of English, a pressure group for the 'new English' movement (*see also* LATE).

neighbourhood council
The city equivalent of the village meeting, a key to improving public participation in neighbourhood and schools (although the two are rarely linked).

NUT
National Union of Teachers. The largest teacher union in England and Wales, dominated by head teachers.

open classroom
Architects' term: a cheap method of building a school without many internal walls to enable children to move about easily and informally. Often very unsatisfactory buildings.

Plowden Report
Education report of 1968 which praised progressive primary education. It urged 'positive discrimination' for the EPA or disadvantaged urban school.

PPB
Planned Programme Budgeting: an approach imported from the US whereby policy choices are reviewed so that the best overall decision is made and money accordingly wisely spent.

Rank and File
A ginger group within the National Union of Teachers active from the early 1970s onwards, with a membership of several hundred young teachers working in inner city schools.

rate support grant
Scheme by which central government helps local authorities with extra money for schools and other services, in theory evening up provision between rich and poor parts of the country.

resources, resource centre
Resources is a catch-all word describing anything on which money is spent, but sometimes more narrowly designated as an audio-visual or curriculum aid which can be bought for the school. Resource centres are modern libraries which include 'non-print' materials like slides, tapes, charts etc.

ROSLA
The raising of the school leaving age to 16 in 1972–3.

sanctuary (unit)
A modern name for 'the sin bin': an increasingly popular form of provision for naughty or disturbed secondary school pupils, usually run by one or two teachers on the school site.

Schools Council
The national teachers' and curriculum centre, which has made some creative contributions to curriculum.

Seebohm Report
An influential report (1968) resulting in the reorganization of social work training along 'generic' and permissive lines.

teachers' centre
A local meeting place, curriculum development and inservice centre for teachers.

team teaching
When several teachers (especially subject teachers) join together to teach a group of children.

ten year rule
A method, discontinued in 1973, of counting black faces in British schools without saying as much. In 1978 there were sensible proposals to revive counting.

tipping
A US phrase used to describe the point at which a neighbourhood and its schools turn from white to black upon, or immediately before 'desegregation' has been legally enforced.

vertical grouping
Also known as family grouping: the practice of teaching children of varied age together in one classroom.

virement
The accountant's phrase for 'the power to switch money from one head of estimates to another' (*see also* AUR).

wedge catchment
A secondary school intake zone in a small city, formed by cutting wedges narrow at the centre and wide in the suburbs, so as to direct a 'range of ability' to each secondary school.

white flight
A US term for the phenomenon of white parents removing their children from desegregated schools.

White Paper
A government paper indicating legislative intention: the final stage before the bill is put before the House of Commons.

Yellow Paper
A memorandum or discussion document, informal or confidential.

Bibliography

Chapter 1

1 SILBERMAN, CHARLES E., *Crisis in the classroom: The remaking of American education;* New York: Random House, 1971.
BOUDY, HARRY S., *The Real World of the Public Schools*; New York: Harcourt Brace, 1972.
Schools in Australia; Australia Schools Commission, Australian Government Publishing Service, 1973.
Improving Learning and Teaching; Educational Development Conference; New Zealand Government Publications, 1974.
BLAIR, T. L., *The International Urban Crisis*; St Albans: Paladin/Granada, 1974.
CLAYDON, L. F., *The Urban School*; Carlton, Victoria: Pitman Pacific, 1975.
FIELD, FRANK, *Education and the Urban Crisis*; London: Routledge & Kegan Paul, 1977.
2 'London has massive numbers of difficult children'; *TES*, 8 Oct. 1971.
RUTTER, MICHAEL, 'Attainment and adjustment in two geographical areas'; *Brit. J. Psych.*, *126*, June 1975.
3 FAIRHALL, JOHN, 'More teachers, but more schools on part-time'; *Guardian*, 23 Jan. 1974.

4 LOWENSTEIN, L. F., *Violence in Schools and its Treatment*; National Association of Schoolmasters, 1972.
DORAN, ANTHONY, 'Schools clash in knife battle'; *Sun*, 5 July 1973.
'Police guard on mob riot school'; *Evening News*, 5 July 1973.
HYAM, JOHN, '100 pupils in knife fight over "stolen loves"'; *Peckham/Dulwich Advertiser*, 6 July 1973.
'Why pupils stabbed the senior prefect'; *Daily Mail*, 10 Aug. 1973.
5 'Drop school leaving age to 14, says Head'; *Evening Standard*, 4 March 1976.
6 CANNON, JAMES, 'Schools on brink of breakdown'; *Teacher*, 27 Sept. 1974.
7 PUGH, G., *Truancy: Abstract of research findings* (Highlight 23); National Children's bureau, Information Service, 1976.
8 'The growing number and cost of fires in schools'; *J. Fire Prevention*, *89*, 1970.
'School fires: a major problem in 1974'; *J. Fire Prevention*, *107*, 1975.
9 'ILEA move to cut down £3·5m repair bill'; *TES*, 4 Jan. 1974.
10 *Vandalism in Schools*; Child Care Department, Save the Children Fund, 1977.
11 BLISHEN, EDWARD, *Roaring Boys: A*

schoolmaster's agony; London: Thames & Hudson, 1955.

TOWNSEND, JOHN, *The Young Devils*; London: Chatto & Windus, 1958.

BRAITHWAITE, E. R., *To Sir with Love*; London: Bodley Head, 1959.

HERNDON, JAMES, *The Way it Spozed to be: A year in the ghetto school*; London: Pitman, 1970.

COX, C. B. and DYSON, A. E. (eds), *The Black Papers on Education*; London: Davis-Poynter, 1971.

KOHL, HERB, *Thirty-six Children*; Harmondsworth: Penguin, 1971.

BOYSON, RHODES and FOX, BRIAN (eds), *Black Paper 1977*; London: Temple Smith,1977.

12 'The Panorama School'; letter to *The Times*, 23 March 1977.

13 BERG, L., *Risinghill: The death of a comprehensive school*; Harmondsworth: Penguin, 1968.

14 DAVIES, HUNTER, *The Creighton Report*; London: Hamish Hamilton, 1976.

15 POSTMAN, NEIL and WEINGARTNER, CHARLES, *Teaching as a subversive Activity*; Harmondsworth: Penguin, 1971.

16 ROWAN, JEAN, *The writing on the Blackboard*; London: Tom Stacey, 1973.

17 ILEA plea for fair reporting of school incidents; *see Press Release*, 9 July 1973. '200-strong bloody race battle'; *Islington Gazette*, 3 Oct. 1975.

18 DOE, BOB, *Shape of a Lesson* (Report of a Cambridge researcher); *TES*, 5 Dec. 1975.

19 DEVLIN, TIM, 'Teachers tell why they play truant'; *The Times*, 28 Jan. 1974.
'Too many weaklings in the classroom'; *TES*, 2 May 1975.

HILSUM, SIDNEY and CANE, BRIAN, *The Teacher's Day*; Slough: NFER, 1971.

20 TROPP, A., *The School Teachers*; London: Heinemann, 1957.
'Comparative pay' (letter); *TES*, 16 June 1967.

21 'Teachers' pay: the widening gap'; *TES*, 1 Dec. 1974.

22 FAIRHALL, JOHN, 'Bleak sums on the blackboard: survey of teacher turnover and pay'; *Guardian*, 25 March 1974.

23 HANNAN, CHARLES, *et al.*, *The First Year of Teaching*; Harmondsworth: Penguin, 1976.

24 BURGESS, TYRRELL (ed.), *Dear Lord James: A critique of teacher education*; Harmondsworth: Penguin, 1971.

25 GRACE, GERALD, *Role conflict and the Teacher*; London: Routledge & Kegan Paul, 1970.

26 'Gay staff fight ban'; *TES*, 14 Feb. 1975.

27 *Statistics of Education: Teachers, 4*; London: HMSO, 1974.

28 MORTON, JANE, 'Housing help'; *New Society*, 26 April 1973.

29 TAYLOR, PHILIP H., *How Teachers Plan their Courses*; Slough: NFER, 1970.
WATTS, JOHN, *Teaching*; Newton Abbot: David & Charles, 1974.

30 'Police enquiring into teachers' political views'; *The Times*, 25 March 1971.
BURKE, VINCENT, *Teachers in Turmoil*; Harmondsworth: Penguin, 1971.

31 'Teacher Unions'; *Education*, 15 June 1973.

32 SMITH, MIKE, *The Underground and Education*; London: Methuen, 1977.
DALE, ROGER, ESLAND, GEOFF and MCDONALD, MADELEINE, *Schooling and Capitalism*; London: Routledge & Kegan Paul, 1977.

33 SEARLE, CHRISTOPHER (ed.) *Classrooms of Resistance*; London: Writers' and Readers' Publishing Co-operative, 1975.

34 BARRELL, G. R., *Teachers and the Law*; London: Methuen, 1966.

35 ETZIONI, A., *The Semi-Professions and their Organization*; New York: Free Press, 1969.
DEEM, ROSEMARY, 'Which teachers strike?'; *New Society*, 20 Sept. 1973.

36 'Bachelors' last fling'; *Education*, 13 Jan. 1978.

37 'Chaos at teachers' rally'; *Daily Telegraph*, 28 Feb. 1973.

38 MACLURE, STUART, *One Hundred Years of London Education 1870–1970*; Harmondsworth: Penguin, 1970.
TIPTON, BERYL, 'The hidden side of teaching: the teachers' unions'; *London Educ. Rev.*, 3, 2, 1974.

Chapter 2

1 GLASS, D. V., *Social Mobility in Britain*; London: Routledge & Kegan Paul, 1954.
FLOUD, JEAN (ed.) *Social Class and Educational Opportunity*; London: Heinemann, 1956.

2 RAYNOR, J. and HARDEN, JANE, *Readings in Urban Education*; London: Routledge & Kegan Paul, 1973.
STUBBS, MICHAEL, *Language, Schools and Classrooms*; London: Methuen, 1976.
RAYNOR, J. and HARRIS, E., *The City Experience* (Vol. 1) and *Schooling in the City* (Vol. 2); London: Ward Lock, 1977.

3 GIDDENS, ANTHONY, *The Class Structure of the Advanced Societies*; London: Hutchinson, 1973.
'Social class'; *Social Trends 6*; London: HMSO, 1975.
SENNET, R. and COBB, J., *The Hidden Injuries of Class*; Cambridge University Press, 1977.

4 WEDDERBURN, DOROTHY (ed.), *Poverty, Inequality and Class Structure*; Cambridge University Press, 1975.
ROBINSON, PHILIP, *Education and Poverty*; London: Methuen, 1977.

5 CLEGG, ALEC and MEGSON, BARBARA. *Children in Distress*; Harmondsworth: Penguin, 1968.
AINSWORTH, MARJORIE E. and BATTEN, ERIC J., *The Effects of Environmental Factors on Secondary Educational Attainment in Manchester: A Plowden follow-up*; London: Macmillan, 1974.

6 General Household Survey Introductory Report; An interdepartmental survey sponsored by the Central Statistical Office; London: HMSO, 1973.
FIELD, FRANK, *Unequal Britain: A report on the cycle of inequality*; London: Arrow, 1974.

7 STOUFFER, S. A., *et al.*, *The American Soldier*; Princeton University Press, 1949.

8 RUNCIMAN, W.G., *Relative Deprivation and Social Justice*; London: Routledge & Kegan Paul, 1966.

9 *Statistics of Education, 1, Schools*; London: HMSO, 1969.
BYRNE, EILEEN M., *Planning and educational Inequality: A study of the rationale of resource allocation*; Slough: NFER, 1974.

10 *Strategic Plan for the North West*; Joint Planning Team Report; London: HMSO, 1973.
Local Authority Needs and Resources: The effect of the Rate Support Grant in the North West; North West Interprofessional Group, Centre for Environmental Studies, 1974.

11 'Rate Support Grant: Education digest'; *Education*, 10 Dec. 1976.

12 PEARSON, P. K., *Costs of Education in the United Kingdom*; Council for Educational Technology, 1977.

13 *Books in School – Needs and Provision*; Educational Publishers Council, 1973.

14 KELLMER PRINGLE, M. L., *et al.*, *Eleven Thousand Seven-year-olds*; London: Longman, 1966.
HUNT, AUDREY, *et al.*, *Families and their Needs*; from the Office of Population Censuses and Surveys; London: HMSO, 1973.

15 WEDGE, PETER and PROSSER, HILARY, *Born to Fail*; London: Arrow, 1973.

16 LOMAS, G., *The Inner City*; London Council of Social Service, 1974.
RUTTER, M. L., 'Why are London children so disturbed?'; *Proc. Royal Soc. Med.*, 1975.
WILSON, HARRIET and HERBERT, G. W., *Parents and Children in the Inner City*; London: Routledge & Kegan Paul, 1978.

17 RUTTER, M. L., *Helping Troubled Children*; Peng, 1975.

18 Literacy Surveys; ILEA, 1968, 1971, 1975.

19 *Children and their Primary Schools* (Plowden Report); London: HMSO, 1967.
SMITH, GEORGE (ed.), *Educational Priority, 4*, 'The West Riding Project'; London: HMSO, 1975.

20 MIDWINTER, ERIC, *Priority Education: An account of the Liverpool Project*; Harmondsworth: Penguin, 1972.
SCOTT, GAVIN, 'Profile: The man who brings Music Hall into the classroom'; *TES*, 22 July 1974.

21 GARNER, NORMAN, *Teaching in the Urban Community School*; London: Ward Lock Educational, 1973.

22 'EPA experiment a success – Halsey'; *TES*, 6 Oct. 1972.
HALSEY, A. H., *Educational Priority, 1*, 'Problems and policies'; London: HMSO, 1972.

23 MAYS, JOHN BARRON, *The School in its Social Setting*; London: Longman, 1967.

24 PETERS, R. S. (ed.), *Perspectives on Plowden*; London: Routledge & Kegan Paul, 1969.

25 YOUNG, MICHAEL F. D., *Knowledge and Control: New directions for the sociology of education*; London: Collier Macmillan, 1971.

KEDDIE, NELL, (ed.), *Tinker Tailor: The myth of cultural deprivation*; Harmondsworth: Penguin, 1973.

26 MARKLUND, S., 'Scholastic attainment as related to size and homegeneity of classes' (1962); in A. Yates (ed.), *Grouping in Education*; UNESCO, 1966.

27 HM Inspectorate, *Ten Good Schools*; London: DES/HMSO, 1977.

28 GINSBURG, H., *The Myth of the Culturally Deprived child*; Englewood Cliffs, NJ: Prentice Hall, 1972.

THORNBURY, ROBERT, 'EPA go away, come again another day'; *Guardian*, 4 Dec. 1973.

LEES, R. and SMITH, G., *Action Research in Community Development*: London: Routledge & Kegan Paul, 1975.

CDP Inter Project Editorial Team, *The Costs of Industrial Change*; Curriculum Development Project, 1977.

29 BARNES, JACK, *et al.*, *Educational Priority, 3*, 'Curriculum innovation in London's EPAs'; London: HMSO, 1975.

Chapter 3

1 CULLINGWORTH, J. B., *Town and Country Planning in Britain*; London: Allen & Unwin, 1977.

2 THORNBURY, ROBERT, 'Dealing with the demographic landslide'; *TES*, 25 Oct. 1974.

3 SHANKLAND, GRAEME, 'London's housing: relieving pressure in the inner city'; address to the LCSS annual meeting, 1976.

'Employment and industry in Greater London: A background document'; LCSS, 1977.

4 HALL, P., *The Containment of Urban England*; London: Allen & Unwin, 1974.

5 TAYLOR, NICHOLAS, *The Village in the City*; London: Temple Smith, 1973.

6 DONNISON, DAVID, *et al.*, *London: Urban patterns, problems and policies*; London: Heinemann, 1973.

7 *Population and the Social Services*; London: HMSO, 1977.

COATES, B. E., *et al.*, *Geography and Inequality*; Oxford University Press, 1977.

8 EVERSLEY, DAVID, *The Planner in Society*; London; Faber & Faber, 1973.

HARVEY, D., *Social Justice and the City*; London: Arnold, 1973.

SIMMIE, J. M., *Citizens in Conflict: The sociology of town planning*: London: Heinemann, 1974.

9 UNGERSON, CLARE and DEAKIN, NICHOLAS, *Leaving London*; London: Heinemann, 1977.

10 LAUWERYS, J. A. and SCANLON, D. G. (eds), *The World Year Book of Education 1970*: 'Education in Cities'; London: Evans, 1970.

RIGHTER, ROSEMARY and WILSHER, PETER, *The Exploding Cities*; London: Andre Deutsch, 1975.

MORGAN, E., *Falling Apart: The rise and decline of urban civilisation*; London: Souvenir, 1976.

11 *Housing in Multi-Racial Areas*; Community Relations Commission, 1976.

12 UREN, TOM, 'Segregation is the shame of the fast growing city complex'; *Australian*, 13 March 1973.

13 THORNBURY, ROBERT, 'Taking the rap'; *TES*, 10 Dec. 1976.

14 CULLINGWORTH, J. B., *Housing and Local Government in England and Wales*; London: Allen & Unwin, 1966.

United States Department of Housing and Urban development, *Freedom of Choice in Housing*; Washington National Academy of Science, 1972.

MANDELKER, DANIEL R., *Housing Subsidies in the United States and England*; Indianapolis, Bobbs-Merrill, 1974.

FUERST, J. S. (ed.), *Public Housing in Europe and America*; London: Croom Helm, 1974.

15 GANS, H. J., 'Urbanism and sub-urbanism as ways of life,' in Arnold M. Rose (ed.), *Human Behaviour and Social Progress*; London: Routledge & Kegan Paul, 1962.

REX, J. A., 'The sociology of a zone of transition', in R. E. Pahl (ed.) *Readings in Urban Sociology*; Oxford: Pergamon, 1968.

16 WILLMOTT, PETER and YOUNG, MICHAEL, *Family and Class in a London Suburb*; London: Routledge & Kegan Paul, 1960.

17 WARD, COLIN, *Tenants Take Over*; London: Architectural Press, 1974.

18 JACKSON, BRIAN and MARSDEN, DENNIS, *Education and the Working class*; London: Routledge & Kegan Paul, 1962.

19 JOBLING, M., *Children in Flats*; Abstract of research findings (Highlight 4); National Children's Bureau Information Service, 1973.

20 WARD, COLIN, *Tenants Take Over; see Note 17.*

21 DAMER, SEAN and MADIGAN, RUTH, 'The housing investigator'; *New Society*, 25 July 1974.

22 ALDERSON, STANLEY, *Britain in the Sixties: Housing*; Harmondsworth: Penguin, 1962.

23 HOGGART, RICHARD, *The Uses of Literacy*; Harmondsworth: Penguin, 1957.
JACKSON, BRIAN, *Working Class Community*; London: Routledge & Kegan Paul, 1968.
PLATT, JENNIFER, *Social Research in Bethnal Green*; London: Macmillan, 1971.

24 WILMOTT, PETER, 'Population and community in London'; *New Society*, 24 Oct. 1974.

25 SAVILLE, DUDLEY, *The Needs for, and Rights of Policing Local Authority Housing Estates*; Association of London Housing Estates, 1973.

26 RAVETZ, ALISON, *Model Estate: Planned housing at Quarry Hill, Leeds*; London; Croom Helm/Rowntree, 1974.

27 BYRNE, D. S., *Problem Families: A housing lumpen proletariat*; University of Durham Department of Sociology and Social Administration Working Paper 5, 1974.

28 GILL, OWEN, *Luke Street: Housing policy, conflict and the creation of the delinquent area*; London: Macmillan, 1977.

29 SMITH, D. J. and WHALLEY, A., Racial Minorities and Public Housing (Bulletin 69); PEP,1975.
Housing in Multi-Racial Areas; Community Relations Commission, 1976.

30 *Records and Information relating to the Housing of Members of Ethnic Groups*; DOE Consultation Paper, 1976.

31 LITTLE, ALAN, 'Class has more influence than racial mix'; *Oxford Rev. Educ.*, 2, 1975.
LEE, TREVOR R., *Race and Residence* (Oxford Research Studies in Geography); Oxford: Blackwell, 1977.
LITTLE, A., *Housing Choice and Ethnic Concentration: An attitude study*; Commission for Racial Equality, 1977.
Housing Need among Ethnic Minorities (Response to the Housing Consultative Document); Commission for Racial Equality, 1977.
The Social Impact of Housing (UN Seminar); London: HMSO, 1977.

32 Housing Act, 1969; Area Improvement Circular 65/69; London: HMSO,1969.

33 HAMNETT, C., 'Improvement grants as an indication of gentrification in Inner London'; *Area, 5*, 4, 1973.

34 *See* TIBBENHAM, ALAN, 'Housing and truancy'; *New Society*, 10 March 1977.

35 TURNER, E. W., 'The effect of long summer holidays on children's literacy'; *Educ. Res., 14*, 3 June 1972.

36 COLLISON, PETER, *The Cuttesloe Wall: A study in social class*; London: Faber & Faber, 1953.

Chapter 4

1 TAWNEY, R. H., *Equality*; London: Allen Lane, 1931.
SILVER, HAROLD, *Equal Opportunity in Education*; London: Methuen, 1973.

2 SIVANANDAN, A., *Role, Class and the State: The black experience in Britain*; Role and Class pamphlet 1; Institute of Race Relations, 1976.
The Role of Immigrants in the Labour Market; Project Report; DOE, 1977.

3 *The Education of Immigrants*; Education survey 13; London: HMSO, 1971.
Population Estimates 1975–1976. Office of Population and Censuses; London: HMSO, 1977.

4 REX, JOHN and MOORE, ROBERT, *Race Community and Conflict*; Oxford University Press, 1967.

5 TOWNSEND, H. E. R. and BRITTAN, E. M., *Organization in Multi-Racial Schools*; Slough: NFER, 1972.

6 TOWNSEND, H. E. R., *Immigrant Pupils in England: The LEA response*; Slough: NFER, 1971.
LITTLE, A., 'The educational achievement of ethnic minority children in London schools'; in K. Verma Gajendra and Christopher Bagley (eds), *Race and Education Across Cultures*; London: Heinemann, 1975.
GILES, R. R., *The West Indian Experi-*

ence in British Schools: Multi-racial education and social disadvantages in London; London: Heinemann, 1977.

7 Race and Council Housing in London; Runnymede Trust; London: Runnymede, 1975.

8 The Education of Immigrants; DES Circular 7/65; London: HMSO, 1971.

9 COARD, BERNARD, How the West Indian Child is made Educationally Subnormal in the British School System; London: New Beacon Books, 1971.
HAYNES, JUDITH M., Educational Assessment of Immigrant Pupils; Slough: NFER, 1971.

10 Report of the Select Committee on Race Relations and Immigration; Education (Vol. 1); London: HMSO, 1973.

11 Educational Needs of Children from Minority Groups; Community Relations Commission, 1974.

12 KEMP, GERARD, 'Black parents blame white on discipline'; Daily Telegraph, 28 May 1975.

13 CONYERS, TONY, 'Coloured youths blamed for 80 per cent of local mugging'; Daily Telegraph, 20 June 1975.
BARRATT, LEONARD LEE, The Rastafarian Dreadlocks of Jamaica; London: Sangsters/Heinemann, 1977.

14 Educational Disadvantage and the Educational Needs of Immigrants; Command 5720; London: HMSO, 1974.

15 SMITH, DAVID J., Racial Disadvantage in Britain: The PEP Report; Harmondsworth: Penguin, 1977.

16 FLOUD, J., HALSEY, P. H. and MARTIN, F. M., Social Class and Educational Opportunity; London: Heinemann, 1956.

17 COLEMAN, J. S., et al., Equality of Educational Opportunity; US Department of Education and Welfare and the Office of Education; Washington, 1966.

18 JENCKS, CHRISTOPHER, Inequality; Harmondsworth: Penguin, 1972.

19 MOYHIHAN, D. P. and MOSTELLER, F., On Equality of Educational Opportunity; New York: Random, 1972.

20 JENSEN, ARTHUR, Genetics and Education; London: Methuen, 1972.

21 JENSEN, ARTHUR, Educability and Group Differences; London: Methuen, 1973.

22 RUTTER, M. and MADGE, N., Cycles of Disadvantage; St Albans: Paladin/Granada, 1975.

23 LECOURT, DOMINIQUE, Proletarian Science? The case of Lysenko; London: New Left Books, 1977.

24 LABOV, W., in C. Reed (ed.), The Learning of Language; Hemel Hempstead: Appleton-Century-Crofts, 1971.

25 TURNER, R. H., 'Sponsored and contest mobility'; Amer. Soc. Rev., 1960.
RAWLS, JOHN, A Theory of Justice; Oxford: Clarendon Press, 1971.
HERNSTEIN, RICHARD J., The Meritocracy; Boston: Atlantic Press, 1973.

26 YOUNG, M., The Rise of the Meritocracy; Harmondsworth: Penguin, 1958.

27 BLOCK, NED and DWORKIN, GERALD, The IQ Controversy; London: Quartet Books, 1977.

Chapter 5

1 'Mixed ability classes can curb vandals'; TES, 18 Nov. 1977.

2 FENWICK, I. G. K., The Comprehensive School 1944–70; London: Methuen, 1976.

3 DEARDEN, R. F., Problems in Primary Education; London: Routledge & Kegan Paul, 1976.

4 JONES DAVIES, OLIVE and CAVE, R. G., The Disruptive Pupil in the Secondary School; London: Ward Lock Educational, 1976.

5 WILSON, B., 'The teacher's role: a sociological analysis'; Brit. J. Soc., 39, 4, 1962.

6 Special Educational Needs (Warnock Report), Command 7212; London: HMSO, 1978.

7 Court Lees Approved School Gazette, 61, Sept. 1967.
Home Office Administration of Punishment at Court Lees Approved School; Command 3367, London: HMSO, 1967.

8 WAKEFIELD, TOM, Special School; London: Routledge & Kegan Paul, 1977.

9 WEBER, LILLIAN, The English Infant School and Informal Education; Englewood Cliffs, NJ: Prentice Hall, 1971.
FOSTER, JOHN, Recording Individual Progress; London: Macmillan, 1971.
SILBERMAN, CHARLES S., The Open Classroom Reader; New York: Random House, 1973.

PLUCKROSE, HENRY, *Open School, Open Society*; London: Evans, 1975.

RINTOUL, K. and THORNE, K., *Open Plan Organization in the Primary School*; London: Ward Lock Educational,1975.

ALLEN, I., *et al.*, *Working an Integrated Day*; London: Ward Lock Educational, 1975.

10 CROSLAND, ANTHONY, *The Future of Socialism*; London: Chatto & Windus, 1956.

12 GULLIFORD, RONALD and WIDLAKE, PAUL, *Teaching Materials for Disadvantaged Children*; Curriculum Bulletin 5; London: Schools Council/Evans/Methuen Educational, 1975.
Cross'd with Adversity; Working Paper 25; London: Schools Council/Evans/Methuen Educational, 1970.

WIDLAKE, P., *Remedial Education Programmes and Progress*; NARE; London: Longman, 1977.

13 LACEY, C., *Hightown Grammar*; Manchester University Press, 1970.
See also HARGREAVES, DAVID H., *Social Relations in a Secondary School*; London: Routledge & Kegan Paul, 1967.

14 ROSENTHAL, ROBERT and JACOBSON, LENORE, *Pygmalion in the Classroom*; Toronto: Holt, Rinehart & Winston, 1968.

15 NASH, ROY, *Classrooms Observed*; London: Routledge & Kegan Paul, 1973.

16 BARKER-LUNN, JOAN C., *Streaming in the Primary school*; Slough: NFER, 1970.
FERRI, ELSA, *Streaming: Two years later*; Slough: NFER, 1971.

17 FORD, JULIENNE, *Social Class and the Comprehensive School*; London: Routledge & Kegan Paul, 1969.

18 Language for Life (Bullock Report); DES; London: HMSO, 1975.

19 KELLY, A. V., *Case Studies in Mixed-Ability Teaching*; New York: Harper & Row, 1975.
WRAGG, E. C. (ed.), *Towards Mixed Ability Groups*; Newton Abbot: David & Charles, 1976.
'Streaming on the ebb'; *Comprehensive Educ. J.*, 25 Feb. 1977.

20 VARNAVA, GEORGE, *Mixed Ability Teaching in Modern Languages*; London: Blackie, 1975.
Modern Languages in Comprehensive Schools; London: HMSO, 1977.

21 Report of the ILEA Inspectorate Survey, *Mixed Ability Grouping*, ILEA, 1976.

22 *Aspects of Comprehensive Education*; HMI; London: HMSO, 1977.
See also ROWLANDS, PETER, *Gifted Children and their Problems*; London: Dent, 1974.
Gifted Children in Middle and Comprehensive Schools; HMI; London: HMSO, 1977.

23 WATTS, JOHN (ed.), *The Countesthorpe Experience*; London: Allen & Unwin, 1977.

24 THOMPSON, JOAN, *Secondary Education for All: An analysis of Local Education Authorities' development plans*; London: Fabian Publications/Gollancz, 1947.
CHETWYND, H. R., *Comprehensive School: The story of Woodberry Down*; London: Routledge & Kegan Paul, 1960
TAYLOR, WILLIAM, *The Secondary Modern School*; London: Faber & Faber, 1963.
ROSS, J. M., *et al.*, *A Critical Appraisal of Comprehensive Education*; Slough: NFER, 1972.
BURROWS, JOHN, *The Middle School: High road or dead end?*; London: Woburn Press, 1978.
BELLABY, PAUL, *The Sociology of Comprehensive Schooling*; London: Methuen, 1977.

25 BENN, CAROLINE and SIMON, BRIAN, *Half Way There; Report on the British comprehensive school reform*; New York: McGraw-Hill, 1970.
SIMON, BRIAN, *The Politics of Educational Reform 1920–40*; London: Lawrence & Wishart, 1974.

26 DALE, R. R., *Mixed or Single Secondary School?: A research study in pupil–teacher relationships*; London: Routledge & Kegan Paul, 1969.
PARKINSON, M., *The Labour Party and the Organization of Secondary Education 1918–65*; London; Routledge & Kegan Paul, 1970.

27 GREY, ELEANOR, 'On the buses'; *TES*, 6 Sept. 1974.

28 IZBICKI, JOHN, 'Parents give false addresses to get better schools'; *Daily Telegraph*, 29 July 1975.

29 CORBETT, ANNE, 'One class schools'; *New Society*, 6 July 1967.

30 VAUGHAN, MARK, 'ILEA direct

bright pupils to "sink" schools'; *TES*, 23 June 1972.

MEDLICOTT, PAUL, 'The hidden A plus'; *New Society*, 4 July 1974.

31 'Banding and the ILEA – time to stop'; *TES*, 23 July 1972.

32 MACK, JOANNA, 'A band of selectors'; *New Society*, 11 March 1976.

MACK, JOANNA, 'A test for ILEA'; *New Society*, 5 May 1977.

33 'A retreat – but not on principle'; *Economist*, 1 Dec. 1973.

34 MEDLICOTT, PAUL, 'The further education vacuum cleaner'; *New Society*, 22 Nov. 1973.

MACFARLANE, E., *Sixth Form Colleges*; London: Heinemann Educational, 1978.

WILBY, PETER, 'Death of the sixth form'; *New Statesman*, 29 April 1977.

ROWAN, PATRICIA, 'Co-operation or separation'; *TES*, 4 Nov. 1977.

Chapter 6

1 SEABORNE, MALCOLM, *The English School: Architecture and organization 1870–1970*; London: Routledge & Kegan Paul, 1977.

WARD, COLIN, *British School Buildings*; London: Architectural Press, 1976.

2 Building Bulletin 7; DES, 1951. *Notes on Procedures for the Approval of School Buildings Projects in England*; London: HMSO, 1972.

The Standards for School Regulations; DES; London: HMSO, 1972.

3 BARRON, DONALD, 'The shrink factor in the classroom'; *Educ.*, 27 Sept. 1975.

4 *New Problems in School Design: Comprehensive schools from existing buildings*; DES: London: HMSO, 1968.

Open Plan Primary Schools; DES; London: HMSO, 1972.

New Problems in School Design: Middle schools; DES; London: HMSO, 1973.

5 *The Story of CLASP*; DES; London: HMSO, 1961.

BINYON, MICHAEL, 'Boom in system built schools keeps costs down'; *TES*, 10 July 1970.

6 CHISHOLM, JUDITH, 'People v. architects'; *Architect*, Jan. 1972.

HELLMAN, LOUIS, 'Be seen and be heard democracy for architects'; *RIBA J.*, Aug. 1973.

7 'MACE loses its largest member'; *Educ.*, 12 April 1974.

8 'New MACE school criticized'; *RIBA J.*, Aug. 1975.

See also Architectural Review, July 1971, complete issue on trends.

The Consortia; DES; London: HMSO, 1976.

9 *Open Plan Primary Schools*; Educ. Survey 16; DES, 1972.

Evelyn Lowe School Appraisal; Building Bulletin 47, DOE, 1972.

Open Planning with Special Reference to Primary Schools; NUT, 1974.

10 BROOK, HILARY, 'New but slum of the future'; *Teacher*, 21 Sept. 1973.

11 WARD, COLIN (ed.), *Vandalism*; London: Architectural Press, 1973.

BRITTAIN, VICTORIA, 'Vandalism'; *TES*, 8 Nov. 1974.

12 'Head slams her new school'; *Evening Standard*, 20 July 1975.

13 'School of closed windows'; *Guardian*, March 1976.

14 *Report on the Collapse of the Roof of the Assembly Hall of the Camden School for Girls*; London: HMSO, 1973.

15 'The failure of roof beams at Stepney School'; *Building*, 5 July 1974.

16 BABCOCK, C. I. and WILSON, R. F., 'The Chicago School fire'; *Nat. Fire Protection Assoc. Quarterly*, Jan. 1959.

SMITH, PETER B, '23 dead in Paris school inferno – did materials and type of construction contribute to fire spread and collapse?'; *Fire*, 1973.

BARCLAY, STEPHEN, *Fire: An international report*; London: Hamish Hamilton, 1973.

BARLOW, PEPPY, 'Preventing fire in schools'; *Educ.*, 27 Aug. 1971.

TAYLOR, H. D., 'Counting the true costs of fires in schools'; *Educ.*, 29 June 1973.

17 For illustration of trend *see* table, *J. Fire Protection Assoc.*, Dec 1970.

18 GRIERSON, MARTIN, 'Furniture and equipment for schools', *RIBA JOURNAL*, Sept. 1973.

19 BLISHEN, EDWARD, *The School I'd Like*; Harmondsworth: Penguin, 1969.

STONE, FELICITY and TAYLOR, JUDITH, 'You would hate it, so do they'; Joint survey by Campaign for Advancement of State Education and *The Observer*; *Observer*, 8 June 1975.

Building Work at Voluntary Aimed and

Special Agreement Schools; DES; London: HMSO, 1978.

20 *A Study of School Building*; DES; London: HMSO, 1977.

21 SMITH, PETER, *The Design of Learning Spaces*; Council for Educational Technology, 1974.

22 NEWMAN, OSCAR, *Defensible Space*; London: Architectural Press, 1973.
'Defensible space – Oscar Newman talks about new housing estates in Britain and America'; Listener, 7 March 1974.
See also The Educational Aspects of Schools Building; Paris: OECD, 1971.

Chapter 7

1 WALLER, WILLARD, *The Sociology of Teaching*; New York: John Wiley, 1932.

2 'Paraprofessional school personnel'; Canadian Teachers' Federation; *Bibliographies in Education*, 35, June 1973.

3 MCGEENEY, PATRICK, 'Teachers and their helpers'; *London Educ. Rev.*, 1, 2, 1972.

4 'Role of non-teaching personnel'; ILEA *Contact*, 29 Nov. 1974.

5 *Ancillary Staff in Secondary Schools*; Scottish Education Department; London: HMSO, 1976.
Non-teaching Staff in Secondary Schools; Scottish Education Department; London: HMSO, 1976.

6 FIELD, FRANK, *The Stigma of Free School Meals*; Child Poverty Action Group, 1974.
FIELD, FRANK, *Free School Meals: The humiliation continues*; Child Poverty Action Group, 1977.

7 'School tuck shops surveyed – a blight or a boon?; *Educ.*, 10 Oct. 1971.
Kellogg Breakfast Survey (1977), British Market Research Nutrition Bulletin 21, 1977.

8 BENDER, ARNOLD, 'Report on the school meal service of Brent'; *Sunday Times*, 11 July 1976.

9 EVANS, JUDITH, 'TVP on the school dinner place'; *Educ.*, 9 Nov. 1973.
'Charting the progress of the soya bean'; *Educ.*, 8 Aug. 1975.

10 BOND, G., *Voluntary Helpers in Schools*; Home and School Council, 1974.

11 'Never say caretaking'; *TES*, 27 June 1969.
'Schoolkeepers'; *New Society*, 10 Oct. 1974.

12 'Attacked by four boys'; *South London Press*, 4 Oct. 1974.

13 *See*, for various examples, issues of the *Schoolkeepers' Circular*, ILEA, 1965–1975.

14 ADAMS, L. J. G., *Schoolkeepers' Circular*; ILEA, 26 Feb. 1976.

Chapter 8

1 WALLER, WILLARD, *see* Chapter 7, Note 1.
See also BECKER, H. S., 'The teacher in the authority system of the public school'; *J. Educ. Soc.*, 25 March 1953.

2 ROGERS, DAVID, *110 Livingstone Street*; New York: Random House, 1969.
BIRLEY, DEREK, *The Education Officer and his World*; London: Routledge & Kegan Paul, 1970.
PETERSON, PAUL E., 'The politics of educational reform in England and the United States'; *Comp. Educ. Rev.*, June 1973.
PETERSON, PAUL E., *School Politics Chicago-style*; University of Chicago Press, 1976.

3 COOK, ANN and MACK, HERB, *The Headteacher's Role*; London: Macmillan, 1971.
CORBETT, ANNE, 'The school bosses'; *New Society*, 15 April 1971.

4 BERG, LEILA, *Risinghill*; Harmondsworth: Penguin, 1968.
MACKENZIE, R. F., *State School*; Harmondsworth: Penguin, 1970.
WILBY, PETER, 'How Scotland's top head rolled'; *Observer*, 7 April 1974.

5 LODGE, BERT, 'Recording of minor offences ends'; *TES*, 13 April 1977.
'Secret crime list bans 50 teachers a year'; *Daily Telegraph*, 3 Feb. 1977.

6 PETERS, R. S. (ed.), *The Role of the Head*; London: Routledge & Kegan Paul, 1976.

7 BERNBAUM, G., 'The role of the head'; in R. S. Peters (ed.), *The Role of the Head* (*see* Note 6).

8 STEINMAN, MICHAEL, 'Survey of primary heads in 3 London boroughs'; *Policy and Politics*, 1, 4, 1973.

9 MARLAND, MICHAEL, *The Craft of the Classroom: A survival guide*; London: Heinemann 1975.

10 THORNBURY, ROBERT, 'Management by mafia'; *TES*, 7 Nov. 1975.

11 BOWELL, C., *The School as a Formal*

Organization; Handbook of Organizations; Chicago: Rand-McNally, 1965.

BARRY, D. H. and TYE, F., *Running a School;* London: Temple Smith, 1975.

JENNINGS, ARNOLD, *Management and Headship Make the Secondary School;* London: Ward Lock Educational, 1978.

12 RICHARDSON, ELIZABETH, *The Teacher, the School and the Task of Management;* London: Heinemann Educational, 1973.

RICHARDSON, ELIZABETH, *Authority and Organization in the Secondary School;* London: Schools Council/Macmillan, 1975.

13 HILSUM, S. and STRONG, C., *The Secondary Teacher's Day;* Slough: NFER, 1978.

14 BIRLEY, DEREK, *Planning and Education;* London: Routledge & Kegan Paul, 1972.

Management in the Education Service: Challenge and response; Society of Education Officers; London: Routledge & Kegan Paul, 1974.

15 BUXTON, L., 'Virement and resources in a secondary school'; *Educ.,* 30 March 1973.

BRIAULT, ERIC, *Allocation and Management of Resources in Schools;* Council for Educational Technology, 1974.

16 Education Estimates 1977–8; Chartered Institute of Public Finance and Accountancy, 1978.

17 SHIPMAN, M. and COLE, H., 'Education indices in the allocation of resources'; *Sec. Educ.,* 1975.

18 LAWRIE, N. and VEITCH, H., *Timetabling and Organization in Secondary Schools;* Slough: NFER, 1975.

Curriculum Analysis and Planning; ILEA Secondary Staff Inspectorate; ILEA, 1976.

19 LITTLE, A. N. and MABEY, C., 'An index for designation of educational priority areas'; in A. Shonfeld and S. Shaw (eds), *Social Indicators and Social Policy;* London: Heinemann Educational, 1972.

20 *See* Note 17.

21 Report of the Committee on the Management of Local Government (Maud Report); London: HMSO, 1967.

JOHNSON, M., 'School chiefs shun management skills'; *Educ.,* 18 Sept. 1970.

The New Local Authorities: Management and structure (Bains Report); London: HMSO, 1972.

WINTER, GEOFFREY, 'Corporate management and the educationists'; *Educ.,* 21 Oct. 1977.

22 HOUGHTON, V., MCHUGH, R. and MORTON C., Open University Team, *Management in Education 1* and *2;* London: Ward Lock Educational, 1975.

23 *Output Budgeting for the DES;* London: HMSO, 1970.

24 Report of the Layfield Committee of Enquiry into Local Government Finance; London: HMSO, 1976.

25 KOGAN, MAURICE, *The Politics of Education: Edward Boyle and Anthony Crosland in conversation;* Harmondsworth: Penguin, 1971.

FOWLER, GERALD, *et al.,* *Decision-making in British Education;* London and Oxford: Heinemann/Oxford University Press, 1973.

MEDLICOTT, PAUL, 'Education in Whitehall: how the DES works'; *New Society,* 22 Aug. 1974.

Kogan, Maurice, Educational Policy Making; London: Allen & Unwin, 1975.

26 'Servants or masters? How the civil servants rule British education'; Text of OECD Report; *TES,* 9 May 1975.

GLENNERSTER, W., 'Forward Planning UK style, evaluation UK style'; in *Social Service Budgets and Social Policy;* London: Allen & Unwin, 1975.

Chapter 9

1 BANTOCK, G. H., *Education and Values;* London: Faber & Faber, 1965.

PETERS, R. S. (ed.), *The Concept of Education;* London: Routledge & Kegan Paul, 1967.

STONES, E., *An Introduction to Educational Psychology;* London: Methuen, 1967.

CHARITY, JAMES, *Young Lives at Stake: A reappraisal of secondary schools;* Glasgow.

HOLLY, DOUGLAS, *Society, Schools and Humanity: The changing world of secondary education;* St Albans: McGibbon & Kee, 1971.

HOOPER, RICHARD (ed.), *The Curriculum: Context, design and development;* Edinburgh: Lover & Boyd, 1971.

BRUNER, JEROME S., *The Relevance of*

Education; London: Allen & Unwin, 1972.

WRIGHT, NIGEL, *Progress in Education*; London: Croom Helm, 1978.

LAWTON, DENIS, *Social Change, Educational Theory and Curriculum Planning*; University of London Press, 1973.

HIRST, PAUL H., *Knowledge and the Curriculum: A collection of philosophical papers*; London: Routledge & Kegan Paul, 1974.

LAWTON, DENIS, *Class, Culture and the Curriculum*; London: Routledge & Kegan Paul, 1975.

HAMILTON, DAVID, *Curriculum Evaluation*; London: Open Books, 1976.

MCDONALD, BARRY and WALKER, ROB, *Changing the Curriculum*; London: Open Books, 1976.

BERNBAUM, G., *Knowledge and Ideology in the Sociology of Education*; London: Macmillan, 1977.

WARNOCK, MARY, *Schools of Thought*; London: Faber & Faber, 1977.

2 ESLAND, G., *et al.*, *The Social Organisation of Learning and Teaching*: Open University, 1972.

PRING, RICHARD, *Knowledge and schooling*; London: Open Books, 1976.

BOURDIEU, PIERRE and PASSERON, JEAN-CLAUDE, *Reproduction in Education, Society and Culture*; London: Sage, 1977.

3 STENHOUSE, LAWRENCE, *An Introduction to Curriculum Research and Development*; London: Heinemann, 1975.

4 CORBETT, ANNE, *Much to do about Education: A critical survey of the fate of the major educational reports*; Council for Educational Advance, 1968.

5 *See for example* Freire, Paolo, *Pedagogy of the Oppressed*; Harmondsworth: Penguin, 1972.

6 *The Right of Teachers to Consultation*; NUT, 1972.
'Wasted work of the Schools Council'; *TES*, 17 May 1974.
Schools Council Project Profiles, Sixth Edition; Schools Council, 1977.

7 THORNBURY, ROBERT (ed.), *Teachers' Centres*; London: Darton, Longman & Todd, 1973.

8 CHURCH, MICHAEL, 'Publishers face a crisis'; Account of confidential report to Educational Publishers Council; *TES*, 14 June 1974.

9 SELLECK, R. J. W., *English Primary Education and the Progressives 1914–1939*; London: Routledge & Kegan Paul, 1972.

ASHTON, P., *et al.*, *Aims of Primary Education*; London: Schools Council/Macmillan, 1975.
See also The Whole Curriculum 13–16; Working Paper 53; London: Schools Council/Evans/Methuen Educational, 1975.
The Curriculum in the Middle Years; Working paper 55; London: Schools Council/Evans/Methuen Educational, 1976.

10 NICHOLAS OTTY, *Learner Teacher*; Harmondsworth: Penguin, 1972.

11 CORBETT, ANNE, 'Is the NFER a waste of money?'; *TES*, 12 Sept, 1975.

12 JENKINS, DAVID and SHIPMAN, MARTEN, *Curriculum: An introduction*; London: Open Books, 1976.
CANE, B. and SCHROEDER, C., *The Teacher and Research*; Slough: NFER, 1970.

13 BENN, CAROLINE, 'Education in committee'; *New Society*, 28 Feb. 1974.

14 *See also* JENNINGS, R. E., *Politics and Policy Making in Local Education Authorities*; London: Batsford, 1977.

15 EDMONDS, E. G., *The School Inspector*; London: Routledge & Kegan Paul, 1962.
COWEN, S., 'Inspectors – useless, abysmal, overpaid . . .'; *TES*, 31 Dec. 1976.

16 From a Chief Education Officer, 'The Inspector's Lot'; *TES*, 14 Oct. 1966.
FEILDEN, RICHARD (letter), 'Her Majesty's Inspectors'; *TES*, 4 Nov. 1966.

Chapter 10

1 CORBETT, ANNE, *Innovation in Education: England*; Paris: OECD, 1971.
WHITESIDE, T., *The Sociology of Educational Innovation*; London: Methuen, 1978.

2 PETERS, R. S. (ed.), *Perspectives on Plowden*; London: Routledge & Kegan Paul, 1969.

3 WARWICK, DAVID, *Integrated Studies in the Secondary School*; University of London Press, 1973.
FREEMAN, JOHN, *Team Teaching in Britain*; London: Ward Lock Educational, 1969.

4 NISBET, JOHN, 'Curriculum

[232] Development in Scotland'; in R. Bell (ed.), *Education in Great Britain and Ireland*; Milton Keynes: Open University, 1973.

5 BERNBAUM, G., 'Countesthorpe College'; in *Case Studies of Educational Innovation*; Paris: OECD, 1973.
MACK, JOANNA, 'A school that works'; *New Society*, 10 June 1976.

6 *Dissemination of innovation: The humanities curriculum project*; Working paper 56; London: Schools Council/Evans/Methuen Educational, 1976.
DAVIES, BRIAN, *Social Control and Education*; London: Methuen, 1977.

7 STENHOUSE, L., 'Innovation and stress'; *TES*, 19 Jan 1973.
STENHOUSE, L., 'The idea of neutrality'; *TES*, 4 Feb. 1975.

8 BENNETT, N., *Teaching Style and Pupil Progress*; London: Open Books, 1976.

9 LACEY, COLIN, *Hightown Grammar*: Manchester University Press, 1970.

10 BOYSON, RHODES, *Oversubscribed: The story of Highbury Grove School*: London: Ward Lock Educational, 1974.

11 ELVIN, H. L., PETERS, R. S. and BERNSTEIN, B., 'Ritual in Education'; *Philos. Trans. Royal Soc.* (B), 251, 1961.

12 ADAMS, PAUL, *et al.*, Children's Rights; St Albans: Panther/Granada, 1972.
BERG, LEILA, *et al.*, *Children's Rights: Towards the liberation of the child*: St Albans: Granada, 1972.

13 PAYNE, SARAH and DEVLIN TIM, 'Schools Action Union switch to all-out revolution'; *TES*, 7 Nov. 1969.

14 'Indoctrination scare after teenagers' trip to the Red House'; *TES*, 13 Feb. 1976.

15 GOODMAN, PAUL, *Growing up Absurd*, New York: Random House, 1956.
KOZOL, J., *Death at an Early Age*; Harmondsworth, Penguin, 1971.
GOODMAN, PAUL, *Compulsory Miseducation*; Harmondsworth, Penguin, 1971.
REIMER, EVERETT, *School is Dead: An essay on alternatives in education*; Harmondsworth: Penguin, 1971.

16 HANSEN, SOREN and JENSEN, JESPER, *The Little Red Schoolbook*; London: Stage One, 1971.

17 LEWIS, IAN, 'Ten Commandments for the schooler and ten for deschoolers'; *TES*, 6 Aug. 1971.

18 ILLICH, IVAN, *Deschooling Society*; Harmondsworth: Penguin, 1973.

19 FREIRE, PAOLO, *Pedagogy of the Oppressed*; Harmondsworth: Penguin, 1972.
DOUGLAS, HOLLY, *Beyond Curriculum*; St Albans: Hart Davis McGibbon, 1973.
HEAD, DAVID, *Free Way to Learning: Educational alternatives in action*; Harmondsworth: Penguin, 1974.
WARDLE, DAVID, *The Rise of the Schooled Society*: London: Routledge & Kegan Paul, 1974.

20 The School of Barbiana, *Letter to a Teacher*; Harmondsworth: Penguin, 1970.
BREMER, JOHN and VON MOSCHZISKER, MICHAEL, *The School without Walls: Philadelphia's Parkway programme*; Toronto: Holt, Rinehart & Winston, 1971.
LISTER, IAN, *Deschooling*; Cambridge University Press, 1973.
RICHMOND, KENNETH W., *The Free School*; London: Methuen, 1973.

21 STEVENS, AURIOL, White Lion Free School'; *TES*, 22 Nov. 1974.
White Lion Free School, *How to Set Up a Free School*; White Lion School, 1975.
NEWELL, PETER, 'A free school now'; *New Society*, 15 May 1975.
'The odd White Lion out'; *Guardian*, 23 June 1977.

22 HILL, BARRY, 'Liverpool free school "Vanguard of Social Change" in depressed area'; *TES*, 18 Dec. 1970.
HILL, BARRY, 'Few friends as yet for free school'; *TES*, 25 June 1971.

23 MIDWINTER, ERIC, 'Stick with the system'; *TES*, 28 July 1972.
JUDGE, HARRY, *School is not Dead*; London: Longman, 1974.

24 SCOTT, GAVIN, '60 children stranded when free school closed'; *TES*, 5 April 1974.
MORISSEAU, JAMES, *The Mini-School*; New York: Urban Coalition, 1975.
'London's £1m to isolate troublemakers'; *TES*, 11 Nov. 1977.
MACBEATH, JOHN, 'Goodbye free school, hello special unit'; *TES*, 9 Dec. 1977.

Chapter 11

1 MORRIS, JOYCE, *Reading in the Primary School*; London: Hamlyn, 1959.
CANE, BRIAN and SMITHERS, JANE, *The Roots of Reading: A study of 12 infant schools in deprived areas*; Slough: NFER, 1971.
Inner London Education Literacy Surveys, 1968–75.

2 START, K. B. and WELLS, B. K., *The Trend of Reading Standards*; Slough: NFER, 1972.
MACKAY, DAVID, *The Initial Teaching of Reading and Writing: Some notes towards a theory of literacy*; London: Longman, 1968.
GOODACRE, ELIZABETH, 'Published reading schemes for the primary school'; *Educ. Res. 12*, 1, 1969.

3 GOODACRE, ELIZABETH, *Children and Learning to Read*; London: Routledge & Kegan Paul, 1971.

4 WARBURTON, F. W. and SOUTHGATE, V., *ita: An Independent Evaluation*; London: John Murray & W. R. Chambers, 1969.

5 *Children with Specific Reading Difficulties* (Green Paper); London: HMSO, 1971.
Report of the Advisory Committee on Handicapped Children, Children with Specific Reading Difficulties; London: HMSO, 1972.
MILES, T. R., *The Dyslexic Child*; Hove: Priory Press, 1975.

6 TOWNSEND, JOHN ROWE, *Written for Children: An outline of English children's literature*; London: Garnet Miller, 1975.
ELLISON, T. and WILLIAMS, G., 'Social class and children's reading preferences'; *Readings*, 5, 2 1971.

7 WHITEHEAD, FRANK CAPEYAC and MADDREN, WENDY, *Children's Reading Interests*; London: Methuen/Evans, 1974.
WHITEHEAD, FRANK, *et al.*, *Children and their Books*; London: Schools Council/Macmillan, 1977.

8 SEYMOUR, JOHN, 'To help people pass exams'; *TES*, 5 Oct. 1973.
'Ronald Ridout: A profile'; *Observer*, 21 Sept, 1975.
BUGLER, JEREMY, 'Golden eggs'; *TES*, 26 Dec. 1975.

9 BERNSTEIN, BASIL, *Class Codes and Control*; St Albans: Granada, 1973.
BERNBAUM, GERALD, 'Sociology's Double Helix: the work of Basil Bernstein'; *TES*, 17 May 1974.
BERNSTEIN, BASIL, *Class and Pedagogies: Visible and invisible*; Paris: OECD, 1975.

10 GAHAGAN, D. M. and D. A., *Talk Reform: Explorations in language for infant school children*; London: Routledge & Kegan Paul, 1970.

11 LAWTON, DENIS, *Social Class, Language and Education*; London: Routledge & Kegan Paul, 1968.
SHAYER, DAVID, *The Teaching of English in Schools 1900–1970*; London: Routledge & Kegan Paul, 1972.
EDWARDS, A., Language in Culture and Class; London: Heinemann, 1976.

12 ROSEN, HAROLD, *Language and Class: A critical look at the theories of Basil Bernstein*; London: Falling Wall Press, 1972.
MEDLICOTT, PAUL, 'Language and class'; *New Society*, 5 June 1975.

13 LABOV, WILLIAM, *Language in the Inner City: Studies in the black English vernacular*; Oxford: Blackwell, 1977.

14 ROSEN, CONNIE and HAROLD, *The Language of Primary School Children*; Harmondsworth: Penguin, 1973.

15 HOGGART, RICHARD, *The Uses of Literacy*; Harmondsworth: Penguin, 1973.

16 CLEMENTS, SIMON, *et al.*, *Reflections: An English course for students aged 14–18*; Oxford University Press, 1963.
MARSHALL, SYBIL, *An Experiment in Education*; Cambridge University Press, 1963.
HOLBROOK, DAVID, *English for the Rejected: Training literacy in the lower streams of the secondary school*; Cambridge University Press, 1964.
A Programme for Research and Development in English Teaching; Working Paper 3; London: Schools Council/HMSO, 1965.
DIXON, JOHN, *Growth through English*; Oxford University Press, 1969.
BRITTON, J., 'Ten years of NATE'; *Eng. in Educ.*, 7, 2, 1972.

17 BARNES, DOUGLAS, *et al.*, *Language, the Learner and the School*; Harmondsworth: Penguin 1969.
BRITTON, J., *Language and Learning*; Harmondsworth: Penguin, 1970.
CLEGG, A. G. (ed.) *The Excitement of Writing*; London: Chatto & Windus, 1970.
MAKINS, VIRGINIA, 'How "useful"

[234] Jimmy Britton broke the language bar-
rier'; *TES*, 10 Oct. 1975.
TORBE, M. and PROTHEROUGH, R.,
*Classroom Encounters: Language and
English teaching*; London: Ward Lock
Educational, 1976.
BARNES, DOUGLAS, *From Communi-
cation to Curriculum*; Harmondsworth:
Penguin, 1976.

18 *See* Chapter 1, Note 33.

19 TRIPP, JOHN, 'A poet in school';
Educ., 5 Nov. 1971.
Writers in Schools; London: Arts Coun-
cil, 1977.

20 MARTIN, NANCY, D'ARCY, PAT and
NEWTON, BRYAN, *Writing Across the
Curriculum 11–16: Language policies in
schools*; University of London Institute
of Education, 1973.
BRITTON, JAMES, *et al.*, *The Develop-
ment of Writing Abilities*; London:
Schools Council/Macmillan Educa-
tion, 1976.
WILLIAMS, JEANETTE T., *Learning to
Write or Writing to Learn?*; Slough:
NFER, 1977.

21 WARWICK, DAVID (ed.), *Integrated
Studies in the Secondary School*; Univer-
sity of London Press, 1973.
ADAMS, ANTHONY, *The Humanities
Jungle*; London: Ward Lock Educa-
tional, 1976.
TORBE, M., *Language Across the Cur-
riculum: Guidelines for schools*; London:
Ward Lock Educational/NATE, 1977.

22 HOYLES, MARTIN (ed.), *The Politics of
Literacy*; London: Writers and Readers
Publishing Co-operative (undated).
'Whose values – social studies'; *Teach-
ing London Kids*, 7, 1976.

23 CROALL, JONATHAN, 'NATE told:
be positive against racism'; *TES*, 23
April 1976.
'English in a multi-cultural society
(special issue); *Eng. in Educ.*, 11, 1,
1977.

24 GOODMAN, KENNETH S. (ed.), *The
Psycholinguistic Nature of the Reading
process*; Detroit: Wayne State Univer-
sity Press, 1968.
SMITH, FRANK, *Psycholinguistics and
Reading*; Toronto: Holt, Rinehart &
Winston, 1973.

25 WAINWRIGHT, PETER H. and
FRASER, M., *English as a Second Language in Multi-racial Schools: A bibliogra-
phy*; London: National Book League,
1977.

26 'Scope', *London Books for Schools*,
Schools Council, 1969.

27 'Concept 7–9'; E. J. Arnold for the
Schools Council, 1973.

28 TOUGH, JOAN, *Talking and Learning*;
London: Ward Lock Educational,
1978.

Chapter 12

1 ADAMS, C. and LAURIKIETIS, R.,
The Gender Trap; London: Virago, 1976.

2 WHITTY, G. and YOUNG, M., *Explorations in the Politics of School Knowledge*;
Driffield: Nafferton, 1976.

3 ZIMET, S. G., *Print and Prejudice*;
London: Open University/Hodder &
Stoughton, 1977.
DIXON, B., *Catching them Young: Poli-
tical ideas in children's fiction; also Sex,
Race and Class in Children's fiction*; Lon-
don: Pluto, 1977.

4 RICHMOND, P. E., *Educational New
Trends in Integrated Science Teaching
(2 vols); UNESCO*, 1973.

5 'Mercury – one lab in three polluted';
TES, 4 July 1977.

6 DUNN, WILLIAM, R., 'Whatever
happened to teaching machines?';
TES, 31 July 1970.
ROWNTREE, DEREK, *Educational
Technology in Curriculum Development*;
New York: Harper & Row, 1971.

7 RICHMOND, KENNETH, *The Teaching
Revolution*; London: Methuen, 1967.
TROWBRIDGE, N. E., *The New Media
Challenge*; London: Macmillan Educa-
tion, 1974.

8 TAYLOR, L. C., *Resources for Learning*;
Harmondsworth: Penguin, 1972.
CRABB, GEOFFREY, *Copyright Clearance: A practical guide*; Council for Educational Technology, 1977.

9 BESWICK, N., *School Resource Centres*;
Working Paper 43; London: Schools
Council/Evans/Methuen Educational,
1972.
EDWARDS, R. P. A., *Resources in
Schools*; London: Evans, 1973.
BESWICK, N., *Organising Resources*;
London: Heinemann, 1975.
LISTER, IAN, *The School of the Future*;
Council for Educational Technology,
1975.
BESWICK, N., *Resource-based Learning*;
London: Heinemann, 1977.

10 HILL, BRIAN, 'CCTV: is the game
worth the candle?'; *TES*, 20 Oct. 1972.

11 BEALE, C. G., 'ILEA cable network for the axe'; *Broadcast*, 21 March 1977.

12 BROWN, RAY (ed.), *Children and Television*; London: Collier Macmillan, 1977.

13 'Report on school children's viewing habits'; National Viewers and Listeners Association; *Guardian*, 24 April 1977.

14 MURDOCH, GRAHAM and PHILLIPS, GUY, *Mass Media and the Secondary School*; London: Macmillan, 1973.

15 DE BONO, EDWARD, 'The dog exercising machine'; *TES*, 20 Oct. 1970.
'The up and coming game of golf'; *Educ.*, 2 June 1972.
HURMAN, ANN, 'Anthropology for 4B'; *TES*, 26 Oct. 1973.
SUGARMAN, BARRY, *The School and Moral Development*; London: Croom Helm, 1974.
WRINGE, COLIN, *Developments in Modern Language Teaching*; London: Open Books, 1976.

16 KOHL, HERB, *Writing, Maths and Games*; London: Methuen, 1977.

17 BERGMAN, JIM, 'Jazz in school'; *TES*, 5 June 1970.
BENTLEY, ARNOLD, Time for Music; Schools Council Project 'Music Education of Young Children'; London: Schools Council/Arnold, 1977.
WILLIAMS, E. M. and SHUARD BODEN, P., *Developments in Geography Teaching*; London: Open Books, 1977.

18 GLEESON, DENNIS and WHITTY, GEOFF, *Developments in Social Studies Teaching*; London: Open Books, 1977.

19 *Multiracial Education: Needs and Innovations*; Working Paper 50; London; Schools Council/Evans/Methuen Educational, 1973.

20 SKIDELSKY, ROBERT, *English Progressive Schools*; Harmondsworth: Penguin, 1969.
GLENNERSTER, HOWARD and WILSON, GAIL, *Paying for Private Schools*; London: Allen Lane, 1970.
PUNCH, MAURICE, *Progressive Retreat*; Cambridge University Press, 1977.

21 THWAITES, BRYAN, *The Schools Mathematics Project: The first ten years*; Cambridge University Press, 1972.
TAYLOR, L. C., *et al.*, *Experiments in Education at Sevenoaks*; London: Longman/Constable, 1965.

22 KITTO, PAT, 'Dartington's other Hall'; *TES*, 12 Oct. 1973.

23 *Environmental Studies 5–13; The use of historical resources*; Working Paper 48; London: Schools Council/Evans/Methuen Educational, 1973.

24 LAWTON, DENIS and DUFOUR, BARRY, *The New Social Studies*; London: Heinemann Educational, 1973.

25 WATERS, DEREK and BRANTON, MARGARET, *A Book of Projects*; London: Mills & Boon, 1972.

26 *People and Planning* (Skeffington report); London: HMSO, 1969.

27 *Choosing a Curriculum for the Young School Leaver*; Working Paper 33; London: Schools Council/Evans/Methuen Educational, 1971.
'History 13–16 Project'; Schools Council, 1977.

28 GOODEY, BRIAN, 'Where are the urban trails?'; *Bull. Env. Ed.*, July 1975.

29 WARD, COLIN and FYSON, ANTHONY, *Streetwork: The exploding school*; London: Routledge & Kegan Paul, 1973.

30 ARKINSTALL, MICHAEL, *Organizing School Journeys*; London: Ward Lock Educational, 1977.

31 NEWSOME, SIR J. H. *Boarders Away*; London: Longman, 1973.

32 PLATT, JAMES, 'Butlin's comprehensive campus'; *Educ.*, 5 May 1972.

33 *Short Stay Residential Experience*; Schools Council Pamphlet 10; London: Schools Council, 1972.

34 *Pterodactyls and Old Lace: Museums in education*; London: Schools Council/Evans/Methuen Educational, 1972.

35 STEELE, IAN, *Developments in History Teaching*; London: Open Books, 1976.

Chapter 13

1 BELL, R. (ed.), *et al.*, *Education in Great Britain and Ireland*; London: Open University/Routledge & Kegan Paul, 1973.
IZBICKI, JOHN, 'Schools Council to be radically reformed'; *Daily Telegraph*, 20 Jan. 1977.

2 *The Curriculum in the Middle Years*; Working Paper 55; London: Schools Council/Evans/Methuen Educational, 1975.

3 *Impact and Take-up: Project Report*; London: Schools Council, 1978.

4 SHIPMAN, M. D., *et al.*, *Inside a Cur-*

[236] riculum Project; London: Methuen, 1974.

5 Dissemination and In-service Training; Schools Council Pamphlet 14, London: Schools Council, 1974.

6 Edited extracts from the Yellow Book, the DES Memorandum to the Prime Minister; TES, 15 Oct. 1976.

7 WICKING, BRUCE, 'An open and shut case'; TES, 14 July 1974.

8 BENNETT, NEVILLE, Teaching Styles and Pupil Progress; London: Open Books, 1976.

9 SHARP, RACHEL and GREEN ANTHONY, Education and Social Control; London: Routledge & Kegan Paul, 1975.

10 See Chapter 10, Note 28.

11 CLEGG, ALEC, 'Hysteria over reading'; TES, 14 April 1972.

12 BRYANT, PETER, Perception and Understanding in Young Children; London: Methuen,1974.

13 ASH, MAURICE (ed.), Where are the Progressives Now?; London: Routledge & Kegan Paul, 1969.

14 MARLAND, MICHAEL, The Craft of the Classroom; London: Heinemann, 1976.

15 CHANAN, GABRIEL and GIL-CHRIST, LINDA, What School is For; London: Methuen, 1974.

16 WHITE, J. P., Towards a Compulsory Curriculum; London: Routledge & Kegan Paul, 1973.

17 AULD, ROBIN, QC, William Tyndale Junior and Infants School: Public Inquiry; ILEA, July 1976
'The Auld Testament'; Economist, 24 July 1976.
Ellis, et al., William Tyndale: The teachers' story; London: Writers and Readers Publishing Co-operative, 1976.
GRETTON, JOHN and JACKSON, MARK, William Tyndale: Collapse of a school – or a system?; London: Allen & Unwin, 1976.

18 'Tyndale: Flather says all six teachers should be sacked'; ILEA Disciplinary Tribunal Report; ILEA, 1977.

19 STIBBS, A. and TURNBULL, E., 'Penniless English'; Eng. in Educ., 9, 3, 1975.

20 'Survey on book purchase'; TES, 18 and 25 Nov. 1977.
WILBY, PETER, 'The educational Gods that failed'; New Society, 22 Sept. 1977.

21 WEINSTOCK, ARNOLD, 'I blame the teachers'; TES, 23 Jan. 1976.
METHVEN, JOHN, 'What industry wants'; TES, 29 Oct. 1976.

22 'How industry has ditched day release'; Educ., 13 May 1977.

23 Young People and Work: A report on the feasibility of a new programme of opportunities for unemployed young people (Holland Report); Manpower Services Commission; report in TES, 20 May 1977.

24 WILLMOTT, ALAN, CSE and GCE Grading Examinations; The 1973 comparability study; London: Schools Council/Macmillan, 1977.

25 Pupils' art 'Not for burning'; (Complaint by National Society for Art Education); Daily Telegraph, 23 May 1976. See also Dore, R. P., The Diploma Disease; London: Allen & Unwin, 1976.

26 KAY, BRIAN, 'The Assessment of Performance Unit'; Educ. 3–13, 4, 2, 1976.
LEONARD, MARTIN, 'Art of the impossible' (on work of the APU); TES, 17 June 1977.

27 Educating our Children; DES; London: HMSO, 1977.

28 Education in Schools: A consultative document (Green Paper); London: HMSO, 1977.
Local Authority Arrangements for the School Curriculum; DES Circular 14/77; London: HMSO, 1977.

29 The Attainments of the School Leaver; House of Commons, Tenth Report from the Expenditure Committee; London: HMSO, 1977.

30 FLETCHER, DAVID, 'Plan to dismiss incompetent teachers at 50'; Daily Telegraph, 14 Jan. 1977.

31 MAYNARD, ALAN, Experiment with Choice in Education; Institute of Economic Affairs, 1975.
Education Vouchers in Kent: A feasibility study; Maidstone: Kent Education Office, 1978.
Admission of Children to Schools of their Parents' Choice; DES Consultative Paper, 1977.

32 A New Partnership for our Schools (Taylor Report); London: HMSO, 1977.

33 EZARD, JOHN, '20,000 teachers line up for the dole', Guardian, 10 Aug. 1976.
See also BRIAN, JAMES, The Advancement of Spencer Button; Sydney: Angus & Robertson, 1950.

34 *Keeping the School under Review: A method of self-assessment for schools devised by the ILEA Inspectorate*; ILEA, 1977.

35 *Ten Good Schools: A secondary school enquiry*; DES/HM Inspectorate; London: HMSO, 1977.

36 CORBETT, ANNE, 'Profile of Sheila Browne'; *TES*, 29 Nov. 1974.
BROWNE, SHEILA, *Spies in the Garden*; Paper to the Conference of LEAS, 1977.

37 'What is JASP?' *TES*, 30 May 1975.

Chapter 14

1 Report of the Committee on Local Authority and Allied Personal Social Services (Seebohm Report); Command 3703; London: HMSO, 1968.

2 Report of the Commissioner for Police for the year 1972; London: HMSO, 1973.

3 FRASER, MORRIS, Children in Conflict; London: Secker & Warburg, 1973.

4 MAIS, JOHN (ed.), *et al.*, *Social Services of England and Wales*; London: Routledge & Kegan Paul, 1975.
MACMILLAN, KEITH, *Education Welfare*; London: Longman,1976.
FITZGERALD, MIKE (ed.), *et al.*, *Welfare in Action*; London: Routledge & Kegan Paul, 1977.
FITZHERBERT, KATRIN, Child Care Services and the Teacher; London: Temple Smith, 1977.

5 BRONFENBRENNER, URIE, *Two Worlds of Childhood: US and USSR*; Harmondsworth: Penguin, 1974.

6 BOWLBY, JOHN, *Child Care and the Growth of Love*; Harmondsworth: Penguin, 1953.
See also BOWLBY, JOHN, *Attachment and Loss*; London: Hogarth Press, 1973.

7 RUTTER, MICHAEL, *Maternal Deprivation Reassessed*; Harmondsworth: Penguin, 1972.
RUTTER, M. and MADGE, N., *Cycles of Disadvantage*; London: Heinemann, 1976.

8 CLARKE, A. M. and CLARKE, A. D. B., *Early Experience: Myth and evidence*; London: Open Books, 1976.

9 WADDELL, K. and RAYBOULD, E. C. (eds), *The Early Identification of Educationally at Risk Children*; University of Birmingham, 1977.

10 Report of the Review Body appointed to enquire into the case of Stephen Meurs; Norwich: Norfolk County Council, 1975.

11 Report of the Committee of Inquiry into the care and supervision provided in relation to Maria Colwell; London: HMSO, 1974.

12 TURNER, ANN, 'Forgive me, Maria, forgive us all' (letter); *Teacher*, 11 Oct. 1974.

13 SHRIGLEY, S. M., *Selected References on non-accidental injury to children*; DHSS Library, 1977.

14 NEWSON, JOHN and ELIZABETH, *Patterns of Infant Care in an Urban Community*; Harmondsworth: Penguin, 1965.
NEWSON, JOHN and ELIZABETH, *Seven Years Old in the Home Environment*; London: Allen & Unwin, 1976.

15 TIZARD, BARBARA, *Adoption: A second chance*; London: Open Books, 1977.

16 Report of the Committee on one-parent families (Finer Report); London: HMSO, 1974.

17 *Fit for the Future* (Court Report); London: HMSO, 1977.

18 *Who minds? A survey of working mothers and child minding in ethnic minority communities*; Community Relations commission, 1975.
Childminding in London: A study of support services for childminders; LCSS, 1977.

19 KELLMER PRINGLE MIA, *The Needs of Children*; London: Hutchinson, 1975.
TIZARD, JACK, MOSS, PETER and PERRY, JANE, *All our Children: Preschool services in a changing society*; London: Temple Smith, 1976.
Working Together for Children and their families; London: HMSO, 1977.

20 SERENY, GITTA, *The Case of Mary Bell*; London: Eyre Methuen, 1972.

21 WEST, D. J. and FARRINGTON, D. P., *The Delinquent Way of Life*; London: Heinemann Educational, 1977.

22 STONES, EDGAR, *An Introduction to Educational Psychology*; London: Methuen, 1966.
MASUD, HOGHUGI and NETHERCOT, SUSAN, *Troubled and Troublesome*; Aycliffe School, 1977.

23 LOWENSTEIN, L. F., *Violence in Schools and its Treatment*; National Association of Schoolmasters, 1972.

24 CAMERON, SUE, 'More girls take to violence'; *TES*, 6 July 1973.

WADSWORTH, N. E. J., 'Delinquency in a national sample of children'; *Brit. J. Criminology, 15,* 2.

25 BELSON, W. A., *Juvenile Theft: The causal factors*; New York: Harper & Row, 1975.

26 DOYLE, PAT, *et al., The Paint House*; Harmondsworth: Penguin, 1972.
JAMES, PATRICK, *A Glasgow Gang Observed*; London: Methuen, 1973.
DAVEY, JO and TIMOTHY, in Peter Denton and Timothy Davey (eds), *An Alternative Childhood*; London: Quartet, 1974.
HALL, STUART and JEFFERSON, TONY, *Resistance through Rituals*; London: Hutchinson, 1976.
MARSH, PETER, ROSSER, ELIZABETH and HARRÉ, ROM, *The Rules of Disorder*; London: Routledge & Kegan Paul, 1978.
Public Disorder and Sporting Events; Sports Council, 1978.
Football Hooliganism; London: Interaction Imprint, 1978.

27 *Raising the School Leaving Age*; Working Paper 2; London: Schools Council/HMSO, 1965.
TIBBLE, J. W. (ed.), *Raising the School Leaving Age: The extra year*; London: Routledge & Kegan Paul, 1970.

28 CAMERON, SUE, 'Attendance figures may hide "alarming" increase in truancy', *TES*, 10 Aug. 1973.

29 'Few LEAs move to ban the cane'; *TES*, 7 April 1972.
NEWELL, PETER (ed.), A Last Resort; Harmondsworth: Penguin, 1972.
TURNER BARRY (ed.), *Discipline in Schools*; London: Ward Lock Educational, 1973.

30 INSALL, ROGER, 'GLC buys 5,400 canes through sex shop'; *Evening News*, 27 Oct. 1977.

31 LASLETT, ROBERT, *The Education of Maladjusted Children*; St Albans: Crosby Lockwood Staples, 1977.
WAKEFIELD, TOM, *He's Much Better, He Can Smile Now*; Newton Abbot: David & Charles, 1975.

32 ROWAN, PATRICIA, 'Short-term sanctuary'; *TES*, 2 April 1976.

33 COPE, CHRISTINE and ANDERSON, ELIZABETH, Special Units in Ordinary Schools; University of London Press, 1977.

34 ERIKSON, ERIK H., *Childhood and Society*: Harmondsworth: Penguin, 1965.
BLACKBURN, KEITH, *The Tutor*; London: Heinemann, 1975.

35 LYONS, KAREN, *Social Work and the School*; London: HMSO, 1973.
MARLAND, MICHAEL, *et al., Pastoral Care: Organizing the care and guidance of the individual pupil in a comprehensive school*; London: Heinemann Educational, 1974.
HAIGH, GERALD, *The Reluctant Adolescent*; London: Temple Smith, 1976.
HARGREAVES, DAVID H., *Deviance in Classrooms*; London: Routledge & Kegan Paul, 1976.

36 *Counselling in Schools*; Working Paper 15; London: Schools Council/HMSO, 1967.
LYTTON, H. and CRAFT, J., *Guidance and Counselling in British Schools*; London: Edward Arnold, 1975.
VAUGHAN, T., *Education and the Aims of Counselling*; Oxford: Blackwell, 1976.

37 LAMBERT, JACK and PEARSON, JENNY, *Adventure Playgrounds*; Harmondsworth: Penguin, 1974.

38 MCGOVERN, BERNARD S., *Play Leadership*; London: Faber & Faber, 1973.

39 BAZELEY, E., *Homer Lane and the Little Commonwealth*; London: Allen & Unwin, 1948.
WILLS, DAVID, *Homer Lane: A biography*; London: Allen & Unwin, 1964.

40 MAKARENKO, A. S., *The Road to Life* (3 vols); Foreign Languages Publishing House; Wellingborough: Colletts, 1951.

Chapter 15

1 APGAR, M., *New Perspectives on Community Development*; New York: McGraw Hill, 1976.
WARD, COLIN, *Housing: An anarchist approach*; London: Freedom Press, 1976.

2 MANN, PETER H., 'The socially balanced neighbourhood'; *Town Planning Rev., 29,* 2, 1958.
GLAZER, NATHAN, 'The school as an instrument in planning'; *Amer. Inst. Planners J., 25,* 4, 1959.
WOOD, ELIZABETH, *A New Look at the Balanced Neighbourhood*; New York: Citizens' Housing Association Planning Council, Inc., 1960.
STRETTON, H., *Ideas for Australian*

Cities; Melbourne: Georgian House, 1975.

SARKISSIAN, WENDY, 'The idea of socialism'; *Urban Studies*, 1976.

3 DOBRINER, WILLIAM M., *Class in Suburbia*; Englewood Cliffs, NJ: Prentice Hall, 1963.

BOYER, BRIAN, D., *Cities Destroyed for Cash: The FHA scandal at HUD*; Chicago: Follet, 1973.

4 BLAIR, THOMAS, *Retreat to the Ghetto*; London: Wildwood House, 1978.

5 COLEMAN, J. S., 'Recent trends in school desegregation'; *Educ. Res., 4*, 1975.

6 LEVINE, D. V. and HAVIGHURST, R. J. (eds), *The Future of Big City Schools*; Berkeley, Calif.: McCutchan, 1977.

7 FUERST, J. S. (ed,), *Public Housing in Europe and America*; London: Croom Helm, 1974.

8 CONNELLY, HAROLD, 'Black movement into suburbia'; *Urban Affairs Quarterly*, Sept. 1973.

9 WALDRIP, DONALD R., 'Alternative programs in Cincinnati'; in D. V, Levine and R. J. Havighurst (eds), *The Future of Big City Schools* (*see* Note 6).

10 ORFIELD, GARY, 'Policy implications of white flight in metropolitan areas'; in *The Future of Big City Schools* (*see* Note 6).

11 ETHERINGTON, WENDY, *The Idea of Social Mix: A critical biography*; London: Centre for Environmental Studies, 1974.

BEACH, MARK, *Desegregated Housing and Rural Neighbourhoods: A bibliographical guide*; Philadelphia: National Neighbour, 1976.

12 HARVEY, D., *Social Justice and the City*; London: Edward Arnold, 1973.

PORTER, PAUL R., *The Recovery of American Cities*; New York: Two Continents, 1976.

13 MORRIS, WILLIAM, *News from Nowhere*; Kelmscott Press, 1892.

HOWARD, EBENEZER, *Garden Cities of Tomorrow* (1902); F. J. Osborn (ed.), London: Faber & Faber, 1946.

KITCHEN, P., *A Most Unsettling Person: An Introduction to the life and ideas of Patrick Geddes*; London: Gollancz, 1975.

14 MUMFORD, L., *The City in History*; London: Routledge & Kegan Paul, 1961.

LOUIS, WIRTH, 'Towards a definition of the local community'; in A. J. Reiss (ed.), *Louis Wirth on Cities and Social Life*; University of Chicago Press, 1964.

MUMFORD, L., *The Urban Prospect*; London: Secker & Warburg, 1968.

15 JACOBS, JANE, *The Death and Life of Great American Cities*; New York: Vintage, 1961.

16 TAYLOR, NICHOLAS, *The Village in the City*; London: Temple Smith, 1973.

17 CASTELLS, MANUEL, *The Urban Question*; London: Edward Arnold, 1977.

18 DONNISON, D. and EVERSLEY, E. (eds), London: *Urban patterns, problems and policies*; London: Heinemann, 1973.

FRANKENBERG, R., *Communities in Britain*; Harmondsworth: Penguin, 1973.

19 *See* Chapter 2, Note 30.

MARK VAUGHAN, 'Labour promise a "Deprivation Index" '; *TES*, 18 Jan. 1974.

20 Report of speech by Hattersley; *TES*, 18 Jan. 1974.

21 CULLINGWORTH, J. B., *Town and Country Planning in Britain*; London: Allen & Unwin, 1976.

22 *London: The future and you*; GLC, 1973. *Thamesmead: Housing a balanced community*; GLC, 1974. *Strategy for the South East*; DOE review; London: HMSO, 1976.

23 *London Docklands: A strategic plan*; Docklands Joint Committee, 1976.

24 DEMUTH, CLARE, *Government Initiatives on Urban Deprivation*; Runnymede Trust Briefing Paper, 1977. *Housing Policy: A consultative document*; London: HMSO, 1977. *Inner Area Studies: Liverpool, Birmingham and Lambeth*; Summaries of consultants' final reports; London: HMSO, 1977. WARD, COLIN, The Child in the City; London: Architectural Press, 1978.

25 BOECHENSTEIN, W., 'The design of socially mixed housing'; *Amer. Inst, Planners J.*, 37, 4, 1971. MANN, P., 'The socially balanced neighbourhood'; *Town Planning Rev.*, 29, 1958.

26 COLLINS, ROSEMARY, 'House owners fear a price slump from council tenant invasions'; *Guardian*, 27 Aug. 1974.

27 HANDS, JOHN, *Housing Cooperative Dwellings*, 1975.

Final report of the Working Party on Housing Cooperatives (Campbell Report); London: HMSO, 1975.

28 Non-profit Housing Associations; London: HMSO, 1975.

29 FOX, DEREK, Tenant Participation; DOE, 1973.
MANDELKER, D., Housing Subsidies in the US and England; Indianapolis: Bobbs-Merrill, 1974.
WARD, COLIN, Tenants Take Over; London: Architectural Press, 1974.
LEES, RAY and SMITH, GEORGE (eds), Action Research in Community Development; London: Routledge & Kegan Paul, 1976.

30 Records and Information relating to the Housing of Members of Ethnic Groups; DOE Consultation Paper, Dec. 1976.
Urban Deprivation, Racial Inequality and Social Policy; Community Relations Commision; London: HMSO,1977.
Inner London Policies for Dispersal and Balance; final report of the Lambeth Inner Area Study; London: HMSO, 1977.

31 FORREST, R. and MURIE, A., Social Segregation, Housing Need and the Sale of Council Houses; CURS, 1976.
FIELD, FRANK, Do We Need Council Houses?; Catholic Housing and Policy Group, 1976.
'Controversial report said council house subsidies cost three times tax relief on private homes'; Times, 19 March 1977.

32 The Poor Man's Guide to Equity Sharing; London: Housing Corporation, 1978.
Housing Association Leasehold Schemes; London: National Federation of Housing Associations, 1978.

33 Policy for the Inner Cities, Command 6845; London: HMSO, 1977.

Chapter 16

1 STONE, JUDITH and TAYLOR, FELICITY, The Parents' Schoolbook; Harmondsworth: Penguin, 1976.
O'CONNOR, MAUREEN, Your Child's Comprehensive School; London: Pan, 1978.
O'CONNOR, MAUREEN, Your Child's Primary School; London: Pan, 1978.

2 STADLEN, FRANCES, 'ACE in stormy waters as director and chairman resign'; TES, 2 July 1976.

3 GRETTON, JOHN, 'Whither ACE without the boss?'; 1 Oct. 1972.

4 DUNCAN, ANN, Where to Look Things up: A–Z of the sources on all major educational topics; Advisory Centre for Education, 1975.

5 CORBETT, ANNE, 'Private stands, public stances'; TES, 29 Sept. 1974.

6 BARON, G. and HOWELL, D. A., The Government and Management of Schools; University of London Press, 1974.

7 LYNCH, JAMES and PIMLOTT, JOHN, Parents and Teachers; London: Schools Council/Macmillan, 1976.

8 Parents and Teachers as Governors and Managers; NAGM, 1973.

9 HUMBLE, S. and TALBOT, J., Neighbourhood Councils in England; A report to the DOE; University of Birmingham, 1977.
A Voice for your Neighbourhood; London: HMSO, 1978.

10 POSTER, CYRIL, The School and the Community; London: Macmillan, 1971.
SHARP, JOHN, Open School; London: Dent, 1973.
MACBEATH, JOHN (ed.), A Question of Schooling; London: Hodder & Stoughton, 1977.

11 TUDOR, DAVID (ed.), The Community Concept: New Approaches to school management in eight local education authorities; London: Councils and Education Press, 1973.

12 REÉ, HARRY, Educator Extraordinary: the life and achievements of Henry Morris; London: Longman, 1973.

13 MIDWINTER, ERIC, Education and the Community; London: Allen & Unwin, 1975.

14 BALL, COLIN and MEG, Education for a change; Harmondsworth: Penguin, 1973.
HAIN, PETER, Community Politics; London: John Calder, 1976.

15 BALL, COLIN, 'Hypermarkets of corporate life'; TES, 29 Nov. 1974.
BESWICK, NORMAN, 'Corner shop or supermarket?' TES, 4 July 1975.

16 BENINGTON, JOHN, 'The flaw in the pluralist heaven: Changing strategies in the Coventry CDP'; in Ray Lees and George Smith (eds), Action Research in Community Development; London: Routledge & Kegan Paul, 1975.
Leisure and the Quality of Life: A report on four local experiments (2 Vols); London: HMSO, 1977.

17 *VCTV*, *21*, Manchester Free Press, Nov. 1973.

NEWMAN, M., *Adult Education and Community Action*; London: Readers and Writers Co-operative, 1973.

HEAD, DAVID (ed.) *Freeway to Learning*; Harmondsworth: Penguin, 1974.

18 *Adult Education: A plan for development* (Russell Report); London: HMSO, 1973.

CLYNE, PETER, *The Disadvantaged Adult*; London: Longman, 1972.

19 *Teachers' Pay*; Switzerland: International Labour Office, 1978.

20 LACEY, C., *The Socialization of Teachers*; London: Methuen, 1977.

'Tories lead in teacher poll'; *TES*, 4 Oct. 1974.

21 NOP Poll; reported in *TES*, 2 Sept. 1977.

22 TAYLOR, J. K. and DALE, I. R., *A Survey of Teachers in their First Year of Service*; University of Bristol, 1971.

Housing Construction Statistics; DOE, 1975.

23 'House owning, Badminton playing Mr Average'; *TES*/NOP Poll; *TES*, 2 Sept. 1977.

24 Report on Family Expenditure Survey; London: HMSO, 1973.

VENNING, PHILIP, 'What do teachers spend their money on?'; *TES*, 22 Nov. 1974.

25 WILKINSON, MAX, 'The headmaster at a comprehensive tells: "Why I'm sending my child to a grammar school" '; *Daily Mail*, 8 March 1976.

See also 'Labour MPs pick grammar schools'; *Evening Standard*, 24 April 1973.

'Callaghan's grand-daughter switches to public school'; *Evening News*, 19 July 1976.

26 '4,000 non-white teachers, but where are they?; *TES*, 18 July 1975.

'Black teacher'; *New Society*, 1 March 1978.

27 'Urban training ground'; *TES*, 13 Dec. 1974.

28 *Teacher Education and Training* (James Report); London: HMSO, 1972.

29 *Young People and Work* (Holland Report); London: HMSO, 1977.

30 LORTIE, DAN D., *School Teacher: A sociological study*; University of Chicago Press, 1975.

Index